**The astonishing story of five hundred foreign workers
lured here from India and trapped in forced labor—told by
the visionary labor leader who engineered
their escape and set them on a path to citizenship.**

IN LATE 2006, SAKET SONI, a twenty-eight-year-old Indian-born community organizer, received an anonymous phone call from an Indian migrant worker in Mississippi. He was one of five hundred men trapped in squalid Gulf Coast "man camps," surrounded by barbed wire, watched by guards, crammed into cold trailers with putrid toilets, forced to eat moldy bread and frozen rice. The men had been enticed from India by the promise of good work and green cards. Worse, they had each scraped up some $20,000 for this "opportunity" to rebuild hurricane-wrecked oil rigs, leaving their families in impossible debt. During a series of clandestine meetings, Soni and the workers devised a bold plan. In *The Great Escape*, Soni traces the workers' extraordinary escape, their march on foot to Washington, DC, and their thirty-one-day hunger strike to bring attention to their cause. Along the way, ICE agents try to deport the men, company officials work to discredit them, and politicians avert their eyes. But none of this shakes the workers' determination to win their dignity and keep their promises to their families.

Weaving a deeply personal journey with a riveting and important tale of twenty-first-century forced labor, Soni takes us into the lives of the foreign workers the US increasingly relies on to rebuild after climate disasters. For readers of Bryan Stevenson's *Just Mercy*, Katherine Boo's *Behind the Beautiful Forevers*, Matthew Desmond's *Evicted*, and Patrick Radden Keefe's *Say Nothing*, *The Great Escape* is the gripping story of one of the largest human trafficking cases in modern American history—and the workers' heroic journey for justice.

THE GREAT ESCAPE

THE GREAT ESCAPE

A True Story of Forced Labor and
Immigrant Dreams in America

SAKET SONI

ALGONQUIN BOOKS OF CHAPEL HILL 2023

Published by
Algonquin Books of Chapel Hill
Post Office Box 2225
Chapel Hill, North Carolina 27515-2225

an imprint of Workman Publishing Co., Inc.,
a subsidiary of Hachette Book Group, Inc.
1290 Avenue of the Americas,
New York, NY 10104

The names and identifying characteristics of some individuals have been changed.
Some dialogue has been re-created.

Library of Congress Cataloging-in-Publication Data

[TK]

10 9 8 7 6 5 4 3 2 1
First Edition

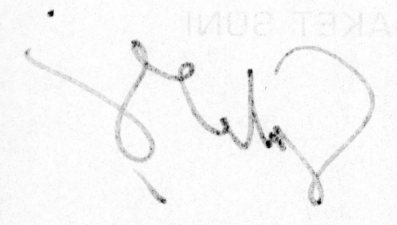

[dedication to come]

[epigraph to come]

CONTENTS

THE GREAT ESCAPE

November 10, 2006
New Orleans, LA

WHEN MY PARENTS called me the night of my twenty-ninth birthday, I was lying in wait for a human smuggler. I pried open my phone, barely feeling my fingers from the cold, and sent them to voicemail with a silent apology. I hadn't called home in months. This was regrettable, irresponsible. But they could sit tight for a few more hours. In Delhi, where they were, my birthday had already passed.

I was in an unheated car parked two blocks from the Home Depot on Claiborne, on an unlit street I couldn't name. In Central City, street signs were still twisted and torn from the flooding after Hurricane Katrina. My sights were trained on Javier Ruiz. He was across the street, standing next to a one-ton dumpster overflowing with construction debris. I squinted to read his expression but could see only his outline, stocky and stoic in a zippered hoodie. He had to be freezing. But he remembered my advice and kept his hands in plain view, holding the plastic bag that contained the ransom money for his kidnapped nephew: $2,000, to be handed over *after* delivery. No nephew, no money.

Javier and I were both new in town. I had been working as a labor organizer in New Orleans for eight months. I met Javier where I met most of the strangers it was my job to help: under a sixty-foot-tall monument to Robert E. Lee.

The city was still reeling. Katrina had hit fifteen months before, in August 2005. The storm surge overwhelmed New Orleans's floodwalls, burst through the levees, killed almost two thousand people, and displaced nearly a million more. The homes left standing were still uninhabitable. Roofs were cracked, walls crumpled, floors piled with mold-caked debris. Katrina had turned the Gulf Coast into a construction site of postwar proportions, with over 600,000 homes to be repaired in Louisiana alone, and nearly as many in Mississippi. The recovery was just now starting in earnest.

The rebuilders were migrant workers like Javier. They came by the thousands—plumbers, roofers, electricians, carpenters, drywallers, painters—arriving from as nearby as Texas and as far away as Brazil and Peru. They lived in tents, in their cars, in dilapidated homes, under the Claiborne bridge. At daybreak, they gathered for work beneath the statue of the Confederate general. Lee Circle was the hiring hub for jobs across the Gulf Coast. Contractors would pull up in vans or buses, pick up day laborers, and drive them out to hurricane-torn places near and far. That's where I went each morning to talk to workers and introduce them to the fledgling local workers' center I had founded.

Organizing migrant workers starts with solving their problems. In most American cities, this means helping day laborers look for contractors who have disappeared before payday, or protecting them when those contractors threaten to call police or immigration agents as a way to avoid paying them. In post-Katrina New Orleans, it could also mean rescuing their relatives from kidnappers.

Javier had migrated to the United States from Honduras after losing his shrimping job in a 2005 drought. After Katrina, he came to New Orleans to find work and learned to fix roofs. He saved up $2,000 to pay for his sixteen-year-old nephew back in Honduras to come join him, and wired it to the smuggler who had arranged his own journey to the US. Weeks later, the smuggler called and said his nephew was being held in Laredo, Texas. If Javier wanted to see him again, it would cost another $2,000. Javier asked if I could help.

"I'll do what I can," I said.

MONEY WAS POOLED. A deal was struck. The smuggler would arrive after dark, here, with the nephew. It suddenly occurred to me that the smuggler might up his price. I'd already contributed $300, which was all

I had. It was the tenth of November, meaning ten days after I paid rent, and five before payday. The workers' center wasn't a volunteer organization—there was a small staff, and we got paid, but not much. If I was lucky, there'd be $100 left in my checking account, not even enough for work expenses on the road, for which I always lost the receipts and never filed for reimbursement. If Javier needed more money, I wouldn't be of any use.

Scenarios I hadn't considered raced through my mind. The smuggler arrives without the nephew. The smuggler arrives with a gun. The smuggler arrives with another smuggler. The smuggler arrives, turns a man over, Javier pays, then realizes it's not his nephew. The smuggler arrives. I lose sight of Javier. A shot rings out. I find Javier in the dumpster. My God.

I could just make out Javier's face. He didn't look scared. Why not? A new scenario played. The smuggler arrives. He shakes Javier's hand. They split the money and disappear. There was never any nephew. My dread tattered into panic. Javier had negotiated this deal, not me. What if I had been drawn into a ruse?

It wasn't out of the question. Just weeks before, another worker had confessed to me that he had been promised a visa by immigration police if he could get me to offer him a false social security card. Apparently, immigration agents weren't content with sting operations against workers—now they were targeting organizers and advocates too.

A man in a baseball cap walked up. No van, no gun, no nephew. The man spoke. Javier spoke. The man motioned—I followed his gesture down the street, into the dead-end darkness. I wanted to shout: *Don't let go of the money until you see your nephew!* Too late. Javier handed over the plastic bag. The man turned and walked back into the darkness. A pause. Then a slender man came up to Javier. They didn't embrace. Javier led him to the car and they climbed in.

"My nephew Julio." Javier beamed. Julio flashed a toothy grin. His face was a younger, brighter version of his uncle's, with a mustache on its way.

"The food's good here, right?" Julio said. "I last ate two days ago."

As we munched on crawfish pies from a corner store, Julio asked his uncle when he could start work.

BACK IN MY APARTMENT, I collapsed on the couch. I could hear the men's soft snoring from my bedroom. They'd be gone the next morning before I woke up. Like most of the workers I sheltered here for a night or two, I'd never see them again.

I poured a glass of Bushmills as a birthday indulgence. Fatigue was weighing on me, but my parents were still waiting for me to call. I played their message first.

"Happy birthday, betoo," my mother said. Her voice, musical and unconditionally forgiving, caught at my heart. I imagined her sitting impeccably upright on the other side of the world, phone in one hand, a steaming mug of tea in the other; my father standing over her, glasses halfway down his nose, fighting his allergy to phone calls. "We know you're very busy with important things," she continued, "but please call us when you have a chance."

By now I was lying flat on the couch, phone on my chest. There was one more message. A man calling from a 228 number: Mississippi. His voice sounded oddly familiar. His entire message consisted of two words—my name.

"Saket Soni," he called out, plaintive. He paused, as if waiting for me to come to the phone. Then he sighed and hung up. I didn't know what to make of it.

I was mustering the strength to call my parents back when the phone rang in my hand. The 228 number again. I had the impulse to send it to voicemail, but then realized what had struck me about that man's voice. He had said my name, Saket, the way it was meant to be pronounced, musical with a soft *t* at the end—the way no one said it in America. I answered.

"Hello?"

"Do you speak Hindi?" said the man, in Hindi.

"Yes," I answered in Hindi, startled. "Who is this?"

"Are you a company man? I need to talk to a company man!"

He launched into a chaotic diatribe. He was owed a green card, he said, and he was a man of his word, and this is what he expected from others. But he had been in America a month already, and still no word on the green card. So he wanted to know: Whom did I answer to? And there is only one correct answer to that question, and it is God, and he had been given my number, and for God's sake, could I give him the update on the green card?

Every few words he would slip from Hindi into the kind of broad-shouldered Punjabi my grandparents spoke. I felt an upwelling of affection for him, but was also mystified. What on earth was this man doing in the ruins of the 228 area code? That was the stretch of Mississippi's coast where Katrina's eye had passed, flattening whole towns. As repairs had gotten underway, some workers had called from the area needing help. Most were from Latin America. There was the rare local worker. The last person I expected to hear from was a Punjabi man—all the more so past midnight. His tirade was finally concluding.

"Well? Say something! What is the update, sir?"

"I'm sorry," I said, "but how did you get here?"

"What sort of question is that?" he barked. "I came from India a month ago. They promised me a green card. But now they tell me I'm on a visa."

"Okay," I said. "What kind of visa?"

"You tell me!" he answered, vibrating with exasperation. "I wasn't told anything about a visa-sheeza."

Visa-sheeza meant, approximately, "Visas et cetera." Fly into Delhi, and a customs agent asks you if you'd like to declare any whiskey-shiskey. Get home, and your family has prepared chai-shai. And this man had been promised a green card, not some kind of visa-sheeza.

"Sir," I said, "Where are you calling from?"

"America," he said. "At least, that's what they tell me." There was a breathless pause. When he spoke next, he was on the verge of tears: "You need to help us, sir. We are growing desperate. Our families—"

The line went dead. I stared at the phone. When I called back, no one answered.

I downed my whiskey-shiskey.

THE MAN'S VOICE stayed with me in the weeks that followed, even as I responded to one worker emergency after another in New Orleans. With repairs to the Central Business District complete, local business owners called immigration authorities to chase migrant workers out of Lee Circle. A delegation of worker leaders and I negotiated for the workers' right to stay there, but lost. They reconstituted their hiring hub in the parking lot of the Lowe's store on Elysian Fields Avenue, but National Guard battalions arrived in full military gear to round them up. Most of my mornings were spent trying to keep the peace between the Guards and the workers. Afternoons, I was doing outreach to hotel workers at shift change, and to the displaced New Orleans residents who were still living in those hotels on government vouchers, waiting for repairs on their homes. Evenings, I knocked on contractors' front doors to retrieve unpaid wages. They would answer with hammers, sometimes guns; the de-escalations could take hours. Saturdays were for worker soccer games, with staff keeping lookout for police and immigration agents.

I dedicated Sundays to solving the mystery of the Indian man in the 228 area code. I drove hours to the Walmarts in Gulfport, Bay Saint Louis, and Moss Point, spent afternoons scouring them for anyone Punjabi-looking. On my way back, I stopped at the only Indian grocery store in the region at the time, the International Market in Metairie. One Sunday evening just before Christmas, I saw a man my age who was unmistakably a new arrival. He glanced around nervously as I engaged him. He said he was on a work visa but wouldn't say where. When I asked him how he was getting home, he said, "A company van." I sensed he didn't want me to walk him out of the store. Whoever had control over him here, they had succeeded in intimidating him. I slipped him a business card as he paid his bill.

"If you ever want to talk," I said quietly.

IN THE FIRST days of January 2007, I got a phone call from a third Hindi-speaking man, also with a 228 number. Unlike my first caller

("Are you a company man?"), this one seemed to think I was an immigration attorney. He spoke in a tense, urgent whisper, as though expecting to be hauled off at any moment.

"I need you to file a case for me."

"What kind of case?"

"A case for a green card," he said. "I will pay you. Just not immediately. The company controls my bank account, you see?"

He wouldn't tell me his name or where he worked, other than "Mississippi." I remembered the first caller had said "*We* are growing desperate," and imagined the three of them together, probably sequestered in a FEMA trailer, parked in the backyard of an Indian restaurant owner—likely a relative who had brought them into the US on tourist visas, then made them work for free as line cooks. It was a sadly common business model among the Indian community in California. It would be easy to replicate in Mississippi, where these workers might be the only Indians for miles around.

In order to help, I explained, I had to be able to understand some basic details. My caller cut me off: he was out of time. I quickly asked him if we could meet. Impossible, he said: the boss only let them off site on Sundays, and only for two hours, for Mass at a Catholic church.

"What if I were at the church praying this Sunday? I could run into you."

"By kismet!"

"Right. How many of you will be there?"

"One other man. Maybe two. You'll mention you're a lawyer, and an Indian one at that."

"I'm not a lawyer," I said. He brushed aside the nuance and warned that they would have to be back in the pew by the time the service concluded.

"I'm sorry to make you miss Mass," I said.

"I'm a Hindu. God is one. See you Sunday."

"Hang on," I said. "What church?"

"The Secret Catholic Church in Pascagoula." With that, he hung up.

IT TOOK A DRIVE through Pascagoula to find it. The Secret Catholic Church was in fact the Sacred Heart Catholic Church. Arriving on Sunday, my heart quickened. I'd be meeting three men at most, for an hour if I was lucky, but I had prepared for days. My Hindi had suffered after twelve years in the United States, so I'd written a two-page opening statement in English and called my parents for help with the translation. (In exchange for a quick turnaround, I promised my mother an uninterrupted hour on the phone after the meeting.)

I'd explain up front that I wasn't a lawyer. *I'm a labor organizer with a nonprofit organization called the New Orleans Workers' Center for Racial Justice. We help people like you improve conditions at work. I know you want to know what I can do for you. But first I need to understand how you got here, whom you work for, and what you're facing. Despite your fears, despite anything they've told you, you have labor rights in America. I can help you act on them. If the three of you sign a petition, you will be protected by US labor law against retaliation. And I will do everything I can to make sure that protection is real.*

As I reached for the doorknob to the church's back room, I imagined how isolated the three men must feel. Pascagoula was a deeply conservative shipyard town with no South Asian community to speak of. No market that smelled and sounded like home. Even in cosmopolitan New Orleans, with a job I loved and friends and mentors, I missed home. Whoever had put them in this position seemed to have near-total control over them. And had them scared.

I opened the door. There weren't three desperate Indian men in the back room of the Sacred Heart Catholic Church. There were almost a hundred.

Who on earth are you, I thought, *and how did you get here?*

PART ONE

DREAMS

1: Schemes

Spring 2006
Kerala, India

THE NIGHT FLIGHT crossed the Arabian Sea. At dawn the plane glinted above the Malabar Coast. It descended into March rain, tilted over a forest braided with rivers, traced a nautilus over Kochi. Wet roofs shone. The back wheels hit the tarmac, unlocking a shudder of applause.

The passengers were Indian laborers and nurses returning from jobs in Bahrain. Most of them came home to see their families every six months. But not Aby Raju, the lanky young man folded into a window seat behind the wings. He unbuckled, clambered over his neighbors, and reached for his bags while the plane was still taxiing. Aby hadn't been home for five years.

He bounded out of the airplane, heaved his luggage off the belt, bribed a customs agent to rescue excess duty-free whisky. Finally he found his parents. His mother cried. His father commandeered the trolley.

Following them out to the curb, Aby was unsettled. His parents were smaller. His mother's gait was more cautious than before, and his father no longer filled his half-sleeved shirt. The taxi driver, a childhood friend, bowed slightly, as if he were picking up a dignitary.

They set off into the drumming downpour, through okra farms and chili fields. Aby's eyes, parched from the desert, were peeled open through it all. From the back seat, his mother dispensed news. There were five years to catch up on! She described the state of his father's bronchioles. Recited an inventory of her own ailments. Reported on the home remodeling project Aby had sponsored with money wired from Bahrain. His father maintained a stoic, wheezy reserve.

By the time the taxi trundled into the Rajus' town of Meenadom, there was only one salient news item that his mother hadn't shared. Last week, Aby's parents had put an ad in the matrimonial pages of Kerala's major paper, the *Manorama*, announcing they were looking for a wife for their only son. He was twenty-seven now and had some cachet as a worker returned from overseas. But an ad is just an ad, not a marriage proposal, so she didn't mention it.

The Raju house approached like an old friend wearing a low hat. Aby's father had bought this land and built this place. It was an improbable accomplishment for a lowly army private. He came into a little money when the army sent him out to Sri Lanka to help quell the Tamil Tigers. He came home with enough hardship pay to start building a house, but not quite enough to complete it. Six-year-old Aby didn't know the difference. The raw cement floor was all the better for cooling his feet. He thought *inside doors* were a curious extravagance of the superrich. Then he grew up, became a builder, reached Bahrain, and started wiring money home so his father could finish what he'd started.

At the front gate, Aby's mother took his hand in hers and threw open the door. There were white tiles on the floor, a finished ceiling, Western toilets, doors for every room. Aby looked for his father to get his approval, but couldn't find him. Maybe he'd stepped out to smoke.

Suppertime brought a gaggle of uncles, aunts, nieces, nephews, neighbors. Children climbed all over Aby. His mother served up bright green parcels: roasted fish wrapped in banana leaves, Aby's favorite. He unwrapped one, inhaled the fishy steam, but the distinct feeling that he was breaking a rule stopped him from touching it. The men ate first in the Raju house. When he lived here last, he had to wait for them to finish before he had a bite, even on the nights he caught the fish. But when he looked around the table, nobody seemed to think Aby was out of place. And, oddly, his father, the biggest eater of them all, was missing from dinner. Aby wolfed down his fish.

After dinner, Aby handed out saris. Cologne. Watches. Jeans and pretty dresses for the kids. He saved the best for last: surround-sound speakers for his parents, with triangular stands that he'd had a friend weld. His dad loved film songs.

"Where is he?" Aby asked his mother.

"On duty," she said. Aby didn't understand. What happened to retirement?

"He took a job at the *Manorama*." His dad was a current affairs buff, but had he become a journalist? "He works the night shift, delivering papers. You'll see him in the morning. Come with me. We got you something too."

She took him out back, held out a set of keys. A beat-up motorcycle was parked on the backstreet. The children squealed. Rides all summer! Aby hugged his mother.

"We don't know much about bikes, but they said this was a good one," she said.

"It's a Hero Honda. The best," said Aby.

"So shall we call it even?" his mother asked. Aby was confused. "The loan you gave us. You'll consider this a repayment?"

A few months ago, his mother had asked Aby for a loan to run the house. He'd sent most of his savings—all but the money for presents. The Hero Honda was pure love, but there was no way it cost even half that amount.

"Of course," Aby said.

"Good boy. Now come inside. You are tired."

AMOROUS PARAKEETS WOKE Aby in the morning, the way they always had. His room faced a grassy hillside, and his gaze landed on a familiar shape: his father walking home from the bus stop on the summit. It hurt to look at him. His father had been up all night, piling stacks of fresh newspapers into a truck, driving around to places like the railway station to stock kiosks. At his age. With his lungs.

Aby's pride over funding the home renovations evaporated. His parents were desperate, and he hadn't seen it. He needed to get right back out there. Find a recruiter to throw him like a dart at the oil economy, into Bahrain, Dubai, Qatar, Abu Dhabi, wherever, for another welding job. It would take him at least two weeks to find a placement, a month to ship out. He had to start looking today.

In the kitchen he ripped the *Manorama* open to the job listings. All the labor recruiters printed ads aimed at men and women in Kerala eager to go where the jobs were overseas. Aby scanned the ads, knowing he faced a tough market. Five years ago, when he first left home, companies in the Middle East were desperate for skilled workers. He had been a hot commodity: at twenty-two, a first-class welder. Recruiters were falling over each other for him. But now he was competing with a glut of young hopefuls willing to work for less. Recruiters were offering wages as low as his starting salary five years ago.

Aby's father came in and collapsed into a seat for breakfast. His mother served plates of steaming appam and poured coffee. But Aby didn't touch either. His eyes were fixed on an ad.

MIGRATE TO USA
On green card/permanent residence visa
In California/New Orleans
Welders. Structural fitters. Fabricators. Marine engine fitters.
Job guarantee provided for 2 to 3 years.
Earn from 4,000 to 5,000 $ per month.

Permanent lifetime settlement in USA for self and family. Aby had seen many fraudulent recruitment schemes aimed at Kerala's young and jobless, but this one, he thought, was admirably bold. Green cards! Any seasoned migrant worker knew that America let in only those with elite educations.

But curiosity overcame him. The landline lived in Aby's bedroom. He went and dialed the number listed on the ad.

An eager woman answered. "Calling about America?" She pronounced the *r* in the word like she had been there, and said Aby was in luck. The recruiter happened to be in the office right now, and could see him personally, if Aby could make it over. The office was in Pampady.

Aby stifled a chuckle. Pampady was right next door, a backwater town named for a large rock. Its biggest attraction was an unlicensed bar. And now it was posing as a springboard for America! He decided to swing by for a laugh. Then he'd ride out to Kochi, where the serious recruiters were, and hunt for a real job in the Middle East. He flung on a jacket and walked out the door. His mother ran after him.

"You haven't finished breakfast! Where are you going?"

"To find work," he said, kick-starting the motorcycle.

"Already?" She sounded hurt. Was she in such a state of denial that she couldn't see it? This was their only path to solvency. "Well, don't be long," she said. "We're having tea with a family. A nice family. A *pastor's* family."

Aby knew what she meant: a girl's family.

"I told you not to look," he said. "I haven't come home to get married."

"We're not *looking*. But people are *calling*. What to do? You're famous!"

"I'm not going."

"Fine, fine," his mother said. "So far, they haven't confirmed. If they don't call, I won't pursue it. But if they call . . ."

He roared on to KK Road, leaving her in a cloud of dust.

THE RECRUITER TOOK Aby for a novice.

"Think of me as a matchmaker," he said. "But not for weddings. For *work*. And I have just the opportunity for you!"

Aby smirked. The "office" was the man's house. The secretary was his wife. Behind the fancy facade, it was another mom-and-pop shop in a sleepy town. The recruiter was in a lungi and had hastily combed hair, as though Aby had caught him napping.

He showed Aby pictures printed from the website of an American company called Signal International: vast oil platforms under repair.

"What's the pay?" Aby asked skeptically.

"Eighteen dollars an hour, forty hours a week, twenty-six dollars an hour overtime." Aby did the math. Almost $54,000 in the first year.

"How much does all this cost?"

The man gave the figure in rupees: just under $20,000. "You recuperate that in four and a half months. Everything after that is in your pocket. But that's not all. Nine months into your job, you get something called a green card. It means you bring your wife and children over. To live with you. It's a family scheme!"

"I'm not married."

"No better time!"

Aby let out a laugh. He was done playing along. He explained that he wasn't a rube—he was a first-class welder who had just returned from Bahrain. He knew what a green card was. A migrant worker's holy grail. And he knew no Kerala recruiter could snap his fingers and produce one all by himself.

"I'm just handling things as the local agent," the man admitted. "My contract is with Sachin Dewan."

Aby's ears perked up. Dewan Consultants was a recruiting empire, with offices in Dubai and Mumbai. But even they could only get people as far as the Middle East. Then the recruiter said the magic words:

"Sachin Dewan is working with *an American lawyer.* He's here with company supervisors to test candidates. There'll be lines around the block. Just take the welding test. You've been to Bahrain, you've built things. I'll tell Sachin to put you in the front of the line."

Outside, Aby got back on his bike. Where to go? The offer he'd come to laugh at had turned out to be real. The test cost 5,000 rupees. He had exactly that, not a paisa more. And if he passed the test, what then? A green card was the chance of a lifetime. But raising $20,000 was unimaginable. Should he still head to Kochi and on to the Middle East? Or to the testing site to meet the Americans?

His phone rang. His mother.

"The pastor's family called. They confirmed. It's just a cup of tea. It's nothing."

He tried to refuse, then agreed to help her save face just this once, on the condition that she suspend all matchmaking.

THE TEA WAS at a house in a placid village close to Aby's. A welcome party waited on the dirt road, all decked out. Aby roared up on his Hero Honda, kicked up dust, pulled off his helmet. His parents followed behind him in a puttering auto rickshaw. The party of relatives ushered them in. The pastor was waiting. Tea was served.

Aby's mother sat across from the pastor and played her opening move. Aby was twenty-seven, 5'7", their only son, an overseas worker, and solvent, having just returned from five years in Bahrain. No firm plans to go abroad again. (Aby grimaced.) Then it was the pastor's turn. His daughter's name was Bincy. She was twenty-five, 5'1", a capable home-maker, and a nurse, so she could stand on her own feet. But she was ready to marry and be a full-time mother.

This was hardly the face-saving chitchat his mother had promised. Aby's eyes met Bincy's. She was pretty. Short. In a green churidar. She seemed nice enough, but that wasn't the point. He had to find a way out. He reached for the newspaper on the coffee table, opened it to the job listings in a show of insolence that he hoped would put off the pastor.

"Very curious about the world," his mother laughed nervously. "Just can't get him to stop!"

The pastor smiled slightly. *Boys these days.* If the *Manorama* was Aby's greatest vice, his daughter would be fine.

They moved into the middle game: negotiating the actual wedding. The pastor went first. They were Seventh-day Adventists, and Adventists marry frugally. A bride can wear a bracelet, maybe a bangle, certainly no earrings. Bincy would not be wearing gold at the wedding.

Aby's mother nodded sympathetically. She knew about Adventists. The Rajus happened to be Syrian Christians. They adorned brides lav-ishly in gold. In a mixed wedding, wouldn't the Adventists respect the somewhat *older* tradition?

The pastor narrowed his eyes. A low blow. The Seventh-day Adventists came to Kerala in 1914. The Syrian Christian Church was founded rather earlier—by Saint Thomas the Apostle, who came from Jerusalem to Kerala soon after the crucifixion of Jesus. His followers had been crow-ing about their origins ever since.

"Bincy won't be wearing gold," the pastor clarified gently.

"Gold is important to Aby," Mrs. Raju said as she smiled back.

Aby lowered the paper. He needed to break through this absurdity. His parents could barely feed themselves. His father couldn't retire. But here was his mother, with her heaviest earrings dragging down her earlobes, playing hardball with a pastor over wedding details. Aby had to end the charade.

"I don't care much for gold," he broke in.

The room froze.

"Don't like it. Never have. Now excuse me, I have to be somewhere."

His mother looked like a swatted bumblebee. Aby's insolence had spoiled any chance of a wedding proposal. Word would spread of his rejection, by an Adventist at that. His price in the marriage market would plummet.

Aby rode toward the test site for the American welding job. He had no idea how he could ever organize $20,000. But he was going to take the damn test. Those Americans wouldn't know what hit them. A fog swallowed the road ahead of him, dissolved the edges of God's own country. Sometimes faces appeared in the blur, sometimes whole bodies: day laborers sitting in highway trucks, appearing to float—nowhere men in search of one last job before the monsoon drowned out their work. Aby was once a nowhere man himself, building warehouse roofs in Pampady for a dollar on a good day, ten cents on a bad one. He felt a rush as he shot past them and disappeared into the mist.

RETURNING HOME FROM the test, Aby braced himself for punishment. But inside, the frying mustard seeds sounded like rain. His mother served up heaps of mutton. Aby sat down to eat with the feeling that he'd been had.

"The girl's family would like to proceed," his mother said.

Aby slammed the table. "Absolutely not!"

"But she's a nurse," his mother said. "And she'll wear gold, by God!"

"We're not a match."

"Too thin? Is that it? We'll feed her cashews!"

Aby finally came out with it. There was an American company that was offering green cards. He had taken their test and passed. More than that.

The American testers had marveled at his weld. They wanted to take pictures of it. They wanted *him*. The next step was payment: $20,000 in three installments—plus the flight. His mother sat down hard, spatula in hand.

"Why are you trying to get so far away from us?"

Aby sat silent, but his stomach churned. *To provide.* The only way was to take a leap like this. Why couldn't she see that?

His mother turned to his father. "Say something to him."

His father spoke for what seemed like the first time in days. "Where are we going to get that kind of money?"

They all knew the beginning of the answer. They were sitting in it. Aby's father would have to take a loan against the house.

Aby's mother pleaded. If only Aby would agree to the marriage, she could leverage the prospect of a green card into a much higher dowry, raise some of the money that way. But he refused, leaving her with the most awful problem of all: telling a pastor that they were leaving his daughter at the altar.

Aby led his mother to the landline. Things that couldn't be avoided were best done quickly. She dialed the pastor. Unexpectedly, it was Bincy who picked up. Her dad was out. Could she take a message?

"We may have to delay the wedding," Aby's mother stammered into the phone, under Aby's uncompromising glare. "I can't say how long. Aby is going away . . . to Uttar Pradesh. My sister lives there, alone and gravely ill. Aby needs to take care of her. Possibly forever."

"I'm sorry," Aby could hear Bincy say. "What happened to her?"

Aby's mother gave up. The only thing harder than lying to a pastor was lying to a nurse about an illness. At her wit's end, she broke protocol. She handed Aby the phone.

"This wedding can't go on," said Aby.

"I'm sorry about your aunt," said Bincy.

"I'll be traveling to be with her. I might not be back."

"I understand. You must love her very much. I'll be right here, praying for you."

Something caught at Aby. Bincy's tenderness slowed down time. In the pause, he imagined her outstretched hands closing the distance between them. To his own surprise, he didn't flinch at her touch. Her breathing comforted him. A new ease opened up in his leaden chest. He wanted to comfort her as well, but Bincy spoke first.

"I'll relay your message."

"My message?"

"Your mother's message. I'll let my father know when he's home."

"No need," he answered, meeting her softness with a gravel sureness.

"But your aunt—" she asked, but did not ask.

"The wedding will move forward," he said. "Okay?"

Will you marry me?

"Okay," she said.

Yes.

They savored each other for a moment, then hung up. Aby turned to his astonished mother.

"Get ready for an Adventist wedding," he said. "No gold."

THEIR SANCTIONED COURTSHIP started after the marriage was set. A courtship conducted entirely by phone, each call a bite from a stolen mango. Bincy rang Aby every day. He always picked up in the middle of some new wedding preparation. Shirtless, painting the house. Erecting a billowing tent in a gale. Firing up a cauldron to braise a goat.

She asked about his hobbies. He couldn't come up with any. What about her? She liked to sing. Would she sing for him now? Of course not. Singing was for church. Later, she slipped out of the house to a shady coconut grove and sang him an Adventist praise song. When she finished, she was quite abashed, and hung up.

One phone call, one praise song at a time, they fell in love. And as they did, Aby's dilemma grew: how to tell his-bride-to-be he would be leaving her right after the wedding.

There had been challenges to the green card plan, but Aby had pushed through. His father's bank refused them a loan against his house, but the local recruiter helped them find another. With that money, and his father's savings, and his mother's jewelry, and cash from relatives, Aby had just under $15,000. The rest came from a moneylender. The American lawyer put in his visa application.

He couldn't tell Bincy on the phone. And he was forbidden from seeing her in person before the wedding. He decided to pay her a clandestine visit on a day he knew she'd be alone. He rode up to her house and called her. As usual, she answered immediately.

"How are you! Where are you?"

"Look outside." He waved to her from his motorcycle. She gave a squeal of delight, then caught herself and switched to a scandalized tone.

"You can't be here!"

"I've brought you food. Biryani, mutton curry—"

She ordered him home. He argued. She scolded back. Eventually, he relented, laughing, and rode off. He hadn't made it to her door, but he was glowing from the rendezvous.

Then it hit him: he'd forgotten all about telling her.

2: Love Marriage

Summer 2006
New Delhi, India

A THOUSAND KITES dotted the Delhi afternoon. Hemant Khuttan's heart soared with them when his girlfriend Shruti arrived. He waved from their table in the back of the restaurant. They couldn't touch or kiss. *Yet.* One day her painted hands could nest in his. She sat, pulled off her sunglasses. Her long eyelashes, lined thick with kohl, caught his breath and tugged at his heart. The kites climbed higher.

Her lips moved. He heard his name. These events, he realized, were related.

"Hemant," she said again, "How's work?"

"First-class, fine-fantastic!" he said. "How's yours?"

She glared. He knew what she wanted. A progress report. They had dreams of a love marriage. But her father's approval depended on Hemant's launching a career—any career. And time for him to do so was running out. Her father was eying other suitors.

"I do have news," he said. "But first, let's have a bite."

Shruti's brow furrowed. A plate appeared without their having ordered. Their usual. He made a spoon with a piece of tandoori roti, scooped a cube of paneer from the glistening sauce, blew on it, and extended his hand. She looked around. Waiters averted their eyes. She took a bite.

"It's good today," she said. "Straight from the tandoor."

Their clandestine romance was the worst-kept secret in all of Rohini Market. He was twenty-six, with a film star's looks, the son of the assistant superintendent of police. She was the intimidatingly beautiful no-nonsense daughter of a top government engineer. In the street below, the golgappa wallah gawked, children teased, and security guards offered sleazy namastes. So they always met at this rickety two-story restaurant called Atithi, from the saying *atithi devo bhava*. "Guest is God." The servers took its name to heart, providing to ordinary people what only the rich get in Delhi: space.

Hemant chewed a runny morsel. He hadn't planned to share the news until he knew more—for now all he had to go on was an ad in the paper: MIGRATE TO USA. But Shruti kept her eyes on him, waiting for him to swallow.

"Okay, so yes: there's an update," he said. "A good one. I mean, great. For us."

"Well?"

"I found an ad for a job—in America! I don't have all the details yet, but I'm going to a seminar right after lunch to learn more."

The lustrous waves framing Shruti's face shook. "America? I don't understand. What about your welding job?"

"I'm not working there right now. But I found—"

"*What?*"

"I lost my job. I mean, I quit. The important thing is—"

"Hemant!" Shruti buried her face in her hands.

"It's part of a bigger plan. At the seminar I'll find out—"

"We're running out of time!"

"I know, I know! That is why—"

She was already fleeing the restaurant. The wind died. The kites fell out of the sky.

AS HEMANT GOT on his motorcycle to ride to the seminar in South Delhi, the whole market seemed to be in glee over the scene. The golgappa wallah brayed. Children screeched. A passing aunty fished her phone out of her bag to tell her friends. The two security guards with full-moon heads rubbed their bellies. *Ladies and gents, namaste-salam-sat-sri-akal! Our hero, Hemant Master, India's future, comedy's king, flops again! Truth told: clean bowled!*

They were right. Ever since he and Shruti had agreed to marry, all he had done was fail. When they first met, he was in twelfth grade, a statue of confidence. Popular. Owned a motorcycle. Gave her rides. When beat cops interrupted their afternoon hangout sessions in the park to angle for a bribe, he baited them till they realized who he was: their boss's son. Then they begged for forgiveness. Afterward Hemant would mimic their whimpering and howl with laughter. His invincibility held Shruti in thrall. And he adored her.

They tried to keep their romance under wraps. But true love can't stay hidden. It must shout like the blackberry vendor! One night, during his first year in college, with three pegs of Johnnie Walker in him, Hemant told his dad about her and revealed their secret plans.

"Love marriage," his father repeated.

"Yes," beamed Hemant, in a whiskey-induced bliss.

"Well then! Let's meet her. And, more importantly, her father."

"Certainly, when the time is right—"

"*Now.*"

The assistant superintendent of police donned his uniform, took Hemant by the scruff of his neck, and rang Shruti's doorbell. Her father answered, nonplussed. It was late for visitors.

"Our children have planned a love marriage," Hemant's father said.

"Is that so?" said Shruti's father, lowering his glasses to the tip of his nose. "Then please, by all means, come in."

THE GUPTAS SERVED tea and pinnis. (Guest is God.) They thanked Hemant's father for his service on the police force. Mr. Gupta was a humble servant of India as well, at the Bureau of Indian Standards, inaugurated by Pandit Nehru in 1947. As an engineer with the bureau, Mr. Gupta certified electric products. That trusted mark on your toaster, on your water heater—that was him. It was difficult, spiritually. Most products fail. And when you fail a product, you disgrace its maker. But modern nations have standards, and India must be modern. And speaking of modern—*a love marriage.* He now trained his eyes on Hemant, who looked like a scared pup.

Mr. Gupta considered the proposal. On one hand, it would be useful to have an assistant superintendent of police in the family. On the other hand, they came from different castes. The Guptas were Banias, merchants from Uttar Pradesh. The Khuttans were Rajputs, the descendants of landowning warriors. Mr. Gupta had, in fact, supported other love marriages in the extended family. But this was his youngest daughter, still in high school. Hemant, with his film-star face, would distract her from her studies. An astrologer had already warned that Shruti might marry straight out of school, and skip college. Not on Mr. Gupta's watch.

"Who are you?" Mr. Gupta asked Hemant, then answered his own question. "Just a boy."

"Yes, sir."

"Go become somebody. Then we'll talk."

So the lovers went underground. For years they met in secret, spoke in low tones, pretended to be strangers in the market. Shruti defied the astrologer, got a bachelor's in education, a second one in the arts, and a master's in economics. She became the headmistress at Shamrock Middle School.

Hemant floundered. He barely graduated college. He failed the police exam—repeatedly, despite his dad's position. Took a law school entrance exam. Failed that. Got a call center job, got fired. Finally, at twenty-six, garlanded in failure, he got a job at a metal workshop. It turned out he had a skill for flux-core welding. Then he saw the ad: MIGRATE TO USA.

Go become somebody.

THE SEMINAR WAS already underway when Hemant entered. He squeezed into a seat in the back between two men with arms like trees. The recruiter described the American job: the company was called Signal International. They needed welders and pipefitters to build oil rigs. Hemant already felt in over his head. The other men in the room were mountains, each one the Prometheus of his hometown. They had built city-sized refineries in the Saudi desert, drilling platforms in the Arabian Sea. What did Hemant build? Vanity projects. Armor plates for politicians' sedans. But oil rigs?

Then something the recruiter said grabbed Hemant's attention. The job started six months from now. And nine months after the start date, the work visa would turn into a green card. Fifteen months total. Which, by Shruti's estimate, was *exactly* the runway they had left. In fifteen months, her older sister would be married off. It would be her turn. If this lined up just right . . .

Hemant straightened. He was a head taller than any other man in the room. Was he not a flux-core welder, a Khuttan, a man? He would talk to his father. Tomorrow morning, as he polished his father's shoes. He'd describe the job, and the cost: $20,000. It would be uncomfortable—they never talked about money. And it was a colossal sum. He guessed it would take the house, his father's pension, and a loan to raise it. But by the recruiter's math, he'd earn it back in six months.

It would be harder to convince Shruti. He'd tell her it was his dad's idea, that he had no choice. She'd wouldn't be happy about it, but it would be for their own good. Because fifteen months from now, there would be another conversation with her father. Hemant would ring the doorbell himself this time, presents from America in hand. A watch. Duty-free whisky. Inside, he'd ask for Shruti's hand. Mr. Gupta, glasses at the tip of his nose, would inspect him.

"Hemant Khuttan! Have you become somebody?"

"Yes, sir."

"Lawyer? Doctor? Engineer?"

"Something better," Hemant would say. "An American."

3: Supplicants

Summer 2006
Chennai, India

MURUGAN KANDHASAMY APPROACHED the US Consulate in Chennai. It had a green shimmer to it, like a dream. The exterior was studded with chips of a milky granite, broken off from the same half-a-billion-year-old rock formations used to build South Indian temples.

Murugan was thirty, with peat-colored skin, a long-sleeved button-down shirt, and a careful dab of cologne. He clutched his bright yellow file and remembered the recruiter's instruction: *You're an applicant, but you're also a supplicant. Stay quiet till you're spoken to. Answer only the questions you're asked. At the end, fold your hands in gratitude and leave.*

Inside, he joined the swollen line that snaked up to the counters. Others stared at the windows trying to read the faces behind the glass. Murugan bowed his head and prayed. Then a voice.

"Next."

He clutched his file harder to steady himself. He faced a ghostly white woman in her fifties, in stern glasses.

"Your name?"

"Muruganathan Kandhasamy," he said. Then he smiled. "You can call me Murugan." He had rehearsed this opening move—an accommodation, an offer of connection. The woman only blinked.

"What are you here for?"

If only he had the English to tell her everything! What was he here for? To rise.

He slid the manila envelope through the slot below the window.

"Work visa for America," he said. She leafed through his papers.

"What's the company?"

"Signal International."

"What's the job?"

"Flux-core welder."

"What's your experience?"

"Five years in Dubai."

"How did you find out about the job?"

The real answer was crazier than Murugan could've explained even if the woman spoke fluent Tamil. This American work visa was *prophesied*.

SIX MONTHS AGO, he had returned from Dubai for what was supposed to be a short vacation. His mother dragged him out to see an astrologer. She wanted his horoscope read. If the time was right, she wanted a wedding.

The timing couldn't have been worse. Murugan was in a hurry to get back to Dubai. His job was the family's only income source. His father had died when Murugan was five. They could barely afford to run a household, let alone a wedding. And the dire straits were Murugan's fault. His older brother had talked him into investing all $10,000 of his savings in an on-demand milk-delivery service, Uber for milk before Uber. Apparently, others had the same idea. Suddenly their township of 100,000 was overwhelmed with rival milk delivery services—more bicyclists carrying bright white milk bags than there were customers. Pretty soon, the milk bubble popped, washing away five years of Murugan's savings and his father's good name.

If I have to get married, Murugan implored his mother, *at least let's bypass the astrologer. Find a girl through a friend or a relative and hold a rush wedding.* That would let him get back to work in three weeks.

She wouldn't hear of it. The traditional method for marriage had worked for her; it would work for him. They got on a bus to Sirkali, the astrologer town.

To his mother's generation, the astrologers of Sirkali were venerated figures, descendants of Agathiyar, the original seer, who had fixed no less a problem than Shiva's wedding. Eons ago, every living being in the world had come to attend the wedding of Shiva and Parvati. With a terrible crack, the weight of the guests had tilted Earth's balance. The great sage Agathiyar volunteered to set things right. He traveled south to Sirkali and knocked Earth back into place with a single blow. Afterward, he settled there and became a full-time prophet. In modern times, his descendants had professionalized: some handled political affairs, some read only children's futures, some worked as wealth managers. Most in demand were the horoscope specialists who handled weddings, like the man who now ushered Murugan and his mother into his windowless office.

"To tape the session, it's fifty rupees extra," he said. "Years later, you play it for your kids. Their wonder is priceless. Shall I record?"

Murugan's mother gave an eager nod.

"Muruganathan Kandhasamy," the specialist said, smiling.

"Yes."

"Of the Moopanar subcaste. Son of Narayan Kandhasamy."

"Yes."

"Who is deceased. Who knew great hardship."

"Yes."

"Which you inherited. You are intimate with hardship."

Murugan was suddenly uncomfortable. What was this about? Could he just get on with the marriage business? The specialist pulled a book from a shelf and presented it to Murugan with a flourish. It was made of palm leaf pages sewn together. The words were punched in with needles. He had Murugan open the book to a random page and read. Then he looked up, smiling with his eyes.

"Welcome to your raj parvai—the auspicious time for a king to take a bride! Now listen carefully. The woman you must marry holds an advanced degree. Probably in chemistry. She is dark, like you. Has a sister. Her father works at a bank. You will find her in a north-facing house within a twenty-five-kilometer radius of your own." He closed the book triumphantly. "Now go! Search her out. Fortunes that are prophesied must still be pursued."

Murugan's mother gushed with gratitude. Murugan paid, grunted his thanks, and headed for the door.

"One more thing," the specialist called. "Something I saw that I want you to know." Murugan turned back. "You will part ways with hardship. You will cross an ocean. In a distant country, you'll come into fortune. In time, you will be the first wealthy man in your family."

Murugan felt a hum, as though a tuning fork had been struck in his heart. For all his skepticism, there was no dream he held more dear.

"Is that part extra?" he said, trying to sound dubious.

"That's a gift," the specialist said.

FOR THREE MONTHS, Murugan surveyed hundreds of summer-scorched north-facing homes looking for a banker's daughter with dark skin, a sister, and an advanced degree. Incredibly, he found her. Her name was Jaya. She was twenty-five, very pretty, and taught sixth grade chemistry. To Murugan's shock, her father rejected him. He didn't want an overseas worker for his daughter, a husband she would see for two weeks twice a year, between his stints in Dubai, or Bahrain, or wherever. Murugan never swore, but that day, he cursed the horoscope specialist.

Then one day he saw Jaya in line at the bank. He steeled himself and walked up to her.

"Our horoscopes match," he began, "and—"

"Outside," she whispered sharply.

He had been on her mind. She liked his pluck. After being rebuffed, he hadn't given up. He had sent emissaries to lobby for him—uncles, aunts, his mother. He'd even managed to recruit her father's boss, a friend of his uncle's, to make his case. But what was he really made of?

They stood under a neem tree. Murugan made his pitch. He'd love her, take full responsibility for her parents in their old age. He leveled with her about his finances. Yes, he had lost his savings, but he could build it back up with just a few years overseas. His body could stand to work at least twenty more years.

"How do you plan to convince my father?" she asked.

Murugan had thought this through. A friend of his was a supervisor at a roofing company an hour away. He would ask this friend to hire him—a ruse to fulfill her father's condition that Jaya marry a boy with a local job. He would work right up to their wedding day, then quit to go abroad.

Revealing his plan to deceive her father was a risk. But she didn't look away. There was a frankness about him she liked. Not ungainly ambition. Just a desire for more.

"Where is it you want to go?" she asked.

"Up," he said. "Somewhere we can live together. Ideally, in a two-story house with a garden and two kitchens, one inside and another outside for frying. And for the kids, swings, a drum set, and a home movie theater. I stopped going to the movies after my father died."

He took a breath. She tilted her head and narrowed her eyes.

"I will finish my studies," she said. Jaya already had a master's degree and was writing a dissertation on industrial water analysis. She continued, "I will eat what I want. Sleep when I want. Visit my parents when I want, for as long as I want."

"Done!"

They were married a month later. Jaya looked stunning in silk and gold. Murugan's mind kept returning to the horoscope specialist. His first prophecy had come true. What about the second? *You will find a fortune in a distant country.* But what country?

If he and Jaya had been allowed to make love, he might have missed the answer. But families in Tamil Nadu separate July newlyweds to prevent their children from being born in April or May, when it's unbearably hot. Murugan was limited to chaperoned visits with Jaya at her father's house each evening. They'd sit in the living room, forbidden to hug or even touch. If Jaya giggled, her father glared. The saving grace was the *Tamil Daily News.* Murugan picked it up when the small talk ran out.

On page twelve was an ad titled MIGRATE TO USA.

He showed it to Jaya. Her eyes widened.

BUT THIS WAS too much to explain at the consulate. So he stuck to the version he'd practiced:

"Advertisement in newspaper."

The American woman set his application down, picked up his passport.

"Did you pay anyone for this opportunity?"

"Sorry, ma'am?"

"At any point in time, did you pay anyone any money for this visa, other than the filing fee?"

A pang of fear ran through Murugan. This was the question the recruiters warned him about. This was where he knew he had to lie.

Of course he paid! The American lawyer named Malvern Burnett had made it painfully clear: they would enter the US on temporary work visas, and while they were working at Signal, Malvern would put in applications for green cards. This would cost $20,000 in three installments. The first would get them on the list. The second was due before the visa interview. The third, when the visa was granted.

Murugan's mother emptied her retirement account. His aunts gave him jewelry to sell. He borrowed from his cousins and their spouses. But it was Jaya who raised the lion's share. She sold her wedding jewelry, convinced her father to lend him his savings and take a loan out on his house. A moneylender made up the gap at 3 percent interest a month.

Murugan had paid the second installment that very morning when he arrived in Chennai, in bank drafts made out to Malvern Burnett, the Mumbai recruiter Sachin Dewan, and an American labor broker named Michael Pol. Burnett was there personally at the Park Hotel, drenched in sweat as he stuffed candidates' manila folders with papers. Sachin gave a pep talk: Murugan's group was the first wave of candidates they were sending to the US Consulate. A lot was riding on them. They were scouting the terrain for hundreds more to follow.

He remembered Sachin saying that the most important thing was not to say a word in the consulate about green cards—those would come later—or the $20,000 recruitment fee. If they did, they'd be denied on the spot, their passports returned. If they were accepted, the official would hold their passports to affix the visa and stamp it later.

Murugan was terrified. But he couldn't pull out now. He was $14,000 deep in the hole. Nonrefundable.

The veins in his neck bulged with fear. The woman would see right through his lie. He could barely get the words out.

"No payment."

"You paid no money?" He could feel it: consular guards were about to snap handcuffs on him and lead him away.

"No payment," he croaked.

He held his breath. She clacked at her keyboard. Then came a whole different question.

"Are you married?"

He broke into a boyish grin. She believed him! The second prophecy was coming true. The hard questions were past, and now she wanted to get to know him personally. He'd heard this about the Americans. They asked about your personal life with ease, even in professional settings.

"Oh yes, married," he beamed. And how! The July wait was long over, and he and Jaya were making love several times a day.

"When were you married?"

"Three months," he said. It was quite a tale. An interpreter would have to be called in.

Then the woman pushed his passport back to him.

"There's no proof of marriage here."

"Proof?"

"Where's your marriage certificate?"

He stood motionless. Unbelieving. Neither Sachin nor Malvern had told him they'd ask for this.

"I can't process your application without proof of marital status."

"I don't understand," Murugan fumbled. But she was already looking over his shoulder.

"*Next.*"

BLUNDERING THROUGH TRAFFIC, crossing the bordering shanties in a daze, Murugan reached the Park Hotel. Inside the ballroom, blind from the sun, he held up his passport and gave a despairing cry. "Rejected!"

He begged to be let back in line. He could run home, come back with his marriage certificate. Everything else was in order.

But merchants don't display their rotten fruit. Malvern Burnett and Sachin Dewan had moved on, and the local recruiter who was there in their place shunned him. And what of his money, the $14,000 he had already paid them? No refunds, the local recruiter said.

Fortunes that are prophesied must still be pursued. Murugan borrowed money to camp out in Chennai. Day after day, he returned to the Park Hotel. If he couldn't count on kindness, he could make himself indispensable. When the next group of workers arrived to prepare for their own interviews, Murugan put out chairs for them to sit in. Helped collect their paperwork. Collated their files meticulously, just like Malvern Burnett had done for him.

The local recruiter took notice. He allowed Murugan to help coach the Tamil applicants. His class of students had a 100 percent approval rating.

Finally the recruiter let him get back in line. Murugan returned to the consulate with his marriage certificate, praying harder than ever.

A month later, the local recruiter called. Murugan's passport had arrived in their Mumbai offices with his US visa in it. There was a group of workers leaving next week. If Murugan could get the last installment together by then—$6,000—he could go to Mumbai, pick up his passport, and leave on the flight.

"Give me an extra two weeks," Murugan said.

"You don't have the money ready?"

"It's not that," Murugan said. "My wife and I are trying to have a baby."

"God bless! There's another crew leaving in a month. I'll put you on the list."

A month later, they still hadn't conceived. The recruiter called again. Murugan asked for more time.

"The last crew leaves next week," he said. "After that, no guarantees."

Murugan agonized.

"Go to America," the recruiter said. "Your wife will join you in nine months, and then you can have all the babies you want. Remember, no refunds."

Murugan hung up the phone.

"Jaya," he called, "Time for me to pack up."

4: Eid

Autumn 2006
Bihar, India

TWO THINGS MATTERED most to Shawkat Ali Sheikh. His word, and his God. And he knew no journey that started with a lie could ever end well. So he decided to call off his trip to America. He dialed Mumbai to talk to Sachin Dewan.

He'd never wanted to lie at the US Consulate. His conscience told him to go in and say he'd paid $20,000 for a promise of a green card and the chance to bring his family to the US. But the American lawyer Malvern Burnett said he had to tell the consulate he'd be returning to India after a ten-month temporary job. What a dilemma! The warning he remembered from Sachin pushed him over the edge: if Shawkat told the truth about paying for the visa and the promise of green cards, they might yank everyone's visas. So he did what seared his conscience. "Did you pay any money for this visa?" "No." Worst of all, he had done it at the beginning of Ramadan. What a way to start the holy month!

But now he'd correct it. He rifled through the receipts he kept in a small airmail envelope. (Thank God he'd held onto them.) *Dewan Sa'ab,* he'd say, *you enrich a poor man like me with even a glance in my direction. But I'd like to withdraw. I have the receipts from my payments, every last one. I'll bring them to Mumbai, and you can refund me the $10,000 I've paid so far.*

Sachin picked up.

"Dewan Sa'ab, it's Shawkat Ali Sheikh—"

"Who? Oh, you," Sachin said. "Your visa's ready."

"But—"

"But what? Flight to America's in three days. Get here by then with the rest of the money. Got it?"

"Yes, sir," Shawkat stammered.

"And bring an extra four hundred dollars. Last-minute surcharge."

"Yes, sir."

Click. He hung up, numb. Put the envelope full of receipts down. Took out his suitcase. Called for his wife.

"Mazda!"

"What's all this?" Mazda said. "Do you have a trip coming up after Eid?" Shawkat was heaving himself against his overstuffed suitcase, trying to get his chunky work boots to fit.

"My visa. Sachin called. I have to leave in an hour. Sit on this so I can zip it shut."

Mazda fell apart instantly. Tomorrow was the festival of Eid, the end of Ramadan, when Muslims returned home to celebrate with family. *Leaving* family on the eve of Eid? It was unthinkable! A breach of faith. Shawkat agreed. But Sachin Dewan had booked the tickets, and he wasn't a Muslim. The train ride to Mumbai was three days long. If he didn't leave tonight, he'd miss the flight to America.

"Then forget the train! Stay for Eid and fly to Mumbai the day after!" Mazda pleaded. "You want to miss your son's first Eid?" Muhammad had just turned six months old. Shawkat was desperate to spend Eid with him. But Sachin had just upped his price. They couldn't spend $120 on a last-minute flight to Mumbai. They needed every penny to run the household.

Mazda grabbed the landline. "We'll borrow from my sisters. Or your brothers. We're in debt already!"

Shawkat yanked the cord right out of the wall. He couldn't carry out the disgrace of an Eid departure in the presence of family—and Mazda knew it. She started to cry in siren-like wails, designed to attract attention. If the neighbors heard, they'd arrive by the dozens to stop him. It was the cost of being a celebrity's son.

"Mazda, enough!" He finally zipped the suitcase shut. Put on his heavy jacket and the knapsack with the money. On his way out, without knowing why, he paused to stuff the envelope receipts into his jacket pocket.

Mazda shook with sobs as she brought the children out to the living room. He kissed his daughters, five and seven, as they rubbed their bleary eyes. When Muhammad gurgled in his arms, Shawkat's heart stopped. On another Eid, he remembered, Allah had commanded Abraham to sacrifice his only son, and Abraham didn't hesitate. Shawkat must not be selfish. He handed the baby back to Mazda, picked up his suitcase, and reached for the door.

"Baba," his son said for the first time.

Shawkat held his breath. If he turned back now, he would never leave. He stepped into the night.

His eyes adjusted to the darkness as he hurried toward the station. At least there was no moon to light his fugitive steps. At the first sighting of the crescent, microphones would blare from the mosque and the streets would burst with the festival. He broke into a sprint toward the station. He was halfway there when lights flashed on and blinded him: the head-lights of a waiting car. Two figures got out: his father's best friends, come to intercept him. Mazda must have tipped them off.

"Shawkat Ali! Where do you think you're going?"

"What Muslim leaves his family before Eid?"

"You think we'd let you leave? You of all people—son of Shaikh Nazeer Hussain?"

Shawkat ground his teeth. Any other man in the village would have been able to slip away unnoticed. Why did he have to be the son of the man who foretold his own death?

RIGHT UNTIL THE DAY he died, Shaikh Nazeer Hussain had been a nobody, a poor shop owner. He made just enough to feed his family once a day. But he had his health. One day, when he was seventy, he called out to his oldest son.

"Hey, you! Ne'er-do-well who still lives at home! Give me a ride on your motorcycle."

The old man gave directions, and they arrived at a store that sold funeral apparel. He picked a pure white tunic and a shroud.

"Who died?" the store owner asked.

"It's for me," Shaikh Nazeer Hussain said. "I'm dying this Thursday at one p.m."

The storeowner was aghast. "There's a no-joke policy about death in this store! You could curse me and my business!"

"I'm dead serious," Shaikh Nazeer Hussain answered and paid his bill.

Back on the motorcycle, he gave new directions. They rode up to a coffin store.

"Can you deliver it to me Wednesday night? I'm due to die this Thursday."

The coffin seller was aghast. "There's a no-joke policy—"

"I would never joke about such a grave affair," Shaikh Nazeer Hussain assured. "Is delivery extra?"

When he was back home, he gathered his relatives and pulled out the tin trunk where he held their precious possessions for safekeeping. He handed back the jewels, the wedding clothes, the ornate boxes for Qurans. When he explained why, the children fell over laughing. The adults shook their heads. *Some jokes aren't funny.*

On Thursday at 11 a.m., Shaikh Nazeer Hussain got a touch of fever. Just before 1 p.m., he went out to the well for water. His son found him out there, collapsed, dead.

News of the old man's prophecy spread like wildfire. The Hindu merchants shuttered their stores to let his funeral procession through commercial streets. Seven thousand people came to the burial, waited for hours as the gravediggers worked. Their spades hit the roots of mango trees and milk flowed from them. Once the coffin was lowered, no amount of wood and dirt would fill the shallow. It still sinks a little, after all this time.

SHAWKAT HAD TEN MINUTES left to make the train. His father's friends were stalling him, arguing, taking turns to wear him out. They spoke in the voice of his own conscience:

"What kind of Muslim are you?"

"Think of your family."

"Your father!"

"Is this what he would want?"

The prophecy had turned his father into a local legend, but his death had plunged the family into crisis. Their little store shut down. Money ran out. Shawkat became the sole provider for seven brothers and their families. And prices were rising even in small-town Bihar. He was a welder in Mumbai, but an Indian salary was no longer enough.

So Shawkat went abroad, farther than any man from his village had yet made it. Each morning for five years, a helicopter picked him up from an Abu Dhabi labor camp and dropped him onto an oil platform in the blinding Persian Gulf. The most dangerous jobs were the ones that came with bonuses. He signed up for all of them. Anything for extra pay.

He crawled through clogged oil pipes. Pressure-tested explosive gases. One day, he nearly died testing a helicopter's emergency system. The chopper flew over the Gulf and dropped *right into* the water, with Shawkat in it. His job was to wait until the propeller slowed down, then yank the door open and swim out. He could have drowned. The propeller could have drawn him into its eddy and chopped him up. He barely managed to reach the surface to flash a thumbs-up sign. At the time he thought he was doing it all for the cash. Only later did he realize he had been grieving for his father.

His daughters were growing up now, and he needed to find a safer way to put food on the table. That's when Sachin Dewan and Malvern Burnett brought their recruitment seminar to Dubai. They offered a miraculous solution: Shawkat could go to America on a green card, and Mazda and the girls would follow nine months later. Shawkat borrowed $10,000 from friends, and the other $10,000 from a Hindu moneylender who gave him the cash wrapped in newspaper, at 17 percent interest. Yes, he had to tell a lie. And that was a sin. But it was one lie, and it let him do his duty as a father and a man.

SHAWKAT LOOKED HIS father's friends in the eye. His leaving wasn't a violation—even on the eve of Eid. It was his deepest act of faith.

"Baba would want me to go," he said. "And he'd want you to give me a ride."

Arriving at the station, his father's friends reluctantly blessed his journey.

"We've picked up so many Muslims from the station the night before Eid," one of them said. "You're the first one ever to leave."

It was true. When Shawkat boarded the train, it was empty. Through his cabin window he watched a full train arrive from the opposite direction. Hundreds of men poured out to make their way home.

Shawkat closed his eyes. His head swam with images of his father, of his son, of Abraham and Isaac. Just as the first crescent of the moon appeared, he fell asleep.

SHAWKAT FOUND SACHIN DEWAN'S MUMBAI office deep inside an industrial sprawl. The line outside was a hundred men deep. The man ahead of Shawkat was short the extra $400 Sachin wanted, and he was scared. *Wish me luck*, he said when it was finally his turn. Shawkat heard barked orders, then a wail. The man came out looking stricken. It was Shawkat's turn.

He found Sachin standing behind a desk piled high with blue passports and bundles of cash. He had a severely clipped mustache and a seemingly permanent scowl, with his shirtsleeves rolled up and his hands on his hips. *Well?* Shawkat produced his money from his knapsack. Sachin counted it all, down to the extra $400. But he was still waiting.

"Sir?"

"The receipts. The ones I gave you for the first two installments. I want them back, or you're not flying. Or getting this." Sachin held up his passport. Shawkat was suddenly flustered.

"I don't have them, sir," he blurted out, even as he felt them in his jacket's breast pocket. He didn't know why he was lying. He never would have chosen to consciously. But something in him made the words come out that way.

Sachin stared at him hard. "Yes, you do. I know your type. You haven't thrown away a scrap of paper in your life." Sachin was right.

"Yes, sir—but not here. They're in my locker in Abu Dhabi." He hadn't quit his job there, he explained, just taken an extended leave until the America thing panned out. The receipts were there, in a small air-mail envelope, along with a Quran and a prayer mat. As soon as work resumed after Eid, he'd call his best friend there, have him send the receipts to his wife, Mazda, and she would travel to Mumbai to deliver them to Sachin personally.

Shawkat's heart pounded as Sachin came around the desk toward him. What if Sachin patted him down?

"You have one month," Sachin snarled.

"Yes, sir."

Sachin had Shawkat sign an affidavit vowing he'd paid no money for the visa, then gave him his passport and dismissed him.

A different kind of man would have left blazing with resentment. But Shawkat felt only shame. He'd told the most elaborate lie of his life—without even knowing why. What kind of Muslim was he? What kind of man? Spinning a web of deceit that spanned continents, entangling his wife and his best friend.

He slipped his passport into his breast pocket. The touch of the receipts burned his fingers.

5: God Bless Malvern Burnett

October 2006
Chennai International
Airport, India

THE NIGHT FLIGHT out of Chennai was raucous with men's voices and laughter. They were America-bound. The visas stamped into their passports bore the name of their employer to be, Signal International. As the plane taxied for takeoff, they cheered. When the seat-belt light went off, men jumped out of their seats and walked the length of the plane, greeting each other like old friends. In fact, they were strangers, but their common hopes bound them. Some rang a constant peal of bells for drinks, as if they were on their way to their daughters' weddings. Flight attendants ferried shots up and down the aisles. It was a transatlantic flight fueled by elation.

Only one man seemed disconnected from the general exuberance. Aby Raju pressed his forehead to the window. His heart was still on the ground, with Bincy.

Their wedding had been transcendent. Even without gold on her, Bincy was a vision. As she walked down the aisle wrapped in six yards of cream silk, a thought needled Aby: *She doesn't know I'm going to America.* When he stepped behind her to tie the wedding pendant around her neck, he wanted to whisper to her right there the reason he had to go. It was for them. All his life he'd had to choose between being with family and providing for them. That's what it is to be a migrant worker: you leave the ones you love to help them live. In America, he wouldn't have to choose. Bincy could join him. It was the one place in the world where an Indian worker could give his family what they needed *and* what they wanted. He hoped she would understand. His welder's fingers fumbled with the golden chain and tied the knot.

Then came the weeks of post-wedding bliss. After that, Bincy's bouts of nausea, and the astonishing news that she was pregnant. He couldn't bring himself to tell her he had to leave. Finally his hand was forced. Sachin Dewan's agent called. The visa was ready. Aby had to fly the next day.

In those twenty-four hours he learned who his wife was. Another woman might have cried, raged, stormed off to her parents' house. Bincy sprang into action. She organized cash, bought a suitcase (bright red so he'd spot it at the airport), stuffed it with a new warm jacket, even packed him a Bible. The bookmark was a pocket-sized notecard with his family's phone numbers on it so he'd have them handy once he got to a phone. In the morning, when the whole family clambered into a three-car caravan, Bincy took a seat in a different car so Aby could ride with his favorite uncle. It was the uncle who stopped the car and insisted that the couple sit together. Bincy fell asleep on Aby's shoulder. The scramble at the airport kept him from saying a real goodbye. Past the glass gates, he turned to catch sight of her one more time, but she was hidden behind his taller relatives.

The thrum of the plane's engines bore into Aby's chest. He would miss the birth of their child! But next year, the day would come when he'd stand waiting in the American airport, see the top of Bincy's head rise into the view on the escalator. And then, in her arms, their baby's smiling face.

"Have a drink, brother?"

It was the man next to Aby. He didn't wait for a response. "Someone get this man a drink!"

Laughter greeted the arrival of another tray of plastic glasses, golden and glowing. Aby peeled himself from the windowpane and joined the party in the sky.

Later, as they crossed over the North Atlantic, a hush fell and their joy turned to wonder. A border was being dissolved. A new world, usually out of reach for all but the wealthiest and most educated of Indians, was opening to them. They praised God, and Jesus, and Rama, and Ganesh, and Allah. They prayed for the wives and children they'd torn themselves away from, for the parents and grandparents and cousins and uncles who'd taken on terrifying debts to launch them on their American adventure. And they prayed for another man: the mysterious American lawyer who'd somehow made all this possible. No one knew where he'd come from or how he'd pulled the deal together, but he'd been there from the beginning, from the recruitment seminars to the coaching sessions for the interviews at the American consulates and embassy. Somehow, he'd engineered their great escape from the stations of their birth, built a golden bridge to an American employer who would change all of their lives.

High above the clouds, drunk on promise, the men's hearts welled over for a man they barely knew. Aby's voice joined a hundred others:

"God bless Malvern Burnett!"

PART TWO

MAN CAMP

1: The Immigrant's Best Friend

1962–2006
New Orleans, LA

MALVERN BURNETT ALWAYS thought of himself as the immigrant's best friend. The last person you'd expect to find in federal court denying his role in one of the largest human trafficking schemes in modern American history.

In 1962, when Malvern was a young boy growing up on a horse farm in the New Orleans suburb of Marrerro, Louisiana, his family took in two refugees from Cuba. They had come as part of Operation Peter Pan, an initiative by a Miami priest, a Havana schoolmaster, and the US State Department to bring thousands of unaccompanied Cuban children to the United States. Their parents, encouraged by US propaganda, decided the threat of indoctrination by Fidel Castro's revolutionary government was worse than the pain of family separation. The US was ready to help with free plane tickets, visa waivers, and resettlement in foster homes— for 14,000 young Cubans in all.

Malvern's mother was a devout Catholic, and she answered the Church's call for the faithful to open their homes. Malvern literally looked up to the two young Cubans: he was still in grade school, while they were college-aged. They spoke no English, so "communicating with them was a chore," he would remember, but baseball bridged the gap. One day one of the Cubans hit the ball so hard that he cracked the bat. The ball rocketed off into the blue, never to be seen again.

Six months later, the refugees disappeared too. But Malvern never forgot them. He carried their memory to college in Kentucky, then the Peace Corps in the Philippines, then law school at Tulane University in

New Orleans. The year he graduated, 1986, President Reagan signed into law an amnesty for the almost three million unauthorized immigrants in the United States. Remembering his refugees, Malvern rushed to set up a one-man immigration law practice, an "amnesty business," out of his house, while still clerking for a judge. He took back-to-back bar exams in two states so he could practice in both Louisiana and Mississippi. And he waited for the flood of amnesty applicants.

It never came. It was true that Reagan's amnesty created millions of customers for immigration attorneys. But most of that business was in California, New York, Texas, and Florida. Louisiana was a tough market—there just weren't that many undocumented people. Still, Malvern doubled down on immigrants. He joined an immigration law firm to have some stability, then in the early 1990s, he launched his own firm.

In the years that followed, millions more unauthorized immigrants arrived in the US, even in the Gulf Coast. Immigrant strivers were working Louisiana's strawberry fields and digging irrigation ditches in the Mississippi Delta. The next amnesty, Malvern thought, might legalize two to three times as many people as Reagan's had. He set up shop in New Orleans's prestigious Garden District, put on his boyish, round-cheeked smile, and waited for the next wave of American generosity.

He was still waiting in 1996 when a prospective client showed up in Malvern's office who would change the course of his life. Not an immigrant. A Mississippi cop.

His name was Michael Pol. He radiated charisma and confidence. He'd been a radio jockey back in college, and was now a sheriff's deputy in Ocean Springs, on the Mississippi Coast. He had a leading man's jawline, an athlete's build, and an immigration question. He needed some Indians, the kind from India. He knew how to find them, but not how to bring them. He'd found Malvern Burnett in the Yellow Pages under *Immigration Attorney*. Could he help?

Pol was more than just a cop. He had recently been elected to the Jackson County Board of Supervisors, which gave him friends in the shipyard industry. One CEO had told Pol that he was desperate to find skilled laborers to finish a big job. The Mississippi labor pool wasn't what it used to be. Permanent workers commanded a high price. Then they got tired, got hurt, got married, wanted breaks, wanted health care— all of which slowed down production. Contract workers were unreliable, and even more expensive. By luck, Pol had a neighbor from India who told him there were thousands of welders in India who worked harder than Americans, for less. Pol sensed an opportunity: What if he became a labor broker? Bring the welders in from India, lease them out to the shipyards, and send them back when the work was done. All he needed was an immigration attorney to handle the paperwork. How soon could Malvern get them here?

Malvern broke it to Pol: *Five years.*

Pol, like most Americans, had no idea how hard the US made it for strivers to come and work. Entering as a tourist was one thing. But virtually the only way for a foreigner to work legally in the US, apart from being sponsored by a US citizen family member, was to have an employer bring you in on a green card. The wait time for that was five years.

Pol pressed on. There had to be a way. It wasn't just any shipyard that needed the workers. It was Avondale, the Gulf Coast legend that churned out tankers for World War II and icebreakers to face down the Russians. Avondale had landed a navy contract to build seven Bob Hope–class sealift ships, each the square footage of ten football fields. Bob Hope himself had flown in for a high-profile keel-laying ceremony. Now the company was under pressure to deliver, all while trying to beat back a nasty union drive. The company would pay top dollar for somebody to solve its labor supply problem. Pol wanted to be that guy.

Then, in a flash, it came to Malvern: *There might be a way.*

In the lonely decade waiting for the amnesty business to take off in Louisiana, Malvern had studied every line of Reagan's 1986 immigration bill. Deep inside it was a hidden pathway into the US, a provision that busier attorneys had ignored. It allowed employers to bring in foreign workers to fill *temporary* labor shortages. You had to prove you had searched for locals to do the work but couldn't find any. Then the government allowed you to bring foreign workers in on ten-month visas.

When the job was completed, the workers went home. Few employers had heard of these visas, known as H-2Bs. Fewer still had applied. And no one had ever tried it at Gulf Coast shipyards. But in theory, it could be done—*if* they could convince labor officials that no locals were available. Pol's eyes lit up. *What are we waiting for?*

Malvern might have done well to pause here. This wasn't even remotely what the H-2B visa program was created for. Welding at Avondale wasn't temporary work. A steady stream of navy and oil contracts made the shipyard one of the most secure sources of long-term employment in the Gulf Coast. (In fact, thousands of workers—white and African American—found their way into the middle-class through their jobs at Avondale.) And there was no dearth of locals to hire, they just didn't come cheap.

But Malvern was in a bind. The outlook for the amnesty business was grimmer than ever. Contrary to expectation, the Clinton Administration wasn't getting any closer to passing another amnesty. Quite the opposite: in Washington, lawmakers were running as far from undocumented immigrants as they could. That very year, 1996, Clinton had signed an immigration bill with the harshest penalties ever for the undocumented, and a provision that even made certain *legal* immigrants deportable.

And it was about more than the money for Malvern. He was born to help strivers find their way to America. Pol wanted to bring in 450 of them. This might be Malvern's chance to serve his purpose.

On most days, the two men would be on opposite sides of America's immigration debate: a liberal attorney and a Mississippi cop. Today, they had a deal.

Could he do it? Pol would remember Malvern's answer as firm and clear.

"Absolutely," said Malvern.

MALVERN DEVISED THE REQUEST for the H-2B welders, using the magic words—a temporary, short-term labor need—and sent it to Washington. While the labor officials mulled it over, he and Pol dashed off to Mumbai. There the duo became a trio. Pol's Indian neighbor connected them to a Mumbai labor recruiter named Sachin Dewan.

Sachin wasn't just any recruiter. He was the scion of the first family of Indian labor suppliers. His father had built an impressive business exporting Indian laborers to build oil rigs in the Middle East. Now Sachin filled Mumbai banquet halls with skilled prospects. Malvern and Pol pitched the American opportunity, and the price for the candidates: a thousand dollars. Malvern wasn't sure they would go for it. But they did, by the hundreds. Malvern submitted their applications to the US Embassy with bated breath.

Sachin had Malvern and Pol over for dinner. The Americans marveled at Sachin's retinue of chauffeurs, live-in servants, and cooks. The men gave each other nicknames. Malvern and Pol called their swashbuckling host "Mafioso." Sachin dubbed Pol, the grimly handsome cop, "Gunwala," the guy with the gun. And Malvern was dubbed "Chacha," the rumpled, affable uncle.

Malvern expressed his astonishment to Sachin: India was a poor country—how had the candidates coughed up a thousand dollars apiece for American visas? Sachin let his partners in on a secret. Indian families stored away savings over generations, waiting for that elusive once-in-a-lifetime opportunity. For many, even a ten-month visa was worth a big chunk of savings. For a really big prize, a green card, say, they might come up with far more.

THE GAMBIT AT Avondale worked. Labor officials approved 450 H-2B visas. Michael Pol cleared $1–2 million, and paid Malvern $100,000–200,000. Back in New Orleans, Malvern was stunned at his success. He had found a key to the golden door that more celebrated attorneys had missed. Thanks to him, 450 souls had reached America.

An epiphany brightened his office. Malvern had been waiting for Congress to pass another amnesty so undocumented immigrants could be his clients. Now he had stumbled onto a new business model, in which his clients weren't just the immigrants—they were the companies looking to bring in temporary workers. Gulf Coast shipyards were humming with the news: Avondale had Indian welders building warships three times faster than Americans, *at a third of the price.* Soon, they'd all want Indians of their own. Malvern could help the shipyards, and the strivers, and make a living—a win-win-*win*. He got ready to file the next round of H-2B applications. Pol opened a new labor recruitment firm with the grand name Global Resources, and started to reach out to Avondale's competitors, asking if they wanted their own Indian workers.

But there was a problem. The secret pathway Malvern had found was now visible to every two-bit immigration lawyer in the bayou. Fly-by-night attorneys came out of the woodwork to offer shipyard companies cheap foreign workers. Some were even applying for H-2Bs for jobs that didn't exist. It was a feeding frenzy. The sudden rush raised red flags in Washington. Labor officials threw all the applications in the trash—including Malvern's pristine ones. Plus the unions jumped into the fray to cry foul. Clinton's labor officials responded with Malvern's worst nightmare: they shut down the H-2B program for the shipyards altogether. If there really is a labor shortage, they said, the solution is to train more locals, not to bring in foreigners.

To lose his new business model overnight—and to be lumped in with fraudsters! He, who'd been inspired by refugees all his life. He, who'd always tried to do right by the strivers. There was nothing to do but wait for his next break.

Five years later, in 2001, it seemed to be at hand. The tide was turning in Washington. President George W. Bush was promising an amnesty *and* an expanded H-2B visa program. That Easter, Malvern prayed for immigration reform. By September, Congress was ready to vote on Bush's proposal.

Then Osama bin Laden intervened.

Every American felt the shock wave. Immigration became the proverbial third rail of American politics: if you touch it, you die. Amnesty was off the table. Malvern had spent his best years—fifteen of them—waiting for his big chance. He was forty-five now, and it had never seemed further away.

Malvern kept an eye on Washington. One day, in 2003, there was a development. Companies that wanted foreign workers on green cards had to wait five years. For most companies, and most workers, that was way too long. But Congress was rewriting the rules and changing the waiting period from five years to two. This new policy was called PERM. Malvern called Pol. Would companies go for it? Pol thought so, and soon found a few who wanted in. Malvern thought back to what Sachin had said that night in India: for the right opportunity, Indians would pay much more. What if the opportunity was a green card in two years? Would they pay? Sachin thought so. He took out blaring ads in the big Indian papers: PERMANENT LIFETIME SETTLEMENT IN USA FOR SELF AND FAMILY.

The trio was back. They went on a recruitment tour that raced from Mumbai to Kochi to Abu Dhabi, where Indian guest workers were employed in big numbers. Throngs of welders and pipefitters crowded wedding ballrooms to watch the trio's Power Point and listen. In two years or less—maybe as little as nine months—they'd have green cards to work at American shipyards. The price: $10,000. The Indians stared. Malvern stared back.

Over 150 of them signed up. A million and a half dollars for the trio to split three ways.

A YEAR LATER, Malvern was speeding forward on open water, his future stretched out like the bright blue sky. He was sailing in the Regatta al Sol, a boat race from Pensacola to Mexico's Isla Mujeres. The PERM candidates' installment payments were rolling in while they waited for their green cards. Malvern had new offices in Gulfport and Bay Saint Louis. He and his family were living in the kind of house they'd dreamed of, blocks from the beach in the Mississippi hamlet of Waveland, nestled among majestic live oaks.

Malvern took a midsea phone call from his office. A young associate of his was leaving to start her own firm. This wasn't a small thing. This associate had accompanied Malvern on the India trip, so she knew the high price he and his partners had charged for the PERM applications. She also knew that Malvern hadn't yet submitted those applications to the government. He couldn't have. Because the PERM program *didn't yet exist.* Congress was *considering* the PERM program but hadn't yet made it law. After paying $10,000 for a promise of green cards in as little as nine months, the Indians were likely to be waiting three years or more. The clock hadn't even started running.

But Malvern wasn't about to reverse course. The new PERM rules were bound to pass soon enough. He'd take on extra help to rush the applications. All would be well. Malvern sailed on, wind in his face, eyes squinting into the brilliant blue.

IN LATE AUGUST 2005, a warm wind rose out of the Bahamas. It grew into a small frenzy in Miami, tearing up trees and killing two people. Exhausted but not extinguished, it lurched west, managing to reach the Gulf of Mexico. There it drew strength, gained speed, got a name. On August 29, 2005, Hurricane Katrina trained its eye on Waveland, Mississippi. Malvern evacuated his wife, Maureen, and their three children north to Lafayette. But Malvern's mother-in-law insisted on staying in Waveland. She was seventy-six, and still worked at Walmart. "I'm not leaving, even if it's a Category Ten," she declared.

When Malvern and Maureen returned in the wake of the storm, the town was a flattened wasteland, covered by thick black mud that felt like concrete. Katrina had lifted homes right off their foundations, flung casino barges into streets, torn caskets out of cemeteries, ripped seacoast oaks out by their roots. Maureen, drenched by rain, ran up to a group of rescue workers.

"My mother, we saw her red Ford Focus under the house," she said. "She might still be alive. We heard knocking."

The rescue workers climbed a pile of debris to reach a roof that lay flat in the middle of Grosvenor Place—no longer with a house underneath it. Maureen caught sight of her mother's dog, Buddy, tangled in branches. The rescue workers untangled him and Maureen scooped him up. "Buddy, you're a miracle," she said. Then the workers noticed a body. They led Maureen away before turning it over. It was her mother.

The destruction was total. On top of the family tragedy for Malvern and Maureen, their dream house by the beach was gone, along with everything they possessed. Malvern's Mississippi office had been destroyed. His main office in New Orleans, on the first floor of a thirteen-story building, had been flooded. Washed away in Katrina's waters, along with everything else, were the unfiled PERM applications.

One night soon afterward, Malvern's phone rang. He answered barely knowing where he was. He'd been in a fog since the storm, his memory and his will both shattered. He slept on a couch in his New Orleans office three nights a week. On weekends he joined his family in Lafayette, where they'd fled. The friend to refugees had become a refugee himself.

"Chacha!" cried a familiar voice.

It was Mafioso—Sachin Dewan, calling from Mumbai. He had been trying to reach Malvern for weeks. He was worried sick. But Malvern was alive, by God! What a relief. And now: What was the update on the green cards?

Malvern mumbled that Katrina had blown away the applications.

Applications?

Malvern came out with it. Although they had collected money from the applicants in 2004, he hadn't submitted the first green card application to the Department of Labor till June 2005. When Katrina hit on August 29, most of the applications had been still sitting in boxes. In offices that were now destroyed. In towns that were washed away.

But why, by God, had Malvern waited so long to file?

Well, to start with, the PERM program had only gone into effect in March 2005. Malvern had been preparing to file soon after. He had even brought in two contract lawyers from India on temporary visas to help. They were gone now too, having fled during the storm.

Sachin was aghast. In India, the pressure kept rising. Nearly two hundred welders were calling his cell phone every day, clamoring for their long-overdue green cards. These men weren't lawyers who worked things out with words. They were industrial welders with powerful fists. How on earth could Sachin tell them their green card applications had been submitted a full two years later than they were led to believe—and the green cards were still years away?

Some of them stopped paying their installments. Others were demanding their money back. When Malvern heard this, he was furious.

"Mafioso," he fired off in an email. "Tell them to pay up or we will substitute for willing candidates. Why can't you make the dolts under-stand? Confused and pissed."

Sachin met with a group of workers in Kochi to relay the threat. "A complete disaster," he reported. The men's frustration boiled over. One worker lost it, screaming that he'd stop payment on his checks and use the money to take out a hit on Sachin. Shaken, Sachin started to pay the workers back out of his share of the payments, and asked Malvern and Pol to pitch in. They never did.

But Malvern and Pol only grew closer. They commiserated about losing their homes. They still called each other by their Indian names, Chacha and Gunwala. One dark day, Malvern emailed Pol a link to a video game from Resist.com, the site of a group called White Aryan Resistance, or W.A.R. The goal of the game was to shoot immigrants as they tried to cross the border.

Would the immigrant's best friend of the pre-Katrina years even rec-ognize the man who sent it?

Pol loved it. He emailed back a review: "Funny as hell."

While Malvern was just trying to get through each day, Michael Pol kept pounding the pavement. One day in early 2006, he called Malvern with news: he'd found a potential new customer. Malvern was already in the process of tracking a slew of new green card applications he'd submit-ted to replace the drowned ones. He was also navigating FEMA and the insurance companies to get his house fixed up. But Pol described a juicy prospect: a rapidly growing oil rig builder called Signal International. Pol had a connection with the top brass going back to his old days as Jackson County supervisor. They had ambitious new management, a load of new contracts, and a shortage of workers after Katrina. They were desperate for welders and pipe-fitters. Pol believed they could sell them on PERM. It might just be what saved them.

Malvern agreed to take the meeting.

THE SHELL LANDING Golf Club sprawled over 120 acres of emerald wetland. Thickets of savanna pine lined the fairways, and swamp maples grew wild. Sandhill cranes walked the grounds in gangly strides. But

Malvern barely registered the enchantment on his way to the meeting. He was still in a fog. His memory wasn't what it used to be. Psychologists were calling this malaise "Katrina brain." Pressed by his family, he was seeing therapists. But part of him suspected he'd never feel normal again.

In the Opus Restaurant on the golf course grounds, Pol made the pitch. Indians, the kind from India, doing repair and conversion on Signal's oil platforms, faster, cheaper, happier than Americans.

The Signal International reps were thrilled. When could the Indians start?

It used to take five years to get them in, Pol said. But now they could come in two.

The company officials traded glances. Signal was already stalled on an upgrade of a set of massive oil rigs. Plus there were other contracts coming in to build new rigs from scratch. This was dirty, dangerous work, and they needed the workers for it yesterday. Wasn't there a way to bring them in quicker?

A memory broke though Malvern's Katrina-brain fog, of the trio's first big score at Avondale with the H-2B guest worker visas. Then the Department of Labor had shut shipyards out of the program. But that was ten years ago, under Clinton. After Katrina, the Bush Administration had relaxed every rule in the book to help businesses get back on their feet. Most labor regulation was suspended. There might be a new opening.

Malvern spoke up. If two years was too long, how about six months? Not for green cards, but for what were called guest worker visas, meant for companies with a temporary need. The company officials listened, but pointed out that their need wasn't temporary. They needed these workers to stay at least three years.

Malvern regained his old deftness as he outlined the plan. The company would have to start by certifying they needed the workers to fill a one-time, short-term need. And they wouldn't be able to apply for green cards concurrently, as that would contradict the company's own claim about temporary need. But what they could do was get the temporary visas *first*, and fast. When those temporary visas ran out, they could apply for extensions. And *after* that, when the extensions ran out, Signal could sponsor green card applications for the workers it wanted to keep. Best of all, it wouldn't cost the company anything up front.

There was just one catch. Malvern didn't say it like this, but for it to work, everyone would have to lie. The company would have to tell the Department of Labor its need was only temporary. Malvern, Pol, and Sachin would have to promise all the workers green cards to get them to pay. The workers would have to tell US consular officials in India that no one had ever promised them green cards—let alone collected hefty fees for them—and that after a ten-month tour of duty, they'd be coming home.

All Malvern said at the meeting was that the temporary visas would be the way in, and after that, he'd help Signal keep the workers they wanted. The company reps picked up the lunch tab. Pol and Malvern had themselves a deal.

It was a risky play. Labor officials might buy it. But if they did, and the workers came, another feeding frenzy would follow, just like it had after Avondale. Malvern warned Pol and Sachin in an email that their new plan was "quite possibly a one-time deal. After all the copycats and fraudsters come out of the woodwork, it will likely shut this process down for India for another 6–10 years."

They'd also be setting off a time bomb. H-2B visas were ten months long and could only be extended for eight months after that. So eighteen months from the day the workers arrived in Mississippi, everyone would find out what Malvern already knew: H-2B visas, by law, could never turn into green cards. The workers would have to return to India even to apply for them. Those applications would take years. Workers who didn't leave the US voluntarily would be deported. Signal's oil rig work would come to a standstill. Once the operation was revealed, it could never be repeated.

But it didn't need to be. Signal International wanted five hundred workers. And Sachin thought they could charge candidates $20,000 apiece. After costs, there would be close to $10 million dollars for the trio to split. The score of a lifetime.

Signal signed a labor provision contract with Michael Pol's company on April 18, 2006. The wording made it sound like an employer's dream come true: "The purpose of this Agreement being, to join together competent Foreign Workers and a US employer for the mutual benefit of both. . . . Global will be responsible for all costs related to the recruitment, transportation, and entry of the 'H2B' and/or 'permanent resident' workers. . . . Global will deliver, at no cost to Signal, the 'H2B' and/or 'permanent resident' skilled Foreign Worker to the airport nearest the city that Signal chooses. . . . Upon the expiration of the authorized period of employment . . . Signal shall have no further obligation or responsibility for the Foreign Worker."

Three trips to India, hundreds of applications, and a flood of recruitment-fee checks later, Malvern got the news that the first group of Indian workers was about to land in the US. A Signal VP named Bill Bingle was on his way to pick them up at the airport.

2: Giani

October 2006
Pascagoula, MS

ON OCTOBER 31, Giani Gurbinder Singh and twenty-nine other Indian men stepped off a plane and into a place called Mobile. Supposedly, this was America. But the airport was puzzlingly small. The man who greeted them at baggage claim was white enough; his name, Bingle, did sound American; and he put them on a first-world-looking bus. This was all reassuring. But as they rode into the dead of night, they were confused. Where were the skyscrapers? The shopping malls? Hours later, the headlights lit an iron gate. It opened. The bus rolled up to the edge of a sea of darkness. They could barely make out the silhouettes of trees.

"Giani," whispered another man, Ranjit, "You sure we're in America?"

Giani, the older of the two, advised calm. "Let's pray that we are."

Bingle led them through a yard to a trailer on stilts.

"You'll sleep here," he said, opening the door. It was fitted with partially constructed bunk beds, missing some mattresses and bedding.

Ranjit, who spoke a little English, approached the American with the question on everyone's mind. "Good evening, sir," he said. "Green card processing okay?" But Bingle just squinted at the words, as if they were in a language he'd never heard. He shrugged and left.

The men unrolled their mattresses. Ranjit insisted on making Giani's bed. It was the least he could do for his guide. Ranjit and five of the other men were Sikhs. "Giani" was Gurbinder Singh's title, not his name. "One with knowledge," an honorific for priests. Sikhs revere their gianis.

While Ranjit and others fussed with his sheets, Giani undid his turban, combed his long hair, and brushed out his tangled jet-black beard.

Before he went to bed, he fixed a picture of his guru on the wall, a man with a beard like his own.

THE HORNS OF SHIPS swelled and woke the men. Giani emerged from the trailer to survey the grounds. In the morning fog lurked a scattering of other trailers: three more for housing (still vacant for now), one with bathrooms, one with washers and dryers, plus a built-out trailer to serve as a cafeteria, and another as a TV room. The facilities were closed in by a chain-link fence with barbed wire on top. Giani and Ranjit walked the perimeter. On one side of it were the company's main offices. On the other was a giant gate with uniformed security guards at a station, separating them from the world outside. A billboard next to it said something in English: MAN CAMP FACILITY.

Walking farther along, they saw a flag billowing. It was the stars and stripes.

"It's America after all," Giani said.

A COMPANY MAN issued them badges and shoes, IDs and bank accounts, took their pictures, took measurements for uniforms. But he didn't say anything about the green cards. Neither did the safety officer who came to speak to them at noon. Instead, he demonstrated the use of a pair of scissors, as though snipping the invisible ribbon of some new public venture.

"What's he saying?" Giani whispered to Ranjit.

"How to shave your beard."

"Ah. Well, not me," said Giani. The safety officer demonstrated the use of an aerosol canister.

"He says that to report for duty, we have to shave."

"I'm not shaving," Giani whispered, definitively. "Sikhs are forbidden."

"Not here," said Ranjit.

A COMPANY MAN arrived at Giani's trailer. Ranjit interpreted.

"Work starts at six a.m. tomorrow. Get yourself shaved by then."

Giani was shaken but stood his ground. He'd simply need to explain to this man. Three hundred years ago, the peaceable Sikhs were fighting off religious persecution in Punjab. Their embattled saint, Guru Gobind Singh, baptized five young disciples. One by one, he brought them into his tent, beheaded them, grew their heads back, had them drink holy nectar. And he made them vow to wear unshorn beards. Sikh men have kept their beards ever since. In contemporary times, younger Sikhs like Ranjit, who left India to become migrant workers, would shave to blend in with other Indians. But Gurbinder Singh wasn't an average Sikh. He was a giani first, a welder second. His holy vows were ironclad. Besides, he'd worked in plants all over India, and his beard had never been a problem. On the contrary. Back home, Giani was an itinerant welder-mystic, employed as a builder, but also venerated as a spiritual guide. Sikh workers would ask him to officiate their weddings. Sikhs in management would call him in from work to help inaugurate new construction projects.

But this history, brisk as it was, surpassed Giani's English. "I don't shave," he said instead. "It's my religion."

The company man's weary look worried him. If only there were an intermediary, someone trusted by the company, ideally from India, who could intercede for him.

"Come with me," said the company man.

Lo and behold! Sachin Dewan, the recruiter Giani had met in Mumbai, sat in the cafeteria, as comfortably as if this were his office.

"Giani," he said, using the honorific. "They told me you won't shave."

Giani started in: perhaps if Sachin explained to the company men the significance, and the origins, of the custom . . . Sachin cut him off.

"You want to work? You'll have to shave. Otherwise, you'll be sent back to India."

"I can't shave. You know that," said Giani.

"Your choice."

He left Giani alone in the cafeteria, staring into a flickering TV.

Back in the trailer, Giani passed on Sachin's words to Ranjit. Ranjit felt awful for Giani. He gathered the others, and they begged Giani to see reason. *Think of your father!* His father had never wanted him to come here. Giani had recruited village elders to prevail on him, and eventually convinced him to sell their farmland to raise the money.

"You want to squander his sacrifice?" the others said. "Work. Get your green card. Then grow your beard back!"

It took them hours to convince him. Giani left the trailer and locked himself in the bathroom, company-issued scissors in his hand. But he couldn't meet his own eyes in the mirror. His hands hung at his sides, leaden. *Arise,* he commanded. They refused. He tried cajoling. *One step at a time. Take the scissors. Tilt your head back. Lift the bristly bush like you're releasing a bird. Then bring the blade to your neck.*

Giani came back out, his face twisted with a coward's shame. The beard still hung impressively, untouched.

"Giani!" the others cried, exasperated. "It has to be done!"

"Then one of you will have to do it," he said.

All their sureness vanished in the shadow of sin. They looked away. No Sikh would cut Giani's beard. No Hindu, either. Nor any Indian Muslim, or Christian.

Finally, in the next trailer, a man named Yeshwant Ghadge, a welder from Pune, agreed to do it. He wasn't easy to convince, but Giani flung himself at Ghadge's feet. By cutting his beard, he said, Ghadge would be saving his life. Ghadge prayed to Krishna for forgiveness. Scissors in hand, he led Giani into the bathroom. Giani's streaming tears moistened his beard and made it difficult to cut.

That night, Giani lay sleepless, feeling the strange cold on his face like a reproach. He stared at the image of the saint he had hung on the inside of his lower bunk. It was Baba Deep Singh on horseback, sword in his right hand, and his own decapitated head in his left. In 1721, Baba Deep Singh was battling marauders who had desecrated the Golden Temple. When an enemy soldier beheaded him, Baba Deep Singh managed to catch his own head. He held it up, using his eyes to see, and kept on fighting. That was courage. Where was Giani's?

He decided to call home. He would tell his father. The company had set up pay phones outside in the muddy yard and issued them phone cards. Giani dialed. His brother answered. Giani told him what he'd had to do. His brother was quiet for a moment.

"Don't call here again," he said, and hung up.

3: Signal

October 2006
Pascagoula, MS

EVEN BEFORE THE Indian workers started arriving in Pascagoula, John Sanders's job at Signal International felt special. Maybe that's why he kept a diary about it.

Sanders was the man camp manager, and his early diary entries were triumphant. "I've already saved the company $3 million dollars," he wrote shortly after Signal hired him that summer. "Nothing like having an immediate impact and putting the cash right where the senior executives want it most—into the bottom line." He had found an alternative contractor for the housing trailers that saved Signal $3 million. His boss, Ronald Schnoor, clapped him on the shoulder and said, "Well, it looks like you've earned your salary!" Sanders beamed. "This will help immensely with salary negotiations down the line," he wrote. In the meantime, he was working twelve-hour-plus days to get the labor camp built before the workers started showing up in October. Without the diary, it would all have been a blur.

Sanders came to Signal International by accident. He had been in Pascagoula doing post-Katrina relief work when he heard that an oil platform builder was looking for a project manager for a very special project: building and managing a labor camp for four hundred Indian workers. (Signal had a second site in Orange, Texas, where there would be another one hundred Indian workers.) How often do you get to work on something like that? Sanders didn't have much experience with man camps, but he did have an MBA from Columbia University, and that helped win him the job.

Signal was one of the biggest oil-platform fabricators in the Gulf, and it was growing fast. They'd started out repairing old oil rigs. Now they were getting contracts to build new ones from scratch—no wonder they couldn't bring in workers fast enough. Everything feels different at a company that's on the rise. The electricity, the possibility. Sanders heard the whispers that the company was on its way to an IPO—one that would make Signal's CEO, Richard Marler, a very rich man.

Still, Signal felt like one big family. They had company picnics where Mr. Marler and Mr. Schnoor and the rest of the top brass were right there with their wives and kids, joking around with the shipyard workers like they were old friends.

Every family has its quirks, of course. The way people talked in Mississippi was . . . different from what Sanders was used to. It wasn't like there wasn't prejudice in Michigan or Massachusetts—or at Columbia, for that matter—but there were still moments at Signal that caught him off guard.

Like in August, when Sanders was trying out Indian food vendors for the soon-to-arrive workers. He let one candidate wheel his cart of sample dishes through the executive hallway. That earned Sanders a talking-to from the CEO's secretary. Sanders was "Mortified," as he told his diary that night.

He caught that same sense of—was *disgust* too strong a word?—when he talked to one of Signal's welding and pipefitting testers who had gone over to India to test the candidates. Sanders asked him what it was like. "[He] told me about India and how it's like another planet," Sanders wrote, "Teeming with hordes of poverty-stricken people clogging chaotic streets and smelling like a hot, humid combination of incense and sweat."

Then there was the name he heard Signal staff using for the labor camp once construction started: "The reservation." A cheap "Indian" joke. "Quite a sense of humor they have," he told his diary.

What was no joke was the site Signal picked to build the worker housing: a big muddy expanse contaminated with toxic levels of lead from an old bayou-dredging project. Not the spot Sanders would've chosen, but

Signal's in-house director of environmental health and safety told him not to worry: they'd lay a "clay cap" on top of the site to keep the lead from poisoning the workers. The housing trailers would be elevated on stilts, as would the walkways between them.

But then there was the question of installing bathrooms for four hundred men. That would require a dedicated sewage lift station, and *that* would require digging down into the clay cap. And a kitchen that could cook for four hundred men would need one hell of a grease trap, and that would mean digging into the clay cap too. Could they be sure they wouldn't breach it? And how were they going to get the okay from the Mississippi Department of Environmental Quality? But Signal's safety director said everything was good to go. (Much later, Sanders would learn that the safety director hadn't even applied to the state environmental authorities for approval until months into construction.)

It was a mad rush to set up the camp. But when the Indian workers finally started coming in October, they made all the hassles of the previous months worthwhile. Sanders felt an instantaneous bond with them—the same way he had with the Africans he'd met after college, when he worked on a charity hospital ship off the coast of Ghana for seven months. Even when he couldn't understand the Indian workers, he loved their big grins, their hopefulness. And even though, being in his midthirties, Sanders was younger than many of them, he felt like an older brother to them. Maybe a trusted uncle. And, he hoped, a friend.

As camp manager, he was their go-to guy for any issues they might have. He liked to stroll through the camp after hours to chat. Ask them how work was going. Give them friendly warnings that they'd be punished for drinking in the man camp.

It wasn't long before they came to him with a concern he never expected. They were all anxious to hear about the progress of their green cards.

Green cards? thought Sanders. *What green cards?*

4: The Mix-Up

November 2006
Pascagoula, MS

THE INDIAN WORKERS kept coming in waves. On his first day, still jet lagged, Shawkat Ali Sheikh was put to work repairing a massive ocean oil rig that had come in after thirty years at sea and was docked at Signal's deepwater harbor. His crew was assigned to clean the pontoons, the hollow steel balls that help rigs float. As Shawkat crawled into the greasy, dark pontoon, the rig bobbed with the water. He felt like he was inside the bowels of a living, breathing beast.

When Aby Raju arrived, he was taken not to Signal's Pascagoula facility, but hours away to the second yard in Orange, Texas, where he was placed high atop the leg of an oil rig being built from scratch. "For George Bush," his American supervisor said.

Murugan was sent to Texas as well and set about building miles-long mazes of pipe to exacting specs.

By the time Hemant Khuttan arrived in Mississippi, the man camp had grown to accommodate hundreds of men. But only Hemant could have shown up with a problem like this.

He'd applied to Signal as a welder. He was trained as a welder. He had worked as a welder. (As long as he'd worked at anything.) But just days before he left India for a Signal welding job, one of Sachin Dewan's men told Hemant there were no more spots open for welders. Hemant's mind reeled. *What do you mean? I paid you $20,000! My dad took out a loan against his pension!* Don't worry, Sachin's man said. We'll put you down as a pipefitter. *But I'm not a pipefitter,* Hemant protested. *They're different jobs. I don't have the training. Pipefitters do a dozen things welders don't.*

Sachin's man shrugged it off as though it were the slightest triviality. *If you want to go to America, get on the plane and figure it out there.*

It was the first thing Hemant planned to do the night he arrived in Pascagoula, just as soon as he dropped off his bags. As he edged his way along the metal walkway that connected a long row of trailers, he glanced at the faces of the men going the other way, alert for any sign of authority or sympathy, the look of someone who could set him back on the right path. But in the Mississippi dark, the most he could make out on their faces was exhaustion.

He reached the housing trailer he'd been assigned for the night. He opened the flimsy door, expecting there might be a temporary trailermate inside. Instead, there were more than a dozen men, scrunched up on bunk beds packed so close there was barely room to squeeze between them.

Well, he thought, determined not to play the privileged policeman's son, *I can stand anything for a night.* Tomorrow he was sure he'd be taken to a proper American apartment before the start of work. Plus, a few of the faces in the trailer were familiar ones: North Indians he knew from Delhi, men who had come a few weeks before. Surely they could help him figure out his pipefitter mix-up.

"How are the apartments here?" Hemant asked, as he did his best to fold his frame into a bunk. All at once he felt how tired he was from the travel.

"Apartments?" came the puzzled answer.

When they understood his mistake, they howled with laughter. There were no apartments. This sardine-can trailer wasn't a temporary stop for the night. It was his new home.

THE NOISE WAS NEVER-ENDING. The trailer wall was only inches from his head, and as substantial as tinfoil. The clanging and craning and drilling of the night shift echoed from the work site. His trailermates snored and muttered in their sleep. When his bunkmate turned over, Hemant's bed shook. At 4 a.m., just as his exhaustion started to overwhelm his nerves, the night-shifters started streaming back to their trailers. Their safety boots clattered along the metal walkway like hammers on steel. The ones with cell phones bellowed into them right there on the walkway, as if their voices had to carry all the way to India. The snatches of conversation that reached him from the Hindi speakers kept returning to green cards. Always green cards. *Where are they? When will they come? No one can tell us.*

He finally dozed off for a moment—only to be awoken around 5 a.m., when his trailermates rose for the day. They had to: that's when the line for the bathroom started. A hundred groggy men waiting to get into the lone trailer with toilets and sinks. Then the line for breakfast. That was the longest one, because the whole day depended on it: you not only needed to grab your breakfast and wolf it down there in the cafeteria, you needed to pick up your lunch from the buffet counter. (He heard the grumbling of the earlier arrivals as he did: *Rice again.* Some days it was parboiled and hard, some days overcooked into a tasteless gruel, but it was all they ever got.) Then you hurried back to the trailer to change into work clothes and safety boots in time to head to the work site.

On top of all of that, Hemant had another morning stop to make: at the administrative line to sign his start-up paperwork. But at least there he could explain to them the job role mix-up. They would sort it out quickly enough. The last thing a big American company would want was a welder masquerading as a pipefitter.

The line to sign the paperwork was nearly as long as the others. When Hemant reached the front he was surprised to see not an American employee of Signal, but another Indian worker, a man named Gaurav. His face was hard, contemptuous. As he pushed a stack of papers forward, Gaurav's look didn't say: *What can I do for you, brother?* It said: *I'm on the company side, and you're not, so don't waste my time.*

Hemant tried to describe the mix-up anyway. Gaurav wasn't interested.

"If you want to work, sign the papers." When Hemant persisted, Gaurav cut him off: "I'm not your foreman. Talk to him. Now are you going to sign or not?"

There were dozens of pages, all in English. Hemant could read them, but he'd need time.

"Look at the line behind you," Gaurav barked. "It's simple: if you want to work, you sign."

It didn't feel right, but what could Hemant do? If he didn't sign, he'd never get to the foreman. No foreman, no solution; no solution, no job. He remembered why he was here. After all the times he'd tested Shruti's faith in him, he was in a place where he could finally make himself worthy of her. He couldn't afford to fail. So he signed.

He joined the crowd of men speed-walking from the man camp to the East Yard, ten minutes away. There he joined another line for the punch-in gate. The Indian faces mixed with white and Black American ones, with Puerto Ricans, Mexicans, Laotians, Central Americans. Above them loomed the rigs.

They were breathtaking. The East Yard was a private Signal dock on the Pascagoula River. Floating on three huge platforms on the river were three oil rigs: two new ones being built from scratch and a third being repaired. Hemant had never seen anything like them. They were carbon-steel monsters, each the size of an eight- or ten-story building. Big enough to hold dormitories, rec rooms, laundry facilities, dance halls, pool tables. All for the offshore oil workers who would eventually travel out to them by helicopter, once the rigs had reached deep-water drilling sites.

Work on the three rigs required a thousand-strong army of welders, pipefitters, structural welders, structural fitters, plumbers, electricians, concrete pourers, sandblasters, and firewatchers, all organized into dozens of crews, crisscrossing each other throughout the day. Hemant and the Indian workers would make up nearly half of the total. That is, if Hemant could find his place.

The men were broken into work crews for their 6:30 a.m. safety meeting. As the American foreman of Hemant's crew detailed the day's work, Hemant's anxiety mounted. They would be crawling down inside the columns—the legs of the rig under repair—to cut away sections of steel that had been corroded by the salt water and replace them with clean steel. Life-or-death work in a crawl space. Filthy. Smoke-filled. Caked in grease. With no room for error.

The meeting ended just before 7 a.m. The crew headed toward their rig. Hemant's stomach churned as he approached his foreman. He was a white American man, and he met Hemant with a smile—something he didn't do with other Indian workers. (Even Americans weren't immune to Hemant's movie-star looks. In the Signal admin office, there would soon be a nickname for him: Hollywood.) But the foreman's smile didn't make it any easier to find the words for the absurd revelation: Hemant Khuttan the pipefitter was actually a welder.

The foreman frowned.

"Look," he said. "You seem like an easy guy to get along with. It doesn't hurt that I can actually understand what you're saying." Hemant was gratified.

"But here's the thing," the foreman continued. "I bring this up to management now, they're going to send you right back to India."

In a flash the scene played out before Hemant's eyes: financial ruin for his family, disgrace for him—and the loss of Shruti's love forever.

"So, you know," the foreman said, scratching under the band of his hard hat, "You might want to find a way to make it work."

HEMANT FINALLY HAD time for a call with Shruti the next day, in the bleak predawn before his shift. She was overjoyed to hear his voice.

"How is the apartment?" she asked brightly.

"First-class, fine, fantastic," Hemant said.

"Good enough for me to join you there, or will we be moving?"

"Oh, it's a start," he said. "A bachelor pad."

"You sound groggy. Are you getting enough sleep?"

"Probably just the jet lag," he said. There was a pause. She could always see through him.

"So how's work?"

"Just fine," he said, as brightly as he could manage. "Speaking of which, I have to go to start my shift." Painful as it was to tear himself away, lying to her any more would be worse. "I'll call you as soon as I can tomorrow," he said.

"I'll sleep with the phone by my side," she said.

5: Rot

November 2006
Pascagoula, MS

JOHN SANDERS WAS trying to keep everybody happy. Really he was. But the Indians weren't making it easy.

One day they were complaining about the food. Next it was the housing. Then overflowing toilets. Then moldy bread. Broken showers. Wet floors that stank like petri dishes. It seemed like every contractor and sub who'd built the camp had cut corners. "We have serious, endemic plumbing problems in the trailers," Sanders wrote to a coworker. "Behind the walls, under the sinks, in the drains—everything is wrong. Pipes can be pulled apart by hand. Showers leak behind the walls, saturating sheetrock, rugs, and wooden subfloors with water. Light pressure on the walls leads to them crumbling in certain places, and the wood will soon begin rotting as well."

The place was falling apart—and so were the workers. "Our Indians have been dropping with sickness like flies," Sanders wrote in his diary. One of them got double pneumonia. Another broke his ankle. Another got a staph infection so bad he nearly had to go to the ER. Somebody else did go to the ER, with what wound up being a viral heart infection that nearly put him in cardiac arrest.

Sanders's diary took a confessional turn: "The Indians are getting worried and believe there are unhealthful conditions in the camp. It is true. The reason is because the plumbing was so shoddily done [that] water has leaked everywhere and stagnated as a result, which serves as a bacterial breeding ground. As I was out at Bunkhouse 16 today, one of the workers came up to me and said many of them are getting sores they had not had before. Even myself, I have noticed between today and yesterday that a couple of pimples have broken out on my legs which appear to have a black center. I suspect it may be a staph infection. It is a very serious matter, most of all because of the impact it will have on the Indians' morale if it continues."

Strange to say, amid the rot and poison seeping through the camp, the workers' biggest complaint was the wait for the green cards. When the new waves of workers showed up, it was the first thing they asked about. Sanders just shrugged. Green cards weren't his department. But then one day, he took a trip to see the second Signal camp in Orange, Texas, and met a worker named Aby Raju.

Aby was sure of himself and spoke a bit of English. And he dropped a bombshell. He told Sanders he'd paid $20,000 for the promised green card. Said his parents put their home in hock to raise the money.

Sanders said it couldn't be true. Aby went trailer to trailer, pulled other men out, translated for them and insisted that Sanders listen. Worker after worker said the same thing: $20,000, ancestral land sold, money borrowed, loan sharks looming.

Finally Sanders understood why they were all so agitated. He knew the recruitment trio of Burnett, Pol, and Dewan—part of his job was liaising with them. Turned out the trio had been lying to Signal all along. They'd said the workers had paid just $2,000–3,000 each in recruitment fees to come. Sanders confronted Dewan in an email.

"Complete bullshit," Sachin wrote back. But Sanders felt it in his gut: this many workers couldn't be lying.

On top of that, Sanders now remembered the other signs that the trio didn't seem to be on the level. Michael Pol had rubbed him the wrong way from the beginning. The first time they met, over Chinese food in a Pascagoula mini-mall, Sanders recalled Pol asking him if he could steer Signal's gravel-buying contract to a friend of his who was a vendor. It was like something out of a mafia movie. Then they got to the real topic of business, the catering to keep the workers fed. Instead of Signal paying an Indian caterer directly, Pol wanted them to pay *him*, then *he'd* pay the caterer—after taking a little off the top for himself. When Sanders tried to negotiate on price—which was his job, after all—he remembered Pol slamming his fist on the table and shouting: "If I'm going to be involved in this, I'm going to make some money at it!" Never in Sanders's professional life had someone talked to him like that.

Then there was the way Malvern Burnett intervened when Sanders wrote to Senator Trent Lott's office asking the senator to put in a good word on their work visas. Sanders mentioned what Signal had said a hundred times: they would need these workers for two to three years minimum. Burnett emailed Sanders: "We do not want to publicize the fact that Signal may have a need for temporary workers for the next two or three years because it could jeopardize the granting of temporary work visas for the requested ten-month period." Was Burnett telling him to lie to an elected official? "No, we're going to say exactly what the issue is," Sanders answered. "We're going to be transparent and forthright."

Now it wound up that this trio had charged the Indian workers *ten times* what they claimed for the right to come work here. And for some green cards that Sanders knew next to nothing about. Signal hadn't hired an Ivy League MBA so he could run to his boss whenever things got sticky. But Sanders also knew when a problem was over his head. So he went to see Mr. Schnoor.

RONALD SCHNOOR HAD a don't-waste-my-time glare and spoke with the slight growl of a former three-pack-a-day smoker. He had a general picture of what life was like in India—from where exactly, he couldn't say—and it wasn't pretty. People living in trash heaps. Scraping by on dollars a day. Eating that food that had you running to the toilet every ten minutes. Here the Indians would be making ten, eleven times what they did back home—even while Signal would be paying them a fraction of what local contract workers would've cost. The Indians should have been over the moon.

Plus, Signal had rolled out the red carpet for them. They'd plowed $7 million into building those labor camps. (True, $3 million less than they would have if not for John Sanders. Bright kid, even if he was a Yankee.)

"All they'll have to do is roll out of bed and walk to work," Schnoor wrote to CEO Richard Marler. Come to think of it, the $35 a day Signal planned to charge the workers for room and board was probably too little, Schnoor said. Why not make it $53 a day instead? "I would think they'll be happy campers."

Marler nixed it, for whatever reason. Some people don't know a good idea when it bites them on the elbow. If Schnoor had been CEO . . . hell, he *had* been CEO of Signal back when it was called Friede Goldman Offshore. But Friede Goldman had gone bankrupt in 2001. A private equity firm out of DC called ACON Investments snapped it up, reconstituted it as Signal International, and named Marler CEO, while Schnoor took a demotion to SVP.

Then the boom times started. Hurricanes Katrina and Rita created a whole world of new opportunities repairing oil platforms in the Gulf of Mexico. By 2006, Signal had all the work it could handle, and two thousand full-time employees. It was positioned, as a breathless feature in *Offshore* magazine put it, to "capture the Gulf." The private equity boys who owned Signal were so excited, they were talking about launching an IPO. The only problem was finding enough workers. The hurricanes had chased away too many locals. Contract workers cost a fortune, and they had gone from 10 percent of Signal's workforce before Hurricane Katrina to 40 percent after.

Hence Schnoor's excitement when his old pal Michael Pol offered him five hundred hardworking Indian welders and pipefitters at a fraction of the cost of locals. There were no up-front costs to Signal to get them.

There was that one red flag. Someone from Signal had to travel to India to explain to the US consulates why Signal needed so many foreign workers. Bill Bingle went, and the lawyer, Burnett, told him he had to say that Signal had a "one-time temporary labor need" for just ten months. Well, that just wasn't true. Signal needed the Indians for at least two to three years—the good ones they'd hang on to as long as they could keep them. Signal might even want more down the road. If Bingle told the consulates the opposite, wouldn't he be lying to the US government?

Burnett told Bingle not to worry: that was just the way the process worked. But Bingle said it didn't feel right. What did Schnoor think?

Well, Schnoor had plenty of other things to worry about. Like five hundred jobs that had to be filled ASAP. Like $7 million sunk into a labor camp that nobody was living in yet. If the lawyer says that's how it goes, then that's how it goes.

Next thing Schnoor knows, Bingle is shuttling workers in from the airport. So far, so good.

Except here comes John Sanders saying the workers are all hot and bothered about their green cards and the money they paid for them. It was time for Schnoor to call that old pal of his in for a come-to-Jesus.

Schnoor sat Pol down and said he knew Pol had lied: the trio hadn't charged the workers $2,000–3,000 apiece; they'd charged $15,000–20,000. No bullshit—he'd seen the receipts. Now they were going to pay the workers back at least half of what they'd overcharged them, or else. Signal couldn't have its labor providers charging the workers five to ten times more than they claimed. And they couldn't have these Indians doing more whining than they were working because they'd paid so damned much to come here.

Pol was stunned. He'd walked in there expecting congratulations on a job well done. He told Schnoor $2,000-3,000 had been an off-the-top-of-his-head estimate, and that had just been what *he'd* planned to charge the workers—what Dewan and Burnett charged was their business. And refunds? Pol stuck out that big square jaw of his and refused. Well, that was his right. And it was Schnoor's right to fire his ass.

As for the lawyer, Burnett . . . that was a little stickier. Schnoor didn't understand all the nuances, but he knew these temporary visas the workers came on would have to be renewed at some point. Then somehow converted into green cards. Burnett had the paperwork, the know-how, and the relationships to do it. Without him—and that Dewan fellow in India—Signal was sunk. They'd not only lose the Indian workers who'd already arrived, just one-third of the total, they might never get the other two-thirds they'd contracted for.

In other words, the lawyer had him by the short hairs. So Burnett would live to fight another day. Burnett refused to refund any of the workers who'd already arrived, but he said he'd try to work out a discount on some of the ones who hadn't come yet.

In the meantime, Schnoor sent Sanders back to the workers. *Start acting like adults*, Sanders told them, *or we're going to shut down the camp.*

6: Tea

December 2006
Pascagoula, MS

FOR JACOB JOSEPH KADAKADAPALLY, it all started with a cup of tea.

He had arrived in the third wave of workers, flying from Kochi to Mumbai to Dubai to Houston to Mobile, Alabama. At baggage claim, a Signal company man named John Sanders greeted him and the thirty other Indian arrivals that day. Sanders was boyish, earnest, like someone Superman saved in an American comic book. He led them to a van parked out in the dead of night. Cramped and cold, knees pressed against his bags, Jacob drew strength from the thought that when he reached Pascagoula, he'd have a cup of tea.

Outside in the still-dark morning the next day, cold hands balled in his pockets, he stood in line behind a hundred others. To brush his teeth. To use the toilet. To shower. To collect his phone card. To call his wife from the man camp's pay phone.

"I'm safe," he told her.

"Did you eat?"

"Yes."

"Did you rest?"

"Yes."

"All well with the green card?"

"Yes."

Then he stood in the next line, for paperwork. When it was his turn, he started to skim the sheaf of documents. But company staff pushed him along, saying there was no time for hundreds of men to read each one. He signed, trudged on like a sleepwalker.

His trance-like state lasted until the next morning. In the cafeteria, just before dawn, he suddenly became aware of his body again. He was staring into a Styrofoam cup. Something wasn't right. What was he drinking? It was cold down his gullet. He had been drinking the only thing the company provided—milk from plastic bottles, chilled in a bucket that leaked water from the card table to the floor. He never got his cup of tea! The deprivation stirred his consciousness into mutiny.

Hell is three days without tea.

He found John Sanders and requested tea. He was rebuffed. He asked again, each day, sometimes several times a day. At the morning safety meetings, he asked the safety manager to put a word in with Sanders "Regarding the tea." In the workshop, when he punched in and punched out, he asked the foreman to remind the safety manager to tell Sanders that "Tea is not yet provided."

A week later, Sanders had had enough. Jacob found tea bags and hot water on a card table in the cafeteria. He sipped the malty brew, savoring his victory. Then he thought about what he needed next.

It was midwinter now. The men worked outside. By lunchtime, the rice they were given would freeze. The men defrosted it by sucking on it. They were going to sleep hungry and waking up ravenous out of dreams of fish curry and goat stew. In the morning, as they dressed, they asked each other what they'd had for dinner in their dreams. But it was no laughing matter. Already a man had fainted from hunger atop a thirty-foot scaffold while he was fixing the leg of an oil rig. He could have fallen to his death.

Jacob hounded Sanders until he relayed his newest request up the company ladder. A week later, the company installed microwaves in the metal workshop. Jacob pressed for something better. Sanders came back with another concession. The Indians could choose a cook from among them. They elected a man from Kerala. He commandeered the kitchen, doing his best with the rations the company provided. There was daal for breakfast. Chicken for lunch.

Jacob: 2—Sanders: 0.

Jacob allowed himself a moderate celebration. From a hideaway bar tucked in the ceiling of the trailer, he pulled out a bottle of whiskey. He had smuggled it past security inside his boxers on his way back from church. He shared it with his roommates, who raised their Styrofoam cups to him and wished him luck.

"For what?" he asked.

"For your next meeting with John Sanders."

"Regarding?"

"Our green cards," they said. "May God grant you all the English you'll need."

7: The Secret Catholic Church

January 2007
Pascagoula, MS

JUST DAYS AFTER Jacob Joseph took on the green card complaints as his latest assignment from his bunkmates, I started getting the calls from distressed Indian workers. A week later I stood at the back door of the Sacred Heart Catholic Church. Having expected three Indian men at most, I found myself staring at nearly a hundred, without a clue who they were or what they were up against.

I drew on my anxiety for momentum, bounding into the room with the energy of an insurgent candidate. The men returned my greetings with solemnity. Some touched their hearts with their palms after they shook my hand. From the front of the room I met their eyes, searching for a knowing smile or a secret signal from my caller. But he had either decided to remain anonymous or not to attend—in the sea of faces there wasn't a flicker of recognition. Most of the men were dressed in collared, half-sleeved shirts, crumpled as if they had slept in them. Most looked bedraggled and exhausted. A few were actually asleep and were now being nudged awake by their neighbors.

"Namashkar," I pronounced for the Hindus. "Salaam walekum," for the Muslims. "Sat Sri Akal," for the Sikhs. "Jai Masih ki," for the Christians. The men stared back at my great sincerity. Some smiled weakly. Many had their arms folded across their chests. Awkwardness is an occupational hazard for organizers in the early stage of a new relationship. I launched into my speech.

"I'm a labor organizer," I began in Hindi. "I work to protect workers from around the world who have arrived to the Gulf Coast in the aftermath of Hurricane Katrina. Workers like you."

Usually when I spoke to new groups of workers, I came in with some research about their company so I could help them make sense of their employer's place, and their own, in the economic order of things. Here, I didn't even know the name of their employer. I wove some basic questions into my prepared speech—where did they work, how many of them were there altogether—but the answers left me increasingly disoriented. I fell back on generic pronouncements and the catechism of my trade. I would do everything in my power, not *for* them, but *with* them. Teach people to fish and they'll eat for a lifetime. Teach them to fight the fishing company, and one day they'll own the means of production.

When it was over, they stared like I was a dud firecracker flaming into failure. I was afraid they'd get up and leave. Then someone said in broken Hindi, "Can you do that in English?"

The room churned as I started over from the top. Most of these men were from Tamil Nadu and Kerala, and their Hindi, if any, was far thinner than mine. Those who knew English interpreted my words into Tamil and Malayalam. When my speech crawled to completion, one man, seated to the right, spoke in English.

"So can you help us?"

"What can you do about the food?"

Another man answered: "Use the microwave."

A third said: "This is a big man, a lawyer. You're asking him about the food? The real problem is the green cards, not the food. What can you do about the green cards?"

I tried to take the issues in order. I explained that the reason the food was bad was because of the power relationship between them and the company. That was the deeper issue. Now if we organized—

"What can you do for us?" asked one man in the back, loudly.

Another answered in my place, "Absolutely nothing!"

I lost control of the room. The meeting broke up and the men streamed out. I had nothing to offer them.

AS I SAID GOODBYES and shook hands where I could, I noticed one man lingering behind the others. I wondered if this was my contact, the one who called me. He waited till the others were out the door to approach me.

"Good speech, Saketji," he said, hooking the respectful suffix to my name with a self-possessed smile. This wasn't my contact. That man spoke Hindi, had very little English, and was North Indian. This man was from the South, with English as clipped and neat as his mustache. He introduced himself. Jacob Joseph, from Kerala. A pipefitter. A Roman Catholic. A husband and a father of two. His half-sleeved red shirt was perfectly pressed. I wondered how he managed that in the cramped, filthy camp the others had described. He was holding a bright manila envelope made of laminated hemp.

He started by solving one immediate mystery for me: How had so many men managed to escape the labor camp for this meeting? He explained that the men were allowed out of the camp on only two occasions: on Sunday mornings, for church, and on company-supervised trips to Walmart every week or so.

He spoke simply and frankly, but the very fact of his staying behind to speak with me while the others hurried back was reason for me to be cautious. In these repressive immigrant labor camps in small Southern company towns, the few immigrant workers who spoke English were the only ones who were in a position to talk directly to their employers. They would translate their employers' barked orders and often become loyal to them. When other immigrant workers started organizing, it was often the English-speaking workers who would give them up.

"I wish the speech had been more successful," I said, guarded.

"They are not angry with you, Saketji," he said in a forgiving tone. "It is their own tension."

In India, the word is deployed to explain away distress. It's imprecise, which is exactly its advantage: *tension* helps maintain strategic ambiguity around difficulties that might threaten one's social status or respectability. No need to specify a terrible diagnosis, or a depleted libido, or a cash flow problem. Whatever your affliction, you can simply call it "Tension."

"And do you share their tension?" I asked.

"Very much," he said gravely.

"Jacobji," I ventured, "Your tension—how did it start?"

It started, he said, with a cup of tea.

As he told me the story of his skirmishes with John Sanders, my suspicion fell away. I understood now why he was talking to me, risking interrogation from the guards back in the camp. Each night in his trailer, the others asked if he had an answer from Sanders about the green cards. Men from other trailers were coming to him too, for "any update." Jacob had none. But he had to offer something. He invited them in, poured whiskey. The liquor coaxed confession. They had all persuaded their families to put the farm in hock, or sell the house, or take wedding bangles and bracelets to the market—all so they could go to America. They'd planned to pay off their debts in a year. Now, banks and loan sharks were about to call their notes due. If the green cards weren't assured . . . the men trailed off. Up in his top bunk, Jacob lay under the weight of their disclosures. Now their burdens were his.

"That's a lot of responsibility," I said.

"They'll ask again tonight."

"What will you tell them?"

He smiled broadly. "That I do have an update. I met a man. I have given him our case. His name is Saketji. Pray for him!"

"Jacob, let me stop you right there. I don't know what I can offer you yet."

He pulled his passport out of his shirt pocket, held it open.

"They told us, 'You will come on this visa. Then we will apply for your green card.'"

"This is an H-2B visa," I said. "These don't turn into green cards."

His self-assured mask melted. He reached back into the envelope, pulled out a photograph, and pressed it into my hands.

"My daughters," he said. "That is Donna. She is five. This is Donya. She is three."

"Jacob," I began. He interrupted, implored.

"You will do something. You must. Because I can do nothing. I am lost."

He took my hands in his. Just then the door opened. Light flooded in. A white woman in her Sunday best stared at us, nonplussed. Her eyes blinked beneath her wide-brimmed hat. Mass was over and she needed to set up for brunch.

I searched for something innocuous to say while she was in earshot. I asked Jacob where he learned his English. In seminary, he said. Years ago, before he was a pipefitter, he had wanted to be a priest.

Outside in the parking lot, Jacob glanced over his shoulder for company men and their wives coming out of Mass. I looked for the other Indians. They were gone.

"You should head back," I said. "Everyone else is back at the camp."

"Saketji, can I tell the men you'll help us?"

"I'll do everything I can," I said. "Meanwhile, you keep doing your part."

"What else can I do? I got tea and bread. But what they really need, I can't give them."

"You already are. You're listening to their fears. Admitting you have your own. Keep doing that. Go to them at night. Trailer by trailer. Ask them how they are. Tell them: however cramped you are, and unclean, and lost, you're good men. Keep the faith."

"Like a priest," he said.

"Yes," I said. "And Jacob—you can be sure that the company is watching you. Be very careful."

"I will, Saketji."

We embraced. He left.

I FELT IT as I drove away: Jacob was carrying the burdens of his coworkers, and now I was carrying his. Donna and Donya, five and three, were watching me with pleading eyes.

After nightfall, I stood across the street from Signal International's infernal gates. I imagined Jacob in there, lying in his top bunk. Propped up on his elbows with his hands clasped in prayer. Tonight, he must have been praying that I would have something to offer.

Something he'd said in our meeting haunted me. He was describing how guest workers transferred from one company to another in other parts of the world, and asking whether it were possible here. But the way he phrased it in his particular South Indian English, the question became a far deeper one.

"In Dubai, in Bahrain, in Baku, we know how to get free," he said. "But how to get free in America?"

8: Winter

February 2007
Pascagoula, MS

JOHN SANDERS COULDN'T catch a break. The complaints kept coming. Especially from that darned Jacob Joseph.

Sanders knew the workers were drowning in debt from the crazy recruitment fees. (At least Michael Pol was fired over that—Sanders didn't shed a tear to see him go.) And he understood why the workers were anxious to get their green card applications moving. It was the only thing that would justify all the money they'd laid out. To understand them better, he even rented the movie *Green Card*, in which an uptight Andie MacDowell marries a roguish French waiter played by Gérard Depardieu so he can stay in the US. (Talk about an odd couple!)

But all that was no excuse for bad behavior. One day in December, things got out of hand. As far as Sanders could determine, some workers showed up for dinner late and got shut out of the dining room. They were so upset, they dragged the caterer out into the hallway and started beating him senseless.

Sanders knew he had to step up. Mr. Schnoor was depending on him. So he called a community meeting. "I was very firm with them," he told his diary that night. "I told them they must act like adults and that there would be no next time: we would shut down the camp."

He didn't like making threats, but everybody needs a little tough love sometimes. "This sort of thing helps me earn their respect, because they see I care a lot about them."

How much did he care? To celebrate Christmas, he gave them their first real taste of American life. For their souls, he took them to a

Pentecostal church service. For the other part, he took them to Bourbon Street. Some workers ended up at a strip club called Barely Legal.

All he wanted in return was respect. But some of them just wouldn't get the message. Especially Jacob Joseph.

To remind them who was in charge, Sanders and the company lawyers wrote up a new set of housing rules: no more drinking in the housing trailers. No more moving furniture from room to room. No visitors in the man camp, period. First violation costs you $250, the second $500. Keep it up and we'll evict you.

But the troublemakers wouldn't let up. By February, Sanders was hearing rumors that Jacob was holding union-type meetings. Maybe even talking to lawyers.

He gritted his teeth and went to break the news to Mr. Schnoor.

To his surprise, Mr. Schnoor already knew. Sachin Dewan had an inside man of his own in the camp, a guy named Gaurav. Dewan had been in touch directly. And Mr. Schnoor was taking it very, very seriously.

Because if restless workers were a nuisance to Sanders, to Schnoor, they were a threat. If this thing blew up on them, Signal would have five hundred unfilled jobs, plus a $7 million hole in their pocket from the man camp. Not to mention that a major workforce disruption could threaten the entire IPO. Signal would go from sitting pretty to leaning off the edge of a cliff.

The troublemakers had no idea what was coming.

9: Captives

March 9, 2007
Pascagoula, MS

BRELAND BUFORD WORKED as a guard at Signal International through a private security contractor. The morning of March 9, he woke up at 4:05 a.m. and struggled out of bed—all six-foot, one-inch, 315 pounds of him. (Even in an industry of big guys, he was the biggest guy he knew.) Anybody would have a rough time getting up before dawn after finishing last night's shift at 11 p.m. But just as Buford had been looking forward to sleeping in, he got a call from Ms. Killeen from Signal's front office. She might have been the most beautiful woman Buford had ever seen in real life. Just the sound of her voice turned him from a twenty-one-year-old man to a weak-kneed boy. She asked him if he could come in for an overtime shift the next morning, starting at 5 a.m. His roommates, too. Buford was on the fence until she said, "We're going to need some muscle." Just you try saying no after that.

Buford's roommates, Trent and Van, worked security at Signal as well. It was still dark when they pulled up to the Signal gates. They were met by Assistant Camp Manager Darrell Snyder. (John Sanders was off that day.) Darrell was a piece of work. Buford remembered one of the first things he ever said to him: *If you ever shake hands with the Indians, you better wash your hands—they don't use toilet paper.* Snyder seemed to think that was hilarious.

Darrell briefed Buford and the other two on the "operation" that was about to go down. He showed them photographs of five of the Indian workers. They were going to round up these men and send them home to

India, Darrell said, and the men were not going to be happy about it. *It could be easy, or it could get real ugly.*

Darrell's eyes were gleaming, and his voice had an edge that Buford didn't like. Buford had gotten to know a bunch of the Indian workers during his year at Signal, and he liked them, felt bad for them even—packed into those trailers like sardines.

But work was work. Darrell told Van to stay outside and man the gate. Trent and Buford were coming with him. They'd round up the five troublemakers and hold them in the community room (a trailer with a pair of TVs) until it was time to take them to the airport and put them on a one-way secret-police-style flight.

The camp was already buzzing when they started their search: men emerging from their trailers, clomping their way up and down the scaffolded walkways, getting ready for their morning shift in the predawn darkness. But as Darrell started waving photos in people's faces, blinding them with his flashlight beam—*Where is this guy? What about this one?*—the strangest thing happened: the whole camp went quiet.

The workers Darrell approached just stared. The sharper his questions got, the blanker they looked. Buford would have rather been anywhere else in the world when Darrell started shouting, veins bulging.

This is America!

IT WASN'T A NOISE that woke Jacob Joseph—it was the silence. As he sat up and tried to understand whether he was dreaming, another worker who lived in his trailer burst in. His name was Sabulal, and he had arrived to work at Signal in the same wave as Jacob. He was from Kerala as well, not far from Jacob's hometown. In Mississippi, they became bunkmates, and Jacob helped Sabulal navigate the company's paperwork. When Jacob went to John Sanders to ask for tea, a microwave, and other improvements, Sabulal was his wingman. Now Sabulal was rambling in a sharp, scared whisper. Something about guards outside and flashlights. They were coming for Jacob, Sabulal said. And for him.

"Stay here," Jacob said. "Stay calm. Let me wake myself up and we'll figure it out."

At the sink at the end of the trailer, he washed himself awake. He had to get out there, find John Sanders, and clear this up. Sure, Jacob had been bringing complaints. But that was no basis for termination. And this was no way to carry it out. As soon as he calmed Sabulal down, he'd go out to talk to the guards.

A terrible wail came from the far end of the trailer. Sabulal lay crumpled in a pool of his own blood. His hand held an industrial blade. He had used it on one of his wrists.

Jacob carried his friend out into daybreak. An already-swirling commotion now swarmed around him. One Indian man pulled his shirt off, ripped it, bandaged the wounded man's arm. Another called an ambulance. Some others carried Sabulal away. Still more surrounded Jacob, asking him if he knew what the guards wanted. He had no clue. Then an American voice cut through the whirlpool.

"Jacob. Come with me." It was Darrell Snyder. Darrell led Jacob into the community room. Good. Now they could focus on helping Sabulal. But Jacob would need his cell phone to call the injured man's family. He told Darrell he'd be right back—he needed to get it from the trailer. But Darrell shut the door.

"Jacob, you sit right here," Snyder said matter-of-factly. "We're sending you back to India."

Jacob's eyes darted across the room. It was about the size of his living room back home. Two couches. On one of them, three other Indian men he didn't know. Frozen in terror, facing the same sentence. Near them stood a security guard, an enormous hulk of a man. Back to India?

"I would like to know the reason."

"We don't need a reason," Darrell said. "There's a flight today. You'll be on it."

Guards would collect Jacob's belongings from his trailer. Darrell would be back in a few hours to drive Jacob and the other deportees to the airport in Mobile.

"That is not going to happen," Jacob said carefully.

He knew something Darrell didn't. Somehow, before he'd left his bunk, he'd known to hide his passport in the pillow of the bed next to his. Without it, he couldn't get on a plane. He prayed the guards wouldn't think to look there.

On the other side of the locked door, Jacob could hear a roiling protest. The other workers were gathering, calling his name, louder and louder. They started banging on the door.

Darrell stared Jacob down. "You're going home, Jacob. You're done." Then Darrell noticed the door being pulled open from the outside. He yelled to the guard.

"Hold that fucking door!"

BUFORD GOT THERE just in time to yank it back shut. He could barely hold on to it. There must have been a hundred men out there, and they were furious. The commotion was terrifying. He'd been in bar fights, the kind where you throw a few fists to loosen up and buy each other beers afterward. But a hundred men—they could literally tear you apart.

Then he heard a voice he knew on the other side of the door, pleading from the middle of the crowd. His buddy Trent. Holy shit.

It was like opening the door on a hurricane. It took all Buford's strength to keep a grip while Trent squeezed his way inside, eyes wild with fear—bodybuilder Trent, tatted-up Trent, shit-kicking good-old-boy Trent—then he and Trent both had to pull as hard as they could to fight the door back shut.

Through the roar shaking the flimsy trailer walls, Buford could barely make out Darrell shouting: "Don't let go of that fucking door!"

THE CALL JOLTED me awake before dawn.

"Hang on," I said, sitting up in bed. "Slow down. Start from the top."

The man on the line was a Signal worker, so agitated I'd missed his name.

"The company has taken some of our men," he said. "They locked them in the community room. There are guards inside. Not police. Company guards."

I pulled on a shirt, stepped onto the cold floor through my trouser legs. I didn't know this man. I had probably given him my business card at the Sacred Heart Catholic Church. To give advice, I needed to know more. I needed to talk to Jacob Joseph.

"If they're locked up, then the company is getting ready to deport them," I said.

A pause.

"To send them back to India."

The guards had stormed in with flashlights, he said, checking their faces against pictures. Whose pictures? He didn't know. They pulled a few men out of bed. In one trailer, a man became desperate. He slit his wrist.

"My God," I said. "Where is he now?"

"In the hospital." He didn't know which one. He was with the others, gathered right outside the door of the community room. "We are thinking that we should not work until they are released. Can they send us to India for that?"

It was possible. The company might punish solidarity. But the only possible protection was in acting together. I told him the company could deport five men. It was harder to deport five hundred. A labor action would give them some small modicum of legal protection. More importantly, it would slow down whatever the company was planning.

With my phone lodged in the hollow of my shoulder, I typed out a petition addressed to company officials, demanding they release the imprisoned workers. I read it to him. He gave me permission to put his name on it, and gathered others to add theirs. I woke up reporters, attorneys, and coworkers as I leapt into a car.

I was five hours from Pascagoula. I dialed Jacob. If the men were planning to refuse work, he would have to act as the on-site organizer, keep morale high, and negotiate the release of the ones in the community room. I could walk him through it on the phone. I dialed again. No answer.

"JACOB! CALL OFF your guys!" Darrell yelled. Men were beating on the sides of the trailer with their fists. There were hundreds of them now.

Jacob looked at his warden. *My guys?* Then he understood.

He walked to the door, which jumped in the hands of the security guards at each tug from the men outside.

"Brothers!" Jacob called, in Malayalam. The commotion died down enough for the men to hear him. "They're sending me back to India."

"We're here," they shouted back. "You're not going anywhere."

"What are they saying?" Darrell barked. Jacob paused.

"I hid my passport in Saji's pillow," he said to the men, still in Malayalam. "It's my freedom. Don't let them take it."

"Say no more," they said. "We found it. We have it."

"Very good," Jacob yelled back. "Now, shake the door. Vigorously. But carefully. Not enough to break it. If you damage their property, they can charge you with vandalism."

The door rattled hard. Darrell's eyes widened.

"They are upset," Jacob said to him. "Be prepared to defend yourself."

"Call them off! We'll fire them! We'll call the police. Let me out!"

"I'll see what I can do," Jacob answered in English. Then, in Malayalam: "Louder. More menacing."

A roar came back. The bigger guard looked at Darrell with desperate eyes.

"I might convince them," Jacob said to Darrell, "*If* you promised to come back with the company president. So I could speak to him directly."

He saw Darrell's mind race. "I can get you a vice president," he said.

They had a deal. Jacob leaned against the door again.

"Great work, brothers," he said in Malayalam. "Now ease up. Let him through."

The men backed away. Darrell slipped out warily, rushed through the tunnel of accusing faces.

While the door was still open, someone handed Jacob his phone. Then the guards pulled the door back shut.

A prisoner again, Jacob sat back down at the card table. He had to call his wife and break it to her. Their American venture was about to crash.

But there was another call that he had to make first. He dialed. Got a shaky connection.

"Good morning, Saketji," he said. "How are you?"

"JACOB," I CRIED. "Thank God! The men inside the community room—how are they?"

"There is tension, Saketji. They will send us to India today."

Only now did I realize he was one of those marked for deportation.

"Saketji, there is one more problem. It is Sabulal. He was very afraid, and—"

"I know. I'll call the hospitals and track him down. What about you? What's happening there?"

"One vice president is coming to talk to me."

If Jacob had become enough of a problem for a VP to come down, then there was hope. Maybe an opening.

"What should I say in the meeting?"

"Your leverage is the men outside. The vice president needs them to get back to work. You need to use that to get what you need. What time is the flight to India?"

"I don't know. Soon."

"Everything depends on you missing that flight. Stall. And get him to admit that you are being deported for organizing. That's what we need: time and an admission that this is punishment."

"Where are you, Saketji?"

"On my way. But I'm four hours out."

JACOB CALLED HIS wife next. He spoke briefly, briskly, like he had when they'd first met through a marriage broker. Ten minutes into the meeting, she had agreed to the marriage, with two words: *Let's proceed.* It was the same two words when he showed her the American ad.

Now, after he told her he was locked in a room and set to be deported, she asked, "How shall we proceed?"

Jacob told her he was about to make his case before a vice president. In the meantime, the other men were refusing to work. There were almost three hundred of them gathered now, chanting, singing, taunting the guards.

"Listen," he said, holding the phone up.

But the men outside had suddenly gone silent. The door opened, and Jacob saw why.

A police officer walked in, gun on his belt and fingers in his belt loops. Darrell was right behind him.

"He's the guy?" the policeman asked Darrell.

"That's him."

"I'll call you back," Jacob told his wife. He tried to stand, but his knees were rubber.

Then another man came in, the kind you never saw on the rigs, in rolled-up shirtsleeves, trousers, and expensive shoes. He introduced himself.

"Bill Bingle, VP."

He and Darrell sat at the card table with Jacob. The officer stayed at the door.

"So, you're Jacob," Bingle said. "Ready to go?"

"Sir," Jacob said, his mouth dry. "I would like to know the reason."

"We both know the reason."

"I have a family," Jacob said. "Think of them."

Family. Yes. Bingle had two families. His own and this company. And Jacob had acted against the company.

"Absolutely not," Jacob said.

"Why've you been inciting them all, then?"

"*Requesting*, sir! For tea. For food that doesn't make us sick."

Problems like that you keep inside the family, Bingle said. But Jacob hadn't. He'd gone to outside groups. Involved others.

"I only want what's best for the company," Jacob said.

"Jacob, we're not dumb. You're drawing workers into complaint after complaint. Stirring up unrest."

"And that's why you're sending me back?"

"Yes," Bingle said.

Jacob sat back. He had the admission he needed.

Bingle turned to Darrell, "Let's get them to the airport."

Darrell checked his watch and cursed. They were already too late to make the flight. And back in the trailer, Signal staff still hadn't found Jacob's passport.

Darrell sighed. "They'll have to go tomorrow," he said.

A NEW RUMBLE came from outside the TV room. The men had been on strike for five hours. They needed to get back to work. One of them called to Jacob: "Brother, what's happening?"

Jacob examined his options. Signal was the only place he could work legally, and there was no way they would keep him. But he couldn't let them deport him. That would mean defaulting on loans, losing the house.

He had to escape. Hide, lie, work. Until he could make back the fortune he had borrowed. Then, and only then, could he even think about going home.

He faced his captors.

"If you let me go," Jacob said, "I will talk to the men. Tell them to get back to work."

"Let you go where?" Bingle asked.

"Out. Anywhere. America. To work. I can't go back to India."

"There's no way," Bingle said. He had his instructions, and they didn't involve letting Signal workers on Signal work visas slip away into the void. But now he stared into his own dilemma. If he kept Jacob till tomorrow, the strike would likely continue. Production would be stalled a full twenty-four hours. They'd fall way behind. On a $300 million contract. Not the kind of thing his boss Ronald Schnoor would easily forgive.

"Who knows what'll happen tomorrow?"

They were all surprised at the source of the voice. It was the police officer. He was leaning against the door, hands on his hips, chewing gum.

"Say, for example, you put him up in a hotel tonight, and take him to the airport tomorrow. Who's to say he'll be waiting when you pick them up in the morning? Who's to say you even remember to pick him up?"

Bingle blinked. If he let Jacob escape now, wouldn't he be illegal?

For the first time, the officer's eyes met Jacob's. Jacob watched the man's jaw work, like a buffalo's. The officer shrugged again.

"He wouldn't be the only illegal in Mississippi."

I PULLED UP hours later. Signal's gates were shut. Jacob was gone. A contact of mine had picked him up and driven him away to safety. A small group of reporters were still outside, with cameras. I'd alerted them to the showdown in Pascagoula, and they had come all the way from Jackson, three hours away.

I launched into an explanation of what had happened. It was important that they report a point of view other than the company's. One reporter complimented my American accent and asked where I was planning to go next. I explained to her that I wasn't one of Signal's Indian workers—they all lived inside. In a labor camp on company property, locked behind those gates. Which was just one example of what was wrong with the temporary worker programs that Congress intended to expand.

"The illegals get free housing?" she asked.

A WEEK LATER, Jacob called. I started at the sound of his voice.

"Saketji. How are you? How's New Orleans?"

"Very good," I said. I wasn't entirely lying. It was a splendid March Sunday. The smell of grilled meat mixed with trombone sounds over Esplanade Avenue. But I was facedown on my couch with the blinds shut, still reeling from the events of the previous week.

Organizers fail, most of the time. The veterans tell you that victory is scarce. You don't take defeat personally. You take the blows. Keep moving. To be honest, I always found this advice difficult to follow. When past campaigns had failed, I *had* taken it personally, probably more than I should have. But I always managed to peel myself off the floor. What choice was there?

This failure felt different. Before Signal's crackdown, I had just been starting to get my head around what the fight there might be—an organizer's heaven-sent, once-in-a-lifetime dream of a campaign. A company worth hundreds of millions, whose customers included global oil giants and defense contractors, running its business on foreign workers trapped in a labor camp. I had hidden my excitement, since I was nowhere near a course of action for the workers. But each time Jacob had called to report the latest headway in his clandestine conversations with the other workers, or some new concession made by John Sanders, I had felt a rush. One day, I thought, the world will meet these workers. Now it seemed I'd been wrong.

Then there was Jacob himself. People had depended on me before, but his life was hanging in the balance, and I had let him down. There was no way he wasn't wishing, right now, that he'd never met me. If it weren't for me, he'd still be paying off his debts.

After he ran away, he wound up in South Carolina. He found work building tugboats in a Charleston shipyard—work way below his skill level, for half of what he'd earned at Signal.

"And how are you, Jacob? And your wife, and Donna and Donya?"

"They are very fine. But there is only one problem, Saketji. One picture has been printed in the newspaper."

When Jacob had emerged from Signal's gates, he had spoken to the reporters outside. One of them worked for an oil and shipyard industry weekly. The newest edition had just arrived at the shipyard where Jacob worked. His face was on the front page, under a blaring headline about labor strife at Signal International. He had been able to get the South Carolina job without papers, under the cover of anonymity. Now it was only a matter of time before a supervisor called immigration police to order up a raid. And Jacob wasn't the only one in danger. About a dozen other workers had made a run for it on March 9. Some were with Jacob, others scattered. Now they were all marked.

"What should I do?"

"Get off the phone right now," I said. "Gather your things and run."

10: Carrot and Stick

March–July 2007
Pascagoula, MS, and
Orange, TX

WHEN SIGNAL CALLED Malvern Burnett in to address a captive audience of workers in the aftermath of March 9, it wasn't calling the immigrant's best friend. It was calling an enforcer.

Malvern shifted uneasily under the eyes of hundreds of men in Pascagoula. (Among them, though he couldn't have picked them out of the crowd, were Shawkat, Hemant, and the clean-shaven Giani.) The workers used to look at him with hope, admiration, even something like adoration. Now they looked anxious. Afraid.

Ronald Schnoor, the Signal SVP, spoke first.

He began by setting the record straight about the men who'd been dismissed on March 9. Forget the rumors about why they'd been fired. The real reason was that they weren't doing quality work. If the others kept their heads down and kept their work up to snuff, Signal would extend their H-2B visas—currently set to expire in July 2007, just four months away. And it would help them obtain green cards after that.

That was the carrot. Next came the stick.

"This company is going to be here for a long time," Schnoor said, with all the steely potency of the heavy-industry SVP he was. "We are being, let's just say, chased by all our competitors in the industry to do their work because we are the best, because we are compliant with the law. The Department of Labor told me so, and I know it anyway."

Schnoor cast his gaze over his listeners while the translator spoke. Did they get the implication? *The government is on our side. So whatever you think you're up to with outside lawyers or whatnot, you better think again.* He went on.

"So I want you to think very, very carefully about suing Signal and about suing us for things that I know are, let's just say, uncalled for. It's what I call a frivolous lawsuit because I know we're fully compliant. We have lawyers too, very good lawyers."

Signal had never paid Malvern a cent directly. It was the workers who had paid him—their life's savings and more. But there was no way to deny it: Malvern was on the company's side now—literally, physically—while Schnoor said something that sent a ripple of alarm through the crowd:

"If we have to spend a lot of energy and effort fighting frivolous lawsuits, then the process will impact all of you. We won't be doing any visa extensions or anything with Signal. This program will be terminated and ended when the visas are complete, and that's July thirty-first. That's not very far away."

No extensions meant no green cards. No green cards meant doom.

Schnoor finished by showing he could play the good cop. "We want to make sure we do the right thing by you. That's how we do our business," he said. "We understand your financial situation. We understand that. And also be advised that when we found that out, we fired the agent that charged you the money you had paid. Signal wasn't part of that. Signal was *not* part of that."

So much bullshit. It was true Signal had fired Pol, but Malvern was as much a part of it as Pol had been, and there he was, still standing. On Signal's side. So was Sachin Dewan—in fact, Sachin was en route from India to do some damage control of his own. The truth was, Signal learned about the workers' debts and barely blinked. It certainly hadn't stopped bringing workers in and getting all it could out of them. Signal was as responsible as Malvern was. No one's hands were clean in this thing.

It was Malvern's turn to speak.

He tried to keep his tone even, to find the sweet spot between reassurance and warning. He started by telling them he was currently filing the extensions for their H-2B visas and would continue to until Signal told him to stop. He was confident the government would approve the extensions. He could see the follow-up question many of them were dying to cry out: *What about the green cards?* Thank God they were too scared to interrupt. That let Malvern deliver his other message.

He had heard the workers had met with an outside lawyer who told them that if they sued Signal, they might get another kind of visa.

"I know a great deal about this visa," Malvern said, his authority rekindled. "The visa that they're talking about is called the T visa—it stands for trafficking visa. I have the application right here, and I will give it to you if you wish." He held it up. The room stared back, totally still.

He spoke slowly, deliberately: "In my twenty years of practicing law, I have never known anyone to get this visa granted. This visa's designed for severe forms of human trafficking." The words sounded absurd even coming out of his mouth. In what possible universe could someone dream that Malvern Burnett, the man inspired by refugees from childhood, the man who'd given his life to opening immigrants' path through the golden door, could be involved in human trafficking?

"You have to prove that you've been subject to involuntary servitude, peonage, debt bondage, or slavery," Malvern said. "This is not meant for people that have problems with the food, with the laundry, with the housing, or with a wage dispute. The way you resolve those issues is you talk to management, talk to your supervisors, talk to your superintendents. Tell them what problems you have."

There were dark looks in the crowd. Some of them *had* been talking to management for months. And what had it gotten them? Where were they now? *And what about the green cards?*

But those looks were the exceptions. Most of the men's faces were different now. Hollow. Crestfallen.

Malvern drove his point home.

"If any of you have any questions about your T visa, I have Indian clients who have applied for the T visa before and had it denied," he said. "You contact me and I'll put you in touch."

FROM THE DAY of the carrot-and-stick meeting, Shawkat Ali could feel the clock ticking. The worry built up like a toxin in his bloodstream. It affected his appetite. His focus. His sleep.

Before he knew it, July had arrived—still with no visa extensions for anyone. Three days before their visas expired, Darrell Snyder told a certain group of workers that their visa extensions hadn't been approved, and they were going to be sent back to India.

Shawkat felt sick. Feverish. What did this mean for the rest of them? Were they all finished? Signal had dangled the carrot of the visa extensions to keep them working as hard as they could up until the last moment. To squeeze them dry. Shawkat had nothing left.

There was only one thing he knew for sure: all hope was lost. Head throbbing, he signed up for a supervised trip to Walmart in the company van, scheduled for one day before his visa expired. He gathered his passport, his welding certificate, and all the cash he had—$50 for food. And from deep inside his suitcase, he pulled out that frayed airmail envelope with the wad of receipts, the ones Sachin Dewan had tried to get him to hand over. He stuffed them in his back pocket and boarded the company van. On the ride to the Pascagoula Walmart, his hands were clammy. Inside, he took a cart and wove through the aisles, bloodshot eyes searching the shelves for some obscure and indispensable item.

When the others got back in the van, Shawkat crouched in the farthest corner of the store he could find. He stayed there until the phantom voices of the coworkers and Signal supervisor who'd accompanied them had died away. When he finally stepped outside, the van was long gone, and the sun was setting. Fatigue and fever overcame him. He collapsed onto a bench in front of the store.

He spent the night there. And the next day. And the next. When he needed the bathroom, he'd stagger back into the Walmart. When he needed to eat, he'd buy the cheapest thing that looked edible in the grocery section. The nights were endless, a delirium of aches and chills and sweats, through which one terrible, inescapable fact blazed before him: he was in hell. And it was no one's fault but his own.

WORD OF THE TURMOIL in Pascagoula quickly reached the other Signal work site, in Orange, Texas. So did Malvern Burnett, who traveled there for another meeting alongside Signal officials.

As Aby Raju listened, he was confused. Wasn't Burnett *their* lawyer? Their advocate with the company, the man who held the key to their futures—to his future with Bincy and the baby on its way? Why, then, did he sound like a prosecutor—who was addressing them like the accused? Aby had a sinking feeling.

There was nothing to do but to keep building that oil rig. For a chance at the visa extension. For any hope of a green card to follow. The moment the shift was over, he went straight to the telephone queue to call Bincy. He tried to pour into his questions all the attention and concern he wished he could have shown in person. What was she eating? (Whatever she could keep down.) Had the nausea gotten any better? (It hadn't.)

She was eight months pregnant on her birthday, May 9, for which Aby wired money so his brother could surprise her with flowers and a wristwatch.

On the morning of June 30, with the visa expiration deadline days away, Aby was twenty feet above the ground, welding torch blazing. He was working on the spud can, one of the rig's gigantic feet. It was shaped like a mushroom cap, as wide as the roof of a house, and would eventually come to rest on the ocean floor to hold up the finished platform.

His phone rang in his back pocket, which it never did during the day. Picking it up on the rig during shift time was against every safety rule there was. But something told him to answer. He released the trigger of the MIG gun to shut off the torch. Lifted his welding hood. Pressed the phone to his ear. It was Bincy.

"I'm going into surgery," she said, her voice bright with alarm. "I wish you were here."

Everything evaporated—the spud can, the platform, the Texas sun, the din of a hundred workers—as Aby's consciousness collapsed into a single searing point of panic. Surgery meant an unplanned Cesarean section. Bincy was in danger. The baby, too.

There was a clamor as someone, a nurse or orderly, pulled the phone from Bincy's hands.

"Bincy!" Aby called. The line went dead.

He sat immobile on the spud can, deaf and dumb, for nearly an hour. Finally the phone rang again. His mother's number. He picked up.

"It's done!" she cried. "Mom and baby are fine. You're a father!"

He still had the phone to his ear, a look of disbelieving elation on his face, when the foreman made his way up a ladder and emerged on the spud can.

"What's going on here?" the foreman barked. "Why aren't you working?"

"I got a baby in India!" Aby cried. The foreman broke out in a smile to match Aby's. "Party in the camp tonight!"

"That's fine, you guys go ahead," the foreman said. "The company doesn't like us going into your camps. I don't want to get into trouble. Get me a cigar tomorrow."

Aby had made friends with the Goan cook who ran the canteen, so that was his next phone call. The cook conjured up a big box of fried chicken, bright with turmeric and red chili powder in the batter—the closest he could get to the deep-fried South Indian delicacy known as Chicken 65. He tossed it over the fence to Aby, who carried it straight to the foremen's office trailer, piping hot.

When Aby burst in, they did a double take. The Indian workers weren't allowed there. But Aby shared his news, and the fried chicken. They clapped him on the back and laughed and said: *Can you bring this every day?*

That night, Aby stole out of the man camp and came back with all the smuggled alcohol he could carry. He invited other workers into his trailer until it was bursting at the hinges. By now, Aby knew the baby's sex. It was a boy. The men drank to his son's birth, and sang like the night would never end, and danced. The trailer shook on its stilts.

PART THREE

ESCAPE

1: Get Out

Summer–Autumn 2007
Pascagoula, MS

EVERY SUNDAY THAT SUMMER I made the three-hour trip out to the Sacred Heart Catholic Church, desperate to keep up my connection with the men inside Signal International's labor camp. But now when I opened the door in the back of the church there was no sea of faces—I was lucky to find five.

The men's H-2B visas had expired, which left them terrified to venture out, even as Signal kept them working. The men who did show up at the church were usually Kerala Catholics come to pray in earnest, not to meet with me. At best they'd talk to me for a few furtive minutes at a time. When I asked what the company was telling them about T visa renewals or green cards, they'd only repeat Signal's promises that there would soon be "Updates." I'd press my phone number into their hands, asking them to call when there was news.

They never did. They all knew I was the one Jacob had been working with, and how his story ended. He was still on the run. Each time he found a new job, usually at a low-paying shipyard, someone would put together that he was the fire starter at Signal, and he'd have to slip away. No one wanted to be the next Jacob. But the next Jacob was exactly what I needed: a new partner on the inside to help me build a movement.

Then one Saturday in September, my phone rang at 4:45 a.m. At that time it had to be a day-shift worker. This was when most called India, before breakfast. It was a man I didn't know, speaking rapid-fire Hindi.

"Saket Soni?"

"Yes-yes. Who is this?"

"Rajan Pazhambadakode, pipefitter." A Kerala man. The eight sylla-
bles of his name went off like firecrackers.

"How can I help you, Rajan?"

"It's you who needs my help. I have an update. It will be useful for
your purposes."

"Not on the phone," I said. "There's a church near you—"

"Yes. I know. I've been to your prayer meetings."

"We've met? I'm sorry I don't remember."

"I sat in the back and listened," he said. "I didn't approach you. It
wasn't the time. It is now. See you at the Secret Catholic Church."

WHEN I CRACKED OPEN the door in the back of the church, a tall, wiry
man was already there, pacing the length of the room in long strides.
He was in brown canvas pipefitter's overalls two shades darker than his
chestnut skin.

"Rajan," I greeted him. "How are you?"

He spun around, sized me up, and pushed past the pleasantries.
"Listen."

Two weeks before, Signal's managers had finally gathered the men
in the cafeteria for the long-awaited "green card update." The men sat
expectantly, waiting for Malvern. But the lawyer who showed up was one
they'd never seen before. She said she used to work for Malvern, and that
he had screwed up their files. That was the reason for the delay in their
H-2B visa renewals. Signal had decided to fire Malvern, but luckily for
them, the company had brought her in to clean up. She had already put
in their paperwork. The government was going to approve their renewals
any day. Once those were through, she'd be putting in the applications
for their green cards. The new lawyer smiled as if there were nothing to
worry about.

They were worried beyond belief. They didn't know this woman.
Malvern was the wizard who had brought them to America, where only
highly educated, upper-class Indians were supposed to be able to enter.
He made the impossible possible. And now he was gone?

A day-shift worker feigned illness and got permission to visit the hospital. Instead, he set out for New Orleans, found Malvern's office, and begged. "If anyone can deliver our green cards, it's you. Don't abandon us." Malvern's reply came as a shock. Signal wouldn't be getting any green cards, Malvern told him. The government had *already rejected Signal's applications for H-2B renewals*, so green card applications were out of the question. But, Malvern said, all was not lost. He was in talks with other companies who were interested in peeling away Signal's workforce for themselves. Malvern made his visitor an offer. For a price, the man could apply for another ten-month-long H-2B visa with a different employer, another Gulf Coast shipyard that needed good hands.

THIS WORKER REPORTED back to the others in the labor camp: Malvern's price was $4,000. They reeled. No one had that kind of cash to spare, and even if they could borrow it, ten months on a new H-2B wouldn't be nearly enough time to shovel out of their debts. And if Signal couldn't get them green cards now, where were they to turn? That night, the men thrashed in their sleep, doomstruck.

But not Rajan. He sat awake all night, remembering what I had said at the meeting months before. There had never been any green cards. The promise of them had been a lie from the beginning. That's when he called me.

"You told us the truth at the Secret Church," he said to me. "You were the only one. So I've come to hear you out. What's your proposal?"

His eyes bored into me. This wasn't an update, but an audience. His tone was frank. The tone of a man ready for action—if he believed in the plan.

"What's the mood in the camp?" I said.

"Forget the *mood*, man! This is the opening you've been waiting for. Signal International's control over us has been destabilized." He spoke like a labor leader himself. It was the first sign that he would become the kind of strategic partner organizers dream of.

"The company's promise has fallen apart," Rajan continued. "Their *workforce* is about to fall apart."

"Which means Signal is scared too," I said.

"Frantically. We're building them two billion dollars' worth of oil rigs, and we're *only halfway done*. You see?" He balled up his fist and pumped his arm.

"That's power," I agreed.

"How do we use it? A strike right now would bring the company to its knees."

I shook my head.

"You only strike for things—"

"That a company can give you," Rajan said, anticipating my thought. "Signal can't give us green cards."

"Only the US government can."

"Then what do we *do*?" He rapped the table with his knuckles. "If it's not a strike, there must be something else."

"There is," I said. "You report a crime. To the US Department of Justice."

"But we're the ones who overstayed our visas."

"You're victims. The crime is human trafficking."

I explained in five minutes the argument my team and I had constructed over six months, and the action plan that went with it.

"You and the rest of the men would come forward to report Signal International and its recruiters to the Department of Justice," I said. "You'd offer evidence that this was an international criminal conspiracy. You'd present yourselves not only as victims, but as witnesses."

Rajan squinted, wheels turning.

"So I get the men on board. You file the complaint. We keep working at Signal and continue to pay down our debts. That's the best of both worlds. How long will the Department of Justice take to come through?"

"No," I said. "You can't stay at Signal. You'll have to escape. All of you, in the middle of the night."

"What for? To hide?"

"The opposite. To show up in every newspaper and TV report we can manage, telling your story. We launch a public campaign to convince the DOJ to open a trafficking investigation."

"And the green cards?"

"Trafficking is a federal crime. You're victims *and* witnesses, so the DOJ needs you here to pursue the case. While it does, it can grant you the ability to stay and work. It's called Continued Presence. That's the first thing we fight for. Then while the DOJ investigates, we apply for another kind of visa, created specifically for victims of trafficking. For all of you. When you're granted this visa, your wives and children get them as well. You can bring them over. Eventually, it converts into a green card. It's called a T visa."

"I've heard of those," Rajan said. "Malvern said that wasn't an option for us."

"Malvern talked to you about T visas?" I asked, startled.

"At the meetings Signal held after March ninth. He warned us not to trust people who promised those. He said the government had never granted T visas to anyone."

"He *what*?" I was outraged at Malvern's audacious claim—and amazed that he had inoculated himself before we'd even made our charges. The prescient motherfucker.

I assured Rajan that the government had indeed granted T visas before—182 of them just last year, in 2006. Another 112 the year before that. And I told him we had some of the best lawyers in the country ready to file the workers' applications.

"Just like in India, there are public interest lawyers in America. They work for free for causes they believe in. They're lining up to join your fight. Attorneys from the Southern Poverty Law Center. The American Civil Liberties Union. The National Immigration Law Center."

Now his brows were knitting.

"But Malvern's right about one thing," I added. "I can't promise you visas. I *can* promise you the fight of our lives. Your best chance to win is if you escape."

"Escape—into a campaign," Rajan absorbed. With two spindly fingers, he made a man suspended in midair, swinging from trapeze to trapeze. "For a DOJ investigation, then Continued Presence, then T visas, then family visas, then green cards."

It was a long, uncertain path. Nothing like the one he'd been sold on when he came. I had an impulse to reassure him but suppressed it. Rajan had to decide to do this on his own.

"And Rajan," I warned, "For this to work, it can't just be some of you."

"Because anyone who stays behind can be a witness for Signal," he said, understanding. I nodded.

He stood up to his full height. "When Signal gets wind of this," he said, "They're going to come at us with everything they've got."

"Right."

"Because a *strike* they would want to settle. Anything to get us back on the platforms. But if their workforce *escapes midproduction* . . . that's a catastrophe for them."

"Not to mention if their top executives are hauled away on criminal trafficking charges," I said.

"In fact," he said, "We might as well call our campaign 'Death to Signal International.'"

I smiled. Rajan had called it "our campaign."

RAJAN WAS RIGHT to worry about Signal getting wind of our plans. By the time I met him, I had put together how Jacob Joseph Kadakadapally was outed. He was given up by Signal management's eyes and ears in the labor camp—another Indian man named Gaurav. Gaurav had come in on the same visa as everyone else, and had managed to get himself promoted soon after he arrived. He was now a "safety officer," but his real job was to inform on the workers and warn Signal managers about any dissent. Gaurav had told Sachin Dewan about Jacob's bedside conversations, and Signal moved to deliver swift punishment. If Gaurav learned of Rajan's involvement with me, they'd deport him as well.

When I told Rajan this, he smiled. He knew Gaurav. They had worked an oil rig job together years ago in Baku, Azerbaijan. "Don't worry," Rajan said. "I'll keep him close, and we'll be careful." Part of that meant making sure Gaurav didn't overhear our phone calls—a risk since Rajan and I spoke in Hindi together, and Gaurav was fluent in Hindi. So when Rajan and I talked on the phone, we'd refer to the great escape we were planning as a wedding. His sister's. (His sister was already married.)

2: Big Man

Winter 2007–08
Pascagoula, MS

RAJAN CALLED ME a few weeks later to set a plan in motion.

"I need groceries. Now that my sister's wedding is set, I'm making dinner to celebrate."

"Sure," I said. "What do you need?"

"Get me a bag of sarson ke beej, the black kind. Also: jeera. And— write this down: methi, dhania powder, shredded coconut, curry leaves, hing."

I had no idea what hing was. But I already knew Rajan well enough now to trust any request, so I raced to keep up with his list.

Our task was to engineer an escape for hundreds of brown men out of two company man camps in two states, 326 miles apart, both guarded at all times. But first, we had to convince them. A union like the United Auto Workers might spend two years organizing a group this size. We had six months at most. By Rajan's estimates, production would be at full force for about that long. Once Signal's rigs were complete, the company was likely to send any workers it no longer deemed essential back to India. On top of that, we had a deadline of March 9, 2008, to file a federal lawsuit on trafficking charges because of the statute of limitations. We were deep in September already. But most of the men were more afraid of leaving Signal than ever. We needed to help them overcome their fear. That's where Rajan's grocery list came in.

I found everything he needed, even the hing. I slipped it all to him in a Walmart aisle, pretending to be a fellow shopper during one of those company-chaperoned trips. Back at the man camp, Rajan commandeered the kitchen. He toasted cumin to an earthy musk. Popped mustard seeds in ghee. Unlocked the floral bouquet of dry coriander seeds. Emptied dime bags of golden hing into woks of velvety coconut paste. Through this artistry, he drew the men in. Over a series of one-pot meals, he pulled them back from the edge of despair. Over seconds and thirds, he said there was an option better than Malvern's. Did they want to hear it?

A few weeks later, Rajan called with a progress report.

"Twenty guests would like to attend the wedding," Rajan said.

"Twenty! That's a start," I said.

A week later, he had twenty more. And in a month, one hundred men were ready to meet. Now we had to figure out how to get them past the guards.

It couldn't be all hundred at once. Rajan needed to be able to come in and out of the camp under the radar, ferrying small groups of men to a nearby hotel room. There I would meet with them a few hours at a time to describe our plan and get them signed up for the DOJ complaint. But we faced the specter of Signal's private security force. Technically, the workers were allowed to venture out between shifts. But the guards wrote up the badge number of any man who set foot outside in a book the bosses scanned every day. They'd notice a sudden spike in foot traffic, interrogate the men, and put Rajan on the chopping block.

Then one night, fate put me on a barstool next to one of the guards. I was at Thunder's Tavern. "Thunder" Thornton had been an Ole Miss lineman, and his bar was a Pascagoula institution. Half the patrons there were Thunder's old friends; the other half worked at shipyards and oil companies around Pascagoula. It was a cozy place. The fist fights were always amiable.

I noticed the man next to me, white, about my age, twice my size, hunched over a miserable plate of fries, in khakis and a polo shirt with the logo of Signal International's private security contractor. I bought him a beer. Six beers later, he was recounting the indignities he suffered at Signal, starting with the crawling skin infection that repulsed his girl-friend ("I wouldn't fuck me either") to, most recently, the barked order to search under the boxers of Indian men for contraband liquor ("They don't pay me enough to sniff ass").

To the Indians, these guards were terrifying wardens. But to judge by this man, the guards themselves were monumentally demoralized. If they didn't need a union, I don't know who did. Signal International was protecting its most valuable asset—a workforce worth millions—with subcontracted, underpaid, degraded men. I realized that they were so deprived of human warmth at the workplace that anyone who smiled at them might feel like a long-lost brother.

Enter Rajan. He launched a charm offensive fueled by tobacco, bourbon, and innuendo. On his way to and from church, he'd slow down to hang out with the guards. He learned their names and attempted to teach them his. (They settled for "Roger.") One Sunday, he returned from church with flavored cigars I had procured from a nearby gas station. "My bird-day," he announced, handing them out to the guards. (It wasn't.) Another Sunday, it was minibar bottles of Wild Turkey. ("Big Man," the guards were now calling him.) They started letting Rajan in and out of the camp without recording his badge number, not just on Sunday mornings, but on weekday evenings after his shift. The bosses didn't need to know. When one guard asked if he had a woman in town, Rajan gave a sly smile. ("Okay, Big Man!") When Rajan tested the limits of the guards' goodwill, taking others out on his jaunts—two or three at a time—the guards waved them by. Rajan vouched for other men, dispensed more Wild Turkey, more cigars. Soon the guards were letting men out without Rajan—to visit bars or women in town, they thought. I'd meet with them in a hotel room right over the river and go over our plans. At the end of the fall, we had about a hundred workers.

But they were all in Mississippi. We also needed to reach into Signal's camp in Orange, Texas, and didn't know how. Then one day Rajan learned that a pipefitter who joined our group in Pascagoula was the uncle of a welder in Orange. The nephew agreed to meet out there and bring others, but where? I started cold-calling churches in Orange to see if there was an analogue to our Secret Catholic Church in Pascagoula: a refuge and meeting spot where men could gather on Sundays. I found a

Catholic priest with a Malayali last name. It turned out he knew the local Signal men already. When the Indians first arrived, he'd gone into the Orange camp to lead prayers, and was shocked at how they were living. When he approached Signal on the men's behalf, they threw him out and shut the gates. He agreed to host a meeting.

By Christmas, a team came together in Orange. We had Aby Raju, the welder from Kerala. He was a natural leader. When others in the Orange camp expressed nervousness about taking on Signal, and asked if it wouldn't be safer to file the trafficking complaint only against the recruiters, it was Aby who turned the tide. Malvern Burnett was the one who brought him to America, Aby said, but Signal was deriving profit from his separation from his newborn son. Signal had to pay. Aby's son became a symbol of what all of the men had lost, and they rallied behind the new father.

We also had Murugan Kandhasamy, the Tamil pipefitter. Early on, Signal supervisors marveled at his skill level, promoted him to foreman, and gave him his own crew: the other Tamils. There was no raise involved, but for Murugan, being their guide, big brother, marriage counselor, and life coach was reward enough. He inducted all sixty into the DOJ complaint.

Back in Mississippi, by the start of 2008, we had all the men from the South Indian states of Kerala, Tamil Nadu, and Andhra Pradesh. The North Indians (Punjabis mostly) hadn't yet joined, but there weren't that many of them, so I wasn't concerned. They'd show up at the meetings soon enough. But Rajan and I *were* worried about a constituency we hadn't broken into—the last major stronghold against our campaign: the unmarried men.

Most of our men were married and were driven by the need to be reunited with their wives and children. Our campaign had given them new hope. But no matter what tack Rajan took with those who weren't married, they remained alienated and unreachable.

Finally he understood. "It is a sex problem," he said. In this regard, Rajan explained, Mississippi was far worse than the Middle Eastern labor camps. In the Middle East, though there were no women, there were outlets that kept you feeling human. You lived four men to a room. On weekends, a local entrepreneur would sell you moonshine and rent you "blue films." At night, you and roommates could sip your drinks from the bunk beds while someone turned the lights out and popped in the video. You could pleasure yourself. There were men who helped each other out. ("Not me," Rajan vowed.) That's how it is for men in labor camps—within the confinement, a small measure of freedom.

But here even that wasn't available. Instead of three bunkmates, you had twenty-three. Skin diseases crawled up your legs, and dysentery ran through the camps. You disgusted yourself and everyone else. You wished you didn't have a body at all. Since they'd arrived in America almost a year ago, the men had barely masturbated. Where would they do it if they even wanted to? In a freezing port-a-potty with a dozen men in line outside? The older men could take it. So could the ones who were married. But the twenty-something singles still woke up with torturous erections. For them, Rajan said, "The sex problem is the most difficult."

"We need more hotel rooms," I told him.

He whispered among the unmarried men: if they joined our clandestine hotel meetings, there would be extra rooms available for anyone who wanted to "Rest."

Two weeks later, we had all the unmarried men.

3: Genius

March 5, 2008
Pascagoula, MS

WE WERE ON TENTERHOOKS. In three nights, if our delicate design hung together, we'd launch our great escape. In two nights, we needed a watertight list of all the men who were "In"—no second thoughts or eleventh-hour superstitions. Tonight in the labor camp, Rajan walked off his anxiety by visiting each trailer, delivering doses of warmth and confidence to inoculate the men against any late outbreak of fear.

Holed up in my hotel room across the river, I pounded my own nervousness into a laptop. Over the past six months, in deep talks with these men, I had scribbled hundreds of pages about the inner workings of Signal's scheme—details only those trapped inside it could know. The totality was dynamite: human trafficking reinvented for twenty-first-century America.

This is how it worked.

Labor trafficking starts with recruitment through "Force, fraud, or coercion." The fraud seemed clear to me from the outset. Malvern Burnett, Michael Pol, and Sachin Dewan charged the men $20,000, led them to expect green cards, and instead delivered ten-month H-2B visas.

Murugan helped me understand the element of force. The recruiters collected their payments in three installments. They waited until after the second installment to reveal that the men were going on H-2B visas, when they were already in line for their interviews at the US Consulate. Murugan described the recruiters' clear instructions: They were to say that they had paid only nominal filing fees for the H-2B visas, and to breathe not a word about $20,000 or the green cards. At this point the men were already out $14,000 each in borrowed money. Lying to the US government was a crime they couldn't afford *not* to commit.

If that was heavy handed on the recruiters' part, the next move was deft. When a consulate stamps your passport with a visa, it's typically mailed back to you. But in this case, Malvern filled out the visa applications so they were mailed to Sachin Dewan. This was leverage: while Sachin held their passports, the workers couldn't back out. Coercion, plain and simple. Numerous men told me that when they'd returned to Mumbai to pay their final installments and recover their passports, Sachin had upped his price and coerced payment: he threatened to burn their passports if they refused, to cross out the visas with a marker and render them useless. He also seemed to grow wary about leaving a paper trail. With one early candidate, the devout and dignified Shawkat Ali Sheikh, Sachin had put a great deal more in writing than he should have, scrawling out receipts for Shawkat's payments that said "Green Card in USA." Shawkat had brought them with him to the US, sensing they might be important one day. He escaped the labor camp with them after the chaos of March 9, and ended up in a Louisiana shipyard town, sharing a cramped apartment with other runaways from Signal. I learned he was there and went to find him. He handed over his trove of receipts.

American trafficking experts focus on developing-nations cartels smuggling bodies across borders. Our recruiter was a liberal lawyer flying the men in on legal work visas. That, of course, was the genius of it: recruitment by force, fraud, and coercion made to look like an orderly line outside the US Consulate. We had to help adjudicators see it.

After that, we'd have to convince them that the men were truly unfree at work—in the language of US law, that they had been recruited "For the purpose of subjection to involuntary servitude." In this, too, the men did not fit the usual mold of the trafficking victim. US investigators look for involuntary servitude in locked hotel rooms, dark restaurant basements, remote farms—not on the work sites of large corporations headed for IPOs. They search for visual cues. Locks and keys.

The emblematic trafficking prosecution up until that point had been *United States v. Kil Soo Lee*. Lee built a garment factory on a remote island of American Samoa, an unincorporated US territory 2,300 miles south of Honolulu. The location allowed him to use the "Made in America" label without drawing attention to the operation. He recruited workers from China and Vietnam, charging them thousands of dollars for a chance at an American job. In this case, the involuntary servitude was clear. The workers lived in a gated compound. Lee ordered guards to beat or even kill workers who weren't sewing fast enough. In one horrific attack, a guard gouged a woman's eye out with a pipe. Lee was sentenced to forty years in prison.

It was quite clear that Kil Soo Lee's workers weren't free to leave. We had to help adjudicators understand that Signal's workers weren't, either, despite the lack of physical constraints. Their bondage was fashioned out of their debts.

As soon as the first wave of workers arrived at Signal's Pascagoula yard, they told Signal officials about the enormous debts they'd taken on to pay the recruiters. And what did Signal do? They didn't stop work. They didn't fire Malvern Burnett. They joined him in making their own promises of green cards. The men had no choice but to keep working for Signal, since by the rules of the H-2B visa, they could only work legally for the employer that sponsored them. And after their H-2B visas expired, Signal manipulated the men's fear of deportation to make them stay inside the labor camp and continue to work.

I had pieced this together in hundreds of interviews with the men. The DOJ would have to hear what I had to see them as unfree. Aby Raju, the father who couldn't meet his newborn son. All the men who were unable to attend their parents' funerals or family weddings. The Sikh man people told me about, a giani who had been forced to shave his beard.

These weren't free people. This was an innovation in American bondage, with a legal guest worker visa as the Trojan horse. And we were going to expose it at the exact time that Congress was set to expand guest worker visas, making countless more workers vulnerable to forced labor.

My phone interrupted my laptop's racing staccato. Rajan.

"You at the hotel?" He sounded grim.

"What's wrong?"

"The wedding's in trouble. The horoscope looks bad. We need to meet."

4: Elders

March 5–6, 2008
Pascagoula, MS

"WE'VE GOT A North Indian problem," Rajan said as he sank into the low armchair in my hotel room. He had spent the evening and much of the night going from bunkhouse to bunkhouse, taking the temperature of the men. Gaunt and angular in his brown pipefitter's overalls, he looked like a quiver full of arrows.

I handed him a cup of tea. "What kind?"

He took a sip and reconsidered. "Actually, we have two. First: this tea. You must use scalding water, or it won't steep enough."

"And the second?"

"The Keralawallas are with us," he said. "So are the Tamils. But they're all watching the North Indians. For this to work, you need to get them on board."

"Rajan, we have two days. We have three hundred men from Kerala. A hundred more from Tamil Nadu and Andhra Pradesh."

"We can't move forward without the North Indians," he insisted. "You said it. For this to work, it can't just be some of us."

"But there are less than twenty North Indians. I wish they'd join us. But they can't hold us back."

"This is about *your* credibility," Rajan said. "The others are watching you. To them, if you cannot convince your own people—"

"My *own* people?" I said, exasperated. Rajan held up his hand.

"Are you not a Delhiwalla?"

"We're in America now. Most Americans don't know Delhi from Dubai. South India or North—what does it matter?"

"India is wherever Indians go," he said. "These twenty North Indians will listen to you if you push them. Do they not call you Soni Sa'ab?"

They did. I hated it, and the relish with which Rajan made his point. Sa'ab was a title for superiors. I'd been glad to leave Indian hierarchies behind when I arrived in the US to attend college twelve years ago, or at least to trade them for less familiar ones. Not these North Indians. A handful of them attended one of our meetings a few months ago. They greeted me with folded hands and made obsequious small talk that ate up precious time. When they found out I wasn't married, they pleaded with me to find a wife, as if my respectability were the subject at hand rather than their precarious future. When I finally laid out the case against Signal, they shrugged and reached for a feudal expression. "We're eating their salt, Soni Sa'ab." How could they bite the hand that fed them? Saddest of all, when they got up to leave (bows again, folded hands) they asked my forgiveness. They couldn't join, but didn't want to make an enemy of me either.

After that meeting, despite my invitations, the North Indians never came back. Eventually, we wrote them off. Why was Rajan suddenly concerned their absence would hurt my credibility with the others?

"Your credibility is only part of it," he admitted. "The other reason is that they're about to wreck everything."

Rajan described a new development from his nightly rounds. He would walk from trailer to trailer, poking his head in, boosting morale. Invariably, he'd run into Gaurav—Signal's eyes and ears in the camp. Gaurav loved making his own rounds after work, teacup full of whisky in hand, aimlessly bullying the others, lording his special relationship with Signal over them. Rajan found Gaurav insufferable. But on the theory that you should keep your enemies closer, he'd shoot the breeze with him for a little while—mostly to be sure Gaurav hadn't caught wind of our plans.

Tonight, though, Gaurav was nowhere to be seen—until Rajan found him sitting alone in the cafeteria, sulking into his teacup. He started venting.

"*I* was Signal's man," Gaurav said. He worked hard for them. But now he was being sidelined. Signal had recruited a broader set of men—one from each trailer—to act as company liaisons. This whole group was ushered into the air-conditioned conference room on the other side of the fence to report on the complaints percolating in the camps. Which was fine as long as Gaurav was at the head of this table. Instead, management was treating another man as the group's leader—a worker with far less experience than Gaurav, and much younger, and with better English. Oh, they loved his English.

Gaurav was furious. It was the same old South Indian story.

"You break your back for the goras. But when it's time for a promotion, they pass you up and pick a North Indian."

"A grave injustice, brother," Rajan agreed. "This new leader, he's a North Indian, then?"

"Oh, the fanciest kind," Gaurav said, knocking back his whisky. "From Delhi."

Rajan didn't know his name. There was no one from Delhi among the North Indians I'd met. But I had described our plans to those men, and they had to have reported back to the Delhi man.

"We need to find him and bring him over to our side, or we're sunk," Rajan said.

"Then we have to build an incentive for him," I said. "These informants—the company's giving them something. Raises, perks."

"Something else, too. You go to a friend's house in India. His grandmother is home. What do you do?"

"Touch her feet," I said, puzzled.

"Why?"

"She's an elder."

"Exactly," he said. "Signal has given this committee of informants a name. The Elders."

Respect: that was the real incentive.

"The escape is two days away," I said. "The North Indians haven't been in the loop. If this top Elder wants to out us to Signal firsthand, he'll need details. My guess is he'll come to us."

"When he does, your job will be to convince him," Rajan said. He sensed my apprehension. "Don't overthink it! You're from Delhi, he's from Delhi. Talk about Delhi stuff—cricket, golgappas, whatever. Get him to trust you."

"Any other advice?" I said dryly.

He gulped back his tea, crushed his cup, and handed me the crumpled Styrofoam.

"Don't fail, Saket Sa'ab."

THE NEXT EVENING, eleven men sat in my hotel room and debated whether sambhar was better with raw mangoes or without. They had just signed up to escape. Their brows were determined, their souls afraid. I made them tea (two bags apiece, scalding). They showed me pictures of their kids. We traded recipes, teased the unmarried men.

"Not unmarried," they corrected, and pronounced the English word they preferred with dignity: "*Bachelors.*"

"Raw mangoes," an older man called them. A wave of laughter crashed against their fear.

Then suddenly, the mirth evaporated. A bachelor motioned: *behind you.* I turned around. Someone new was standing in the narrow hallway, deciding whether to come in. He was deadly handsome, with slicked-back glossy hair, a tight T-shirt, and frayed jeans. This was our Delhi Elder.

The other men set their Styrofoam cups down and filed out without a word. A sheet of butcher paper I'd taped up fell to the floor with a rustle.

"Come in, please!" I said. I switched on my warmest smile and asked his name.

"Hemant."

"Let me guess—you're from Delhi."

"I've heard you are too," he said.

I initiated the New Delhi tea ceremony. I offered "chai-shai," and he politely declined. I poured it; he protested. I set the cup in front of him; he resignedly accepted it. All the while I racked my brain for what to say next. Rajan's counsel rang in my head: *Delhi stuff.* It wasn't that easy. I was born in Delhi, but my father was an Indian foreign service officer, so I had a nomadic childhood: first in Amman, then Delhi, then Singapore, then Delhi again, then Karachi, then back in Delhi, then Kingston, Jamaica. At eighteen, I came to the United States. In Delhi, I felt like an outsider.

Hemant, I could see, was an insider. The kind who'd grown up mastering Delhi's gullies (alleys) and galis (swear words). He would have played back-alley cricket with a splintery laundry plank for a bat, while I was indoors playing chess. His school lunches would have been parathas and pickles, while mine, to my classmates' amusement, were my mother's perfect "Ribbon sandwiches" (ketchup, pudina chutney, mustard). I spoke Hindi chiefly with my teachers and grandparents, and when I tried to strike up conversations with kids like Hemant, I didn't get far before they snickered, "English medium," with derision dripping like syrup from a jalebi.

Still, we were both in Pascagoula now, and I needed to find a way to break through to him.

"So, Hemant," I said, "Where in Delhi do you live?"

"Rohini." He sipped his tea.

"Rohini, sure!" I said brightly, though I had never been there. "My family lives in Greater Kailash. In M-block market, behind the Minar restaurant." Surely he had fond memories of it: M-block was a teeny-bopper mecca. I'd go to the market there for Michael Jackson tapes, and books from the pavement lender.

But Hemant rolled his eyes. I was an upmarket snob after all. I grasped for another approach.

"Did you stay in Delhi for college?" I asked.

He replied curtly, in English this time, that he'd studied "History honors at Delhi University." A humanities major! Well, I'd studied English literature at the University of Chicago, and took a lot of history. I decided to mine this connection, forgetting that in Delhi's mercenary education system, a history degree was for those who failed at everything else.

"History! Wonderful! What college?" Delhi University contained many colleges—my father had gone to the prestigious Saint Stephen's.

Hemant's look darkened. "Khalsa College," he said through gritted teeth. Decidedly *not* prestigious. I had extracted a confession that he was right at the bottom of the barrel. To make matters worse, I now exclaimed that my uncle taught at Khalsa College. *Physics.* Hemant grunted with mock admiration. A subject he could never qualify to study.

There was nothing to salvage from my attempt to build rapport. I had to cut to the chase.

"Hemant, you're aware of our plans." His face flickered. "So tell me, what do you think?"

His look shifted from contempt to calculation.

"How many people do you have?"

It was the right question. But why was he asking? To tell the company, or for some reason of his own?

"You've made it to America," I said. "And this company has invited you in. They see something in you. That's a credit to you." Hemant eased up, took another sip of tea. "But here's the thing," I continued. "They can promote you, give you a raise, but they can't change the law for you. The visa they brought you on doesn't turn into a green card. Your visa's long expired, and now you're undocumented. I'm sure they want to help you. You're their man. But they can't."

"Look, Saketji," he interrupted. "There's something about me you need to know. No one tells me what to do. I come to my own conclusions. *I'm my own man.*"

I had tried to appeal to Hemant's pride at being an insider. But what I had missed was that it was also a sore spot. He was a company man, yes, but a part of him longed to forge his own path. *That* was my opening, the part of him I needed to appeal to.

But it was too late. He was already out my door and down the hall.

Later that night, I was draining the cheerless Styrofoam cups in the bathroom sink when Rajan called.

"Did you solve our North Indian problem?"

"I think I made it worse," I said.

BACK IN THE man camp, Hemant followed the blurry light from the trailers. In the night fog they looked like stranded boxcars. He knocked on the door of one bunkhouse. A man he knew was bent over his open suitcase, folded clothes in hand. In the next trailer, too, men were packing. They froze when they saw Hemant, smiled feebly, made excuses. *Just tidying up! Keeping things clean.* But he knew, and they knew he knew: they were preparing their escape. Everyone was going somewhere but him.

Hemant walked in the slick mud between the trailers, slower now.

Time was running out. For others, the green card was an end in itself. For Hemant, it was a path to a piece of paper far more dear—an invitation stamped with vermillion letters: HEMANT WEDS SHRUTI. Every night, Shruti hounded him for an update. It had been sixteen months already, and Signal had promised a green card in eighteen at most. If it were up to her, she'd wait nine lives. But her older sister's wedding was now set, and she was next. Her father was getting ready to advertise her. Hemant imagined the Banias—bankers, accountants, and the rest—sauntering into Shruti's house and looking her over greedily.

He had made the best of a bad thing at Signal so far. He had even used his good relationship with his foreman to get reassigned from pipefitter to welder, solving the absurd job role mix-up he had arrived with. Now it was time for action. He had to pick a winning side—tonight. Either join the freedom movement that had swept Signal's workforce, or help the company destroy it.

Signal was still promising him a green card. The question was: Could he trust them?

He remembered that morning a year ago, when Signal's armed guards pulled his friend Krishan out of bed, practically naked, unwashed, without as much as a cup of tea, and locked him up in the TV room to deport him. That shook Hemant and made him reassess the company. Days later, a supervisor pulled Hemant off the rig. Management wanted to see him. *I'm next*, Hemant thought. *I stood up for Krishan, and now they're deporting me.*

Darrell Snyder was sitting at a shiny conference table. Next to him was a man he introduced as Ronald Schnoor, Senior Vice President. Hemant winced, but Darrell delivered a compliment. Hemant's English was an asset, he said. So was his levelheadedness. Signal wanted him on a new worker committee. It was going to be called the Council of Elders.

Hemant sat stunned. He wasn't being deported. He was being promoted. He knew this path. He was the son of the Assistant Superintendent of Police. It's how he got ahead in school. It's how he got into college. Now, in America, he was on the inside track again. Not a great welder, but nonetheless, an Elder.

Hemant agreed to serve. He got a $2 an hour raise. And who wouldn't trade an oil rig scaffold in the Mississippi sun for an air-conditioned boardroom each Wednesday afternoon?

He took his responsibilities seriously, deploying his Delhi English to convey to the Americans the peculiar cultural needs of an Indian workforce, such as cooked food and bathroom breaks. He diligently gathered suggestions from the others to bring back to the boardroom: repair the coin laundry, clean the bathrooms.

In the meetings, Snyder usually took notes and asked follow-up questions. Schnoor was silent on all matters except one: the green cards. Whenever Hemant asked for an ETA, it was Schnoor who replied, always giving the same answer: updates soon.

One afternoon, Hemant explained that people were getting impatient with that line. *Who?* Schnoor barked. He demanded badge numbers.

Another time, Hemant brought up the bathrooms again. Four hundred men shared half a dozen portable toilets lined up in a stretch of mud. The wind carried the stench day and night. This time Darrell Snyder exploded. *Who's complaining?*

"It's me," Hemant said. "I'm the one complaining."

"You don't clean your own toilet in India?" Snyder said.

Hemant took a moment so he could respond calmly.

"I do," he said. Then, for the first time, he pushed back. "But in India, apart from the toilet, I have a bedroom, a living room, a kitchen, and a whole family. And I don't pay a thousand dollars a month in rent like I do here."

Snyder just snorted. Trying to stay constructive, Hemant offered an alternative. Why not allow the Indian men to live outside the labor camps, in Pascagoula or nearby Ocean City, and commute to work, like the Americans? Now Schnoor spoke up. Signal had put $7 million into building this labor camp for the Indians, and they intended to break even. Hemant said nothing to that.

He stayed silent, too, about the so-called freedom movement taking root in the labor camp. Some men seemed to think that if they couldn't get green cards from the company, they could get them by protesting the company. Evidently, Snyder and Schnoor were aware something was afoot. But they had no idea of its scale. They ordered random searches. Guards would come into the camp, pat men down, look under mattresses for God knows what—pamphlets? All they found were stashes of alcohol. They confiscated it. When groups of Indians were talking, the guards would sidle up to listen. The Indians would pause, then go right ahead discussing their plans to escape, in Hindi, Urdu, Punjabi, Tamil, Malayalam, and Telugu.

The other Indians did fall silent, though, when Hemant was near. They didn't know how he advocated for them in the boardroom. All they saw was a snitch. Among all but the tight-knit North Indians, he had become a pariah. It hurt. But it would all be worth it, if Signal kept its promise.

Hemant arrived at his bunkhouse. The other North Indians were all inside, waiting for him.

"What have you decided, Hemant? Do we stay or leave?"

They gathered around him expectantly. They would all follow his lead.

Hemant sat in his lower bunk, reached underneath, pulled out a bottle of whisky the guards hadn't confiscated. One of the perks of being a company man. There were many reasons not to trust Signal. But what did protests ever win, apart from firings and beatings? If he told Signal about the movement, he'd be saving the company from an enormous crisis. That would make him indispensable. If they got a green card for anyone, it would be for him.

All eyes were on him. "Well?" said one man.

Hemant cracked open the bottle.

5: Freedom Papers

March 7, 2008
Pascagoula, MS

THE NEXT NIGHT, the ballroom of my Pascagoula hotel was crammed for a mass meeting—our biggest yet, a feat of stealth. The Gujarati hotel owner, who'd been expecting a wedding party, poked his head in and noted the absence of a cake, drinks, women, children, festive outfits, decorations, music, and alcohol. I improvised. Rajan's sister was actually getting married in Delhi, I said. Since he was missing the wedding for a Pascagoula oil rig job, he was throwing his coworkers a party. This seemed to satisfy him. He left.

I looked out at the jittery assembly. A sea of faces with perfectly clipped chevron mustaches, like boats waiting to sail.

The plan was for the men to return to the man camp tonight as if for bed. Throughout the night, they'd trickle back out in groups of four or five. Rajan had already provided excuses and bribes to the guards. Outside, we'd organized a massive car pool and dozens of hotel rooms under aliases.

At 9 a.m., we'd gather in this room. Then we'd march back over to the company gates. There, invited media would watch us deliver the one-two punch we had been preparing for months. We'd report Signal and its agents—Malvern Burnett, Michael Pol, and Sachin Dewan—to the Department of Justice, alleging human trafficking, and we'd sue them in federal court, bringing claims of trafficking, racketeering, and racial discrimination.

I had to describe these logistics to the men in a way that would leave them electrified rather than terrified. To supply them with courage, I'd invited Ted Quant. Ted had been a friend and mentor since I arrived in New Orleans. He was a long-time labor organizer made of pure conviction. It was Ted who had connected me to the Black tradition in Southern labor organizing—the tradition I now wanted these workers to connect to. New Orleans had once been a union town, but African Americans were shut out of most union jobs. Ted and others before him had fought for a multiracial labor movement. It was a risky venture. When Ted became the first Black shop steward for the Amalgamated Meat Cutters Union in Louisiana's largest sugar plant, he'd carried a pistol into union meetings for protection—not from the bosses, but from the Klansmen among his own white coworkers, men he represented at the work site. Eventually, Ted won them over through his moral clarity. That's what I would call on today, to help the men overcome their fear.

Just as I stepped forward to address the men, Rajan motioned frantically from the back. He jerked his head in the direction of the door. I didn't understand—until I saw Hemant. I froze.

I was sure he wouldn't fall on our side. I'd been praying he'd at least remain neutral and claim afterward to the company that he knew nothing of our plans. But here he was, and from the looks of it, his intentions weren't friendly. He stood in the doorway scowling, arms folded. If he was planning to turn us in, he had arrived at precisely the right moment, to get precisely the information he needed. We were finished.

Others started noticing him too. A murmur vibrated through the room. In just moments it would destabilize the assembly's precarious resolve. I had one move. I had no idea if it would work.

I leaned into the front row and whispered in Ted's ear: "Change of plans. You're up."

Skipping the escape logistics altogether, I introduced Ted. He lunged to the front of the room. The men applauded, happy for any outside support.

"And to translate for Ted into Hindi," I said, "Hemant Khuttan!"

The crowd was bewildered. Hemant stared too. Then, slowly, as though unsure of why he was doing so, he walked up to the front. Ted hugged him like a proud father, confusing him even more. Then Ted faced the audience.

"It is not immoral to break an unjust law," he said. He paused, waiting for the interpretation.

Hemant was silent. His eyes were squinted in concentration—either confused by the double negative or trying to decide whether to translate at all.

Ted filled the vacuum: "Indeed, it is sometimes the only moral option."

Hemant translated the first line but stumbled on the second. I could see it on his face: he didn't believe in the truth of Ted's words. No son of an assistant superintendent of police would. But he *could* translate them into Hindi. He found a casual equivalent to Ted's, indeed: *Kabhi kabhi. Sometimes, you just got to.*

Ted gave him an encouraging nod, then pushed off into soaring oratory. *You've got a world to win.* Hemant struggled, but somehow kept up. Ted put people at ease, speaking their fears out loud, increasing their confidence in their campaign, in me, in their ability to win. In Ted's warmth, Hemant found confidence. And Hemant was noticing that the audience—his audience—was starting to lean in.

Then Ted paused, and his tone shifted as he issued a challenge.

"Before you set out on this freedom journey, tell me this. Who are you doing this for? To answer that, think of who did it for you."

Hemant pronounced the words but didn't seem to grasp their meaning. Ted went on. For as long as there's been an America, men and women have been brought over to work on the Mississippi River, just as they were now. Ted himself had worked the river once, loading boats dockside for $50 a week. Escaping river work to get free was a dream as old as America. If you have a way out now, Ted explained, it's because people died to make the road for you. Southern trade unionists. Black longshoremen. Enslaved Africans.

I studied Hemant. He was now clouded by confusion. Even as his translation grew more facile, his tone grew more remote. The further Ted reached into history, the less it all seemed to have to do with him. His reason for being here was as intimate as his own heart. As for the trade unionists and the rest, he pronounced their names tentatively, almost distastefully, and retreated into himself.

Then Ted asked, "They fought for you. Some died for you. Why?"

A pause. The room hung on Hemant for the answer. Hemant turned to Ted.

"For *dignity*."

Ted pronounced the word like it was a name for God. Hemant swallowed, then translated. Saying the word unlocked something in him. Ted had tapped into his deepest need.

"There is *dignity* in making a way for the future. There is *dignity* in fulfilling your responsibility. There is *honor* in that." His voice rose to a thunder: "There is *dignity* in running, if you're running toward freedom!"

Hemant's chest expanded, and his voice deepened, until he matched Ted's voice word for word. In Ted's thunder, the two men were fused. Together they summoned the crowd into one of the oldest human struggles and rang the name for its prize in unison: "Freedom!"

The crowd's silence was taut as steel—then it snapped. The room erupted. The fear inside the men ignited into raw courage. One man, a welder from Kanniyakumari, leapt to his feet and declared: "I thought I was coming to America to work. Now I know why I was sent: for freedom!" He drew a chorus of cheers. Another man, the brother of the first, rose and cried, "You are all as much my blood as this man here!" From the back, a song burst out.

Hemant stumbled, as if in a dream, to the back of the hall. I followed him there, watched him fumble for his phone. He called another North Indian, a welder working the night shift on Signal's rig.

"Forget your job. Get over here," Hemant said. "We're getting our freedom papers."

6: The Last Cashew

March 7, 2008
Pascagoula, MS

UPSTAIRS IN MY ROOM shortly before midnight, still elated, I steadied my hand to pour Rajan a cup of tea. In return, he reached into a pocket. Out came a pouch made of a bright green handkerchief.

"I've been saving these for a special occasion," he said.

I untied it with care. It was full of eggshell-colored cashew nuts. As we munched and washed them down with malty Lipton, I shared the latest news. Hemant's conversion wasn't the night's only miracle.

Here in Pascagoula, with Hemant joining, we now had all the Mississippi workers. In the other camp in Orange, Texas, Aby Raju and Murugan Kandhasamy had succeeded in convincing most of their coworkers to escape. Of the initial one hundred workers there, about seventy were left after some were fired and others ran away. But how would dozens of Indian oil rig builders cross Louisiana and travel three hundred miles to get to Pascagoula, Mississippi, by morning, in time for our protest and press conference?

As it turned out, while Ted and Hemant were setting the workers on fire in Pascagoula, Signal had solved the Orange problem for us. A supervisor had gathered the Texas-based men and told them to pack their bags. Production was ramping up in Pascagoula, and they were being sent there as reinforcements. The Orange Indians (as one supervisor called them) would be in Pascagoula by morning. The most confounding logistical difficulty of the escape had just been solved—by the company.

Rajan believed in omens, and this was a good one. With a flourish, he spread the green handkerchief on the desk. Then he laid the last seven cashews in a line on it, perfectly equidistant.

"It's nighttime," he said. "There's jungle all around. Your only road is narrow. You come upon a boulder." He pointed to the cashew nearest to me with a spindly finger. "You say, how unlucky I am, to face a boulder! Then an unseen hand comes down and clears it." Rajan picked up the cashew and held it up. "Divine intervention changes your perspective. You say, how lucky I am to be able to face the next boulder!" He popped the cashew in his mouth.

A wave washed over me, of love for Rajan and gratitude for our friendship. We had started out wary of each other, uneasy allies. Now we were brothers in arms. There had been dozens of moments like these: he knew just when to slow us down to marvel at the campaign's vicissitudes. I thanked him for the cashews. We each insisted the other eat the last one.

I hated to rush on from this moment, but there were still details to iron out about the morning's protest and press conference. I started to run through the order of speakers, including him.

"There's just one thing," Rajan said. "I'm not speaking tomorrow."

"Of course you are," I said, confused.

"Look. I can't be a public face of this campaign."

"What on earth do you mean? You're essential. We've built this campaign together, every step of the way."

Had he been threatened? Rajan was very protective of his wife—had Sachin called her at home to send a warning?

"I'm as committed as ever," he said. "I'll be your organizer behind the scenes. I just need to stay out of the press."

Now I understood. "Who is it you're trying to hide this from?"

His eyes dropped. "My wife. It's best if she doesn't know."

Behind the scenes, Rajan could be bolder than anyone. But once the news was out, he was afraid of having to admit that he was out of work and undocumented, to be seen by family as a shirker or deserter. If he could at least stay out of the press, he could get away with a temporary cover story, like a dry spell or illness.

But the campaign ahead would be months-long at least. I needed Rajan clearheaded for the whole thing—which meant I couldn't have him living a double life. I knew what that came with: the fear, the sleepless nights, the drinking to bear the weight of the dishonesty. I knew from having done it myself.

"Rajan," I said, "I understand. I told you I knew what it was like to be undocumented. That was because I was. It was one of the hardest things I ever did. Looking back, I wish I had told my family. It's the one thing that would have made it easier."

Rajan's eyes suddenly turned hard, unkind.

"We're not the same," he said. "You could pass as American. I never will."

My cheeks were hot. Solidarity aside, to him, we were from different worlds. Which meant that despite the hours we'd spent working side by side, he didn't fully trust me. And of all the workers, he was the one I was closest to. For all I knew, in the labor camps tonight, there were many more doubts swirling about me.

I needed to give my closest ally a deeper reason to trust me.

"Rajan," I said, "I have to tell you something no one else knows."

I CAME TO THE UNITED STATES at nineteen, to study literature. My love of books started with my father. At the beginning of each summer he'd reach into a dusty, deep cupboard and pull out yellowed paperbacks from his college years. I spent vacations inhaling those sweet vanilla pages. Then we'd talk about them. My father was a reserved man, not given to much conversation, but we connected through those books, and I peered into a part of him that wasn't fully realized. Those pages held a promise he wasn't able to pursue. And since they meant something to him, they came to mean a lot to me. So I announced plans to study literature in college.

My parents were about as distraught as they ever let on. Do anything else, they implored. Economics! Architecture! Something that affords you time to read on the weekends. I upped the ante by applying to American colleges. It was a foolhardy venture. On my father's civil service salary, we could barely even afford the application fees. As a foreign student, I couldn't get federal financial aid. So with zero notion of how a US education might get paid for, I sent off my applications.

The gamble paid off. The University of Chicago, my top choice school (with the semiofficial motto "Where fun comes to die"), offered me a full scholarship. That was largely unheard of for a foreign applicant. There was still the problem of room and board—a $10,000 a year expense. But my parents saw the scholarship as a sign that I might have a financially stable future, maybe as an academic. And it stirred something in my father. At my age, he'd been offered a prestigious Rhodes Scholarship to study at Oxford University, but his parents were too poor to afford the plane ticket and living expenses. So he decided he'd move heaven and earth to let me take the chance that he had missed. His parting advice for me:

"When you get to America, focus on Shakespeare. Master it. Get better at it than the Americans."

I graduated with an English degree and a new ambition. I wanted to become a theater director. I worked sixteen-hour days as an unpaid theater intern ("assistant to the director"). Nights and weekends, I worked odd jobs—some research for former professors, some copywriting. I had very little money, but I was the happiest I'd ever been, part of a tribe of young artists and actors that ranged from charismatic to tragically beautiful, all Americans, mostly funded by their parents. I was out of place, but that was my distinction, my badge of honor, the material for my plays.

Then I became undocumented. My crossing over was nothing as dramatic as escaping a labor camp. At first, I wasn't even aware of it. I was volunteering at a refugee services organization, and convinced its director to hire me to create a theater program there. But then they couldn't hire me. They said I didn't have the paperwork I needed. I called the advisor to international students at the University of Chicago. He said I had missed a deadline to apply for the temporary work permit the government gave to foreign students after graduation. He didn't make it sound much worse than an unreturned library book, and I had several of those. He referred me to an immigration lawyer downtown.

To afford the lawyer, I sold a prized possession: a 1940 first edition of a book called *My Name Is Aram*, by William Saroyan. I had read an excerpt from it in my eighth-grade reading textbook, an enchanting story about an Armenian American boy named Aram growing up among immigrants in Fresno, California. I grew up dreaming of acquiring a copy of *My Name Is Aram*. When I arrived in Chicago, I saved for a year to buy a first edition. Then I sold it to buy an hour with the lawyer.

The meeting ran ten minutes. The lawyer pronounced me out of status. He said President Bush was getting ready to give an amnesty to the undocumented, like Reagan did in '86. It was expected to happen in months, maybe weeks. I asked if I'd qualify.

"You got any problems?" he asked.

"Problems? Plenty."

He pursed his lips, as though trying to be patient with a slow student.

"*Crimes*," he said.

"No."

"University of Chicago?"

"Right."

"If you were coming from Dunkin' Donuts, I'd be worried," he said. "University of Chicago, you'll be fine."

I bounded out of his office. My future in America was secure. I now set about pursuing my dream: a theater company of my own that would tell the stories of immigrants and refugees. I recruited actors from restaurant kitchens, car washes, English classes. I found an unlikely rehearsal spot: the glorious, sprawling bungalow of renowned Shakespeare scholar David Bevington, whom I convinced to let me housesit while he and his wife, Peggy, were summering in Italy, in return for gardening and cleaning.

Most weeknights and each weekend at the Bevington home, I played host to exiles from around the world, refugees without papers who arrived at the back porch to turn their odysseys into art. Afterward, sitting in the verdant backyard, we dreamed of our futures in America.

There was the trade unionist couple from Quito, Ecuador, who'd told their little daughters to pack for Disneyland, then fled paramilitaries in the middle of the night. They dreamed of one day winning elections for expatriate seats in Ecuador's parliament. There was the Kurdish poet-judge from Iraq awaiting asylum, who said he was "Fed up of grief," and dreamed of falling in love. There was the Togolese human rights activist who'd left twelve children behind. He waited to be reunited with his "Football team." The Bevington house, spacious as it was, burst with our American hopes.

Then one Tuesday morning in September, I got on a train, my backpack bulging with plays from the summer, headed for a theater in Evanston that I hoped would stage them. The car was oddly empty. In the noisy rush, a woman's voice sounded behind me. "Is that a bomb?"

It wasn't until I turned around, right into her wide stare, that I realized her question was addressed to me. I grasped for composure. "No, ma'am, it's a backpack," I said, and then, absurdly, "It has these plays I'm working on."

She wasn't reassured. "It's a bomb," she concluded. I stood frozen in place. Others were staring. The train lurched forward unbearably. It was a long way to Evanston. I got out at the next stop. Only once I reached the theater did I learn that terrorists had flown planes into the World Trade Center.

Suddenly I went from scaling a peak to scrambling for a foothold. The professors who hired me for cash before now told me they couldn't risk it. We were still friends, they said as they fired me.

I traded one community for another. The people who could stand with me now were others who were stranded, without papers. My theater company, made of exiles, became my American family.

Meanwhile, without money coming in, I was evicted from my apartment. I desperately needed a job. My trade unionist friend from Quito introduced me to a man in Chinatown who printed me a fake social security card.

"What's your name?" he asked me. I told him.

"No, your new name. For the card." I thought for a second.

"Aram Saroyan," I said.

I WAS ON EDGE all the time. Law enforcement officials were rounding up undocumented immigrants. I furiously rehearsed to open a bold new play, about the myriad ways 9/11 had exploded our already complicated lives into a state of constant crisis. But it all started to feel meaningless. One night in early December, after rehearsal, my friend from Quito broke down. He decided he'd had enough, and jumped into Lake Michigan to drown in it. As I helped pull him out of the frigid water, turning his life into a play suddenly seemed futile, even foolish.

The night that defeated me came not long after. On my way home from a kitchen job, I stopped at a bar near the Cubs' Wrigley Stadium to use the restroom. I was standing at a urinal when the door swung open and two white men, both very drunk, came in. One of them came up next to me, turned to me, unzipped, and pulled himself out. "Scared of this, Osama?" I stepped back, startled. The other one pushed me to the floor. "Fucking Osama!" They urinated on me, all in good fun, then zipped up, laughed, swore some more, and left. I lay there in the warm pool for a while. When I picked myself up and used the sink to wash, I thought, oddly, that I looked nothing like Osama bin Laden.

A few days later, I packed up my few possessions, sold my remaining books, borrowed money from a friend, and bought a plane ticket to New Delhi for Christmas Eve—the cheapest day to fly to India. With my bags already packed, I dialed my parents to tell them I was coming back. It was my first call to India in months; they didn't even know I was undocumented. They answered brightly, relieved to finally be hearing from me. My sister got on the phone and I wished her a happy birthday. She paused, and then said a feeble thank you. Her birthday wasn't until the next day, but she didn't correct me. The awkward moment hung in the air. My parents sensed something was wrong, but I couldn't bring myself to share my news. I told them I had been busy, but that all was well. I decided it was better to just get on the flight and show up at their doorstep. Then I hung up and took the Blue Line train to O'Hare Airport.

As I stood in the departures terminal, a sense of failure washed over me. I remembered my father's send-off at the Delhi airport five years earlier. *Don't let the Americans know what hit them!* The only future he could imagine for me was success. I couldn't leave like this.

I wish it was the memory of his ringing voice that made me turn around, violins swelling behind it. The truth was that standing in the TSA line, I sighted a phalanx of immigration police agents headed in my direction. I was petrified. The TSA agent motioned to me. *Your turn.* She'd be able to see that my visa had expired years before. What if she called the agents over and they pulled me out of line? I told her weakly that I had forgotten something, turned around, and sprinted back to the train.

My ticket to Delhi was nonrefundable, so this was a $1,000 train ride back to the South Side of Chicago. As the worn and beaten car squealed along the elevated tracks, I stared out into the darkness and steadied my nerves. I had to make this ride worthwhile. If I was going to stay in America, it couldn't be to produce plays. It had to be to change things. That was the beginning of my transition from theater to community organizing.

I LOOKED UP at Rajan as if from the bottom of a well. He was the first person I had ever shared this with. He regarded me without pity, then smiled, slightly but warmly. He slid the last cashew toward me.

"You need this more than I do," he said.

Then he took out his phone and dialed. A woman's voice sounded. His wife.

"Shamitha," he said. "You'll never believe what I'm about to do tomorrow." He flashed his heavy eyebrows at me. "I'm going to be famous."

7: The Day Time Stopped

March 9, 2008
Pascagoula, MS

THAT NIGHT, WE PULLED OFF the impossible: the escape of hundreds of men from a guarded labor camp, essentially unnoticed.

The day-shift workers waited until Darrell Snyder and the Signal admin workers were gone for the day, then took full advantage of the months of softening-up work Rajan and others had done with the guards. They trickled out four or five at a time over the course of the next few hours, getting ferried by staff members of mine and the few workers who had cars to the Pascagoula hotel, for the next day's "Wedding." They took only the bare minimum of belongings with them, so that even if a guard had snooped through their housing trailers in their absence, he would see nothing that suggested a mass escape.

The night-shift workers walked from the work yard to the Signal parking lot, with more drivers ready to whisk them away.

In all, three hundred men escaped in Pascagoula, joining the seventy who'd been transferred from Orange. This was nearly all of Signal's remaining Indian workforce after the firings, runaways, and self-deportations of the last six months. Fewer than two dozen Signal loyalists stayed in the camps.

The perpetually dozing guards noticed nothing that night—until the strangest sound of all hung over the camp the following morning.

Silence.

Meanwhile in our hotel, chaos reigned. Every day for a year, I had spent every ounce of energy helping these men lose their fear of the company. I hadn't anticipated their fear of daylight saving time, which fell that very day. Daylight saving time was not observed in India, and the men took it as a bad omen in the United States. To make matters worse, no matter how many times we'd confirmed and reconfirmed our start time—for the press conference for local journalists, for the bus drivers who'd take workers to the kickoff march—everyone seemed to have gotten it wrong.

Rajan stepped up as only he could. He gathered the men for a pep talk that turned daylight saving time from a troubling omen to a symbol of world-changing power.

"The day time stopped!" he cried. "Remember this day!"

The buses took the buoyed men to the starting point of their march. With camera operators scrambling to keep up, the men set off in a noble procession along Pascagoula's Port Road. Their destination: Signal's gates. They would march right up to the site of their captivity to show the company, and the world, that they were free.

The sun poured elation on them. Their iridescent hard hats reflected the clear blue sky. Rajan led the column in blazing orange overalls. They moved along the road like a pulsing, singing river. But when Signal's gates came into view, the men halted, momentarily hushed.

"Will they come out to talk to us?" asked a man next to me. As if to answer him, the gates rumbled shut.

"They're busy," another man said. "Busy looking for us."

The laughter spread. I shouted a protest call I had learned in Mumbai and taught to the men: "Awaaz do!" (Give me your voices!)

A chorus of men shouted the response: "Hum ek hain!" (We are one!)

The chant swelled into a crescendo and rose above the iron gates, drowning out their fear. But not mine. I had posted lookouts along the US 90 highway and on the main streets nearby to watch for police cars. Once on the highway, they could reach us in minutes.

I signaled Rajan. He ran like an orange blur from one man to another, pulling together the stage picture we had rehearsed. The men were lined up at the company gates, fingers on the brims of their hard hats. The press hurried into place with their cameras. At my signal, the men would fling their helmets over the gates in a symbol of liberation.

A lawyer whispered into my ear. Police had been sighted.

I gave the signal. And gave it again. The men just stood there. No hard hats flew.

"What's going on?" I asked Rajan. The men were stalling. A loud discussion was brewing, in Malayalam.

"There's a split between helmet-throwers and helmet-keepers," Rajan said. "Helmets aren't cheap."

"We need to move. Can we settle this?"

"Why not let them work it out? Debate increases political confidence, as you say."

"The police are coming," I hissed. Rajan's face changed. We brokered a quick compromise.

While the cameras rolled, the men threw their hard hats straight up into the sky. It was one of the most beautiful sights I'd ever seen.

The helmet-keepers collected theirs, and I rushed the men into the caravan of getaway cars and buses. As we roared onto US 90, the keepers waved their helmets out windows.

The police reached Signal minutes later and puzzled over the pile of hard hats in the dust.

OUR NEXT STOP was Malvern Burnett's law office in the Garden District of New Orleans. We spilled out of the buses a block away. Ted Quant and I ran ahead, with the rest following. I had called Burnett's office ahead of time and secured an appointment, posing as an employer looking to bring in H-2B workers. A scout had confirmed that Malvern was there that morning. He was in for a surprise.

In deciding on how to confront Malvern, we faced a dilemma. It was one thing to convince liberals in New Orleans that a giant Mississippi oil fabricator had trafficked workers and held them in forced labor. It was quite another thing to convince them that respectable Malvern was at the heart of the scheme. He was the immigrant's best friend.

I'd learned this while looking for local counsel for our lawsuit. We needed a New Orleans–based attorney, as the case was in the Fifth Circuit. Our prospects were initially excited at the chance to be "Atticus

Finch for the immigrants," as one put it. But Burnett's name brought the conversation to a stammering halt.

"I hope Mal didn't do anything wrong."

"Mal? No, not Mal."

And my favorite: "Human trafficking? Mal? He probably didn't mean it."

It was Ted Quant who knew how to dislodge Malvern's halo. The usual forms of protest wouldn't work—a candlelight vigil outside his office, pastors locking arms. We accessed a more radical tradition. After the end of slavery, white vigilante groups unleashed violence on the recently enslaved. Abolitionists turned a racist tactic on its head to defend against the terror. They interrupted vigilante crime by conducting citizen's arrests.

Ted and I had sprung citizen's arrests on Southern bosses before. Usually it was figures like "Bimbo" Relan, a cigar-chomping farmer in cowboy boots whom I confronted after his Mexican workers told me he'd held them captive at his strawberry fields. Bimbo denied it and fended us off with a shotgun, even as he shared all kinds of colorful views ("The Jews are the only people who like to work"). Malvern Burnett was a stark contrast: a well-heeled immigration attorney. It took Ted to see the continuity. *Looks to me this guy took captives with a visa program instead of a gun*, he said of Malvern. *Why should we treat him any different?*

So Ted, as the citizen, was going to conduct a citizen's arrest of Malvern Burnett. We planned to announce who we were, inform him that this was a citizen's arrest, and recite our allegations. Forced labor. Trafficking with respect to peonage. Unlawful conduct with respect to documents. After Ted read him his rights, we'd ask him to stay until law enforcement arrived.

The farmers who'd faced this were stunned, angry—as we imagined Malvern would be. In case he had a gun, we planned to stay close to the door. And we couldn't hold him against his will. If he asked us to leave, we'd step outside—at the very moment the workers would converge on the office, chanting.

We reached Malvern's office, a two-story white shotgun house with an imposing iron gate and an American flag hanging from the balcony. We tried the gate. It was locked shut.

I could already hear the workers' chanting from half a block off. But they wouldn't have the satisfaction of confronting Malvern. He was long gone.

"Someone tipped him off," Ted said.

Only a few trusted people knew we were coming. Somehow word had leaked out. It was the first sign of the trouble to come.

8: Paradise

March 9–10, 2008
New Orleans, LA

THE FAILURE OF our quixotic action on Malvern Burnett did nothing to dampen the men's exuberance. From their perspective, he ran away. *From them.* They were invincible. Some wanted to stay outside his office to confront him, even camp there overnight. But several hundred brown men couldn't stay out in the open for too long. We needed to hide.

Thankfully, we had just the place: the Canal Street Hotel. The hotel had sustained heavy wind damage during Hurricane Katrina. When it was repaired, it had roared back to business housing out-of-town contractors and their crews. The lobby swarmed with disaster entrepreneurs. Men ran unlicensed bars out of their rooms. Police officers looking to pick up rebuilding work on the side played poker with contractors. I had been there many times to rescue immigrant workers who had been crammed into rooms by labor brokers, then abandoned. But two and a half years after Katrina, the hotel's business had dried up, so it was empty. It was also the only place we could afford to put up so many men indefinitely.

We gathered in the hotel ballroom. First, I presented my staff—the half-dozen bedraggled, sleep-deprived young organizers who'd carried out the logistical feats leading up to the escape. I had been worried about their exhaustion and flagging morale. While I had the benefit of seeing the men in person and drawing energy from them, my team had been working in a blur booking hotel rooms, finding buses, coordinating press, all on an impossible timeline. On top of that, they were worried about our workers' center's finances. They were right to be.

We were a tiny organization. At that moment, we had $1 million on hand that was meant to last us for the next nine months, until our funders, organizations like the Ford Foundation, cut their next checks. But our budget hadn't included providing room and board for hundreds of welders and pipefitters. My finance director gave me the back-of-the-envelope math: even the leanest costs (dozens of cut-rate rooms at the Canal Street Hotel, plus $10 per man per day in food costs, with wholesale ingredients) would add up to a bill of $7,000 a day, almost $50,000 a week.

I was frantically trying to raise money and recruit new donors, but the clock was ticking. At this burn rate, we'd run out of money in five months. Then we'd be finished. We had nothing to sell. Our most valuable physical asset was a Xerox machine. And it was broken.

So when I introduced my team, it was more for their sake than for the men's. The newly freed Indian workers greeted the staff with the kind of cheers usually reserved for champion football teams. My young idealists took pride in scorning praise. But today the applause and affection of the strangers they'd helped moved them deeply. It was the tonic they needed. Even my finance director teared up.

I laid out our next steps. We had submitted our official complaint to the DOJ and would be pushing them to open an investigation quickly. When they did, their first step would be to interview victims. We'd wait for them here in New Orleans. And we'd urge them to grant us Continued Presence, the special status designed for immigrant trafficking victims to protect them during the course of an investigation. Continued Presence came with work permits. So as soon as the DOJ recognized the men's allegations as credible and worth investigating, the men would be able to take jobs and pay down their debts.

In the meantime, their greatest vulnerability was their undocumented status. The press and the defense attorneys for Signal and Malvern might look to blame the men, cast their trafficking claims as a ploy by people who chose to overstay their visas and now wanted to duck punishment. I'd already heard the men insisting that they "came in legally," straining to distance themselves from being defined as undocumented. I told them they needed to do the opposite. They needed to come out as undocumented. Own it and explain why they were fighting for status now. Not just to the press and the DOJ. They needed to come out to the hardest audience they had, the ones they wanted to protect from the news: their families.

"Get ready to tell your stories," I told them. "Call your families tonight. Your wives, your brothers, your sons and daughters. Tell them what you've been through. Without veneer or gloss. Without apology. Without shame. Tell them what's happened, and what you're doing about it." In the coming months, in interviews, in depositions, and in the press, the men would be forced to revisit every humiliation they faced in the labor camps with great specificity. If they had already narrated these to their families, they could face other interlocutors unashamed.

Then I delivered news. When the DOJ opened investigations like these, it partnered with a law enforcement agency to investigate. That could either be ICE—Immigration and Customs Enforcement, an aggressively anti-immigrant agency we definitely didn't want on the team—or the FBI, which we did. And, in fact, the Mississippi FBI had just called us. It looked like our complaint had reached them. New cheers went up.

On cue, the doors of the ballroom swung open. I'd teed up a brass band for this moment, and it burst into golden sound. The men started dancing, wildly, joyous in their bodies for the first time since they left India. The room was a riot of hope. Men embraced each other. Some embraced me. One man, a barrel-chested Tamil pipefitter, approached me. It looked like there were a hundred things he wanted to say, but he put it all in one word:

"Freedom."

THE CANAL STREET HOTEL became a workers' paradise. I arrived there each morning with a bucket of coffee and a civil rights figure. Ted Quant taught Southern labor history. Reverend James Orange drove in from Atlanta to connect the Indian workers' struggle to Dr. King's. John O'Neal taught freedom songs. Lolis Elie told of defending Black Panthers from being evicted for their politics, and suing President Nixon on behalf of African American women on welfare. Brother Don and Sister Lillian from the New Orleans Hope House offered teachings from the Catholic worker movement.

The managers gave us the keys to their unstaffed, empty kitchen, which Rajan commandeered. He and his helpers did massive grocery runs, then cooked. Biryani. Lamb kebabs. Egg curry. Breakfast and dinner were communal; lunch was delivered door to door on a luggage dolly. After dinner, men gathered in the ballroom to drink and entertain each other with talent shows.

The breakout star was a quiet man from Kerala with soft eyes and a kind face. He announced that in addition to being a pipefitter, he was also a "Mimicry artist." When he perched atop a stool, the room fell silent to his exquisite presence. He cupped his hands to his mouth. We heard a bird wake up in a Kerala town. Its wings flapped. It flew in search of food. Alighted by a river. The water gurgled. Children splashed. They swam to a village. Ran into a market. Drove off on a scooter. Night fell. Crickets chirped. The bird came back to nest.

Home.

9: Restless

March 11–16, 2008
New Orleans, LA

A WEEK WENT BY. From the Department of Justice, there was radio silence. The FBI had vanished after that first call. And at the Canal Street Hotel, hope had soured. Restless and desperate to work, the men were breaking open the whisky earlier and earlier. When I arrived there each evening, the sea of faces was more pleading than proud.

Even Rajan's mood was turning dark. One night, he had decided to deliver meals himself on the luggage dolly. He'd made skin-on chicken legs, pan-fried to a golden crisp. When certain men opened their doors, he offered them an extra drumstick for a small bribe. The men gleefully agreed. As they fished in their pockets, Rajan announced that this was a sting operation, "an assault on corruption, conducted by the union on behalf of the common man." His victims would be exposed in an evening meeting. He was serious. I spent a very difficult hour talking him out of publicizing the "chicken bribery scandal."

Meanwhile, the vultures were circling. The men's labor was a precious commodity, and all manner of people wanted to profit from it. I was getting phone calls from labor brokers, shipyard operators, temp agency owners, and recruiters. They'd heard that Signal's legendary workforce had bolted, and that I knew where they were. One caller insisted he could get work for them at the Port of New Orleans if they paid him $500 each. Another wanted to pay me $10,000, as if they were my property. ("I'll take 'em off your hands.") A Houston-based Indian American real estate entrepreneur proposed we go into the worker-leasing business together. Most of them promised fantastical work-arounds for the legal status issue. And they pleaded that I tell them where the workers were. I refused, of course. If the vultures started showing up at the Canal Street Hotel, the men might have to leave.

One evening, I squeezed in a call to my parents, my first since the escape from Signal. They were getting news of me from the front pages of Indian national dailies, which had been blaring their outrage at each new detail about Signal's labor camps.

"We've been saving every paper, every day," my mother said proudly.

"The Indian parliament will probably be taking this up," my father added. We had set off an international incident. Through my exhaustion, I savored the moment. My parents had always been supportive of my work, but it was so far and apart from them. This campaign was bridging our worlds.

I told them the latest. The Indian Embassy in Washington, DC, silent for ten days, had just contacted us. I had written to the Indian ambassador asking him to come meet with the men himself. He was now sending a pair of staffers to New Orleans. I wanted the ambassador to join our call for an investigation.

"I very much doubt he would do that," said my father.

"But it's his job to advocate for his countrymen in the US," I said.

"Well, if I were with the embassy, I would ask: Did these workers register before they left for the US?"

"Register?" I felt myself getting defensive. "Register with whom?"

"The Indian authorities. Before they leave, they are supposed to inform the authorities. If they don't, they forfeit the advocacy of the Indian government."

I gritted my teeth.

"Well," I said, "The workers need their government to show some concern for their welfare."

My father said matter of factly that the government had bigger fish to fry than five hundred migrant workers. "India's negotiating a nuclear deal with the US. You may be heroes to the press, but to the government, you're a distraction. For the ambassador, the best outcome would be that all these workers return to India."

In an instant I was back at my family dinner table, my naive idealism colliding with my father's ridged brow and formidable worldliness. He had been a diplomat, and often spoke from the point of view of people in power, instructing me on "The difference between *is* and *ought*."

"They'd gladly return to India," I said, "If not for their debts. How about the Indian government just pay to make them whole?"

But I knew he was right. In fact, the Minister of Overseas Indian Affairs, Vayalar Ravi, had called my cell phone a few days ago in the middle of the night (his afternoon). He'd yelled his demand that the workers drop their "Drama T.V. show" and come home. Soon after, a story in the Indian press quoted an embassy official about the "greedy, illiterate Indians" who decided to run away, and left their employer "Holding the can."

Another call came through. I put my parents on hold to take it. It was Rajan.

"Police are here," he said. "Lots of police."

I ran toward the Canal Street Hotel, fearing the worst. That Michael Pol had found them. That he was there with a police squad to recapture his investment. Indian men whom Pol had brought in past years told me he had done this before. Once, they said, Pol had gotten word that dissatisfied workers were meeting after hours, and he'd gathered police officers and burst into the workers' quarters, compelling them to be silent. I imagined Pol in the lobby now, Rajan in handcuffs, police officers following the scent of roasted spices to men's rooms. Hauling them away, terrified, in their underwear.

When I got there, the lobby was empty except for Rajan—sweating, crumpled, waiting on the seedy velour couch.

"What happened?"

"I came down to prep tomorrow's breakfast. That's when I saw them. There were a dozen of them," he said wearily. "They looked around. Woke up the guy behind the desk, asked him some questions, and left."

"How are you doing?"

"Recovering from a heart attack. But it might be the ghee I've been cooking in."

"You should get to bed," I said. "We have an early morning. The embassy men will be here at nine."

"Listen," Rajan said. "The police aren't our only problem. The men are at their wit's end. It's been two weeks since they've worked. They can't just keep sitting here. They need to move. Reporters and civil rights are fine, but they need to talk to decision makers. Otherwise, they're staring into the abyss. They're bleeding hope."

Rajan disappeared into the cavernous Canal Street Hotel. I sank into the seedy couch, in case the police returned. They didn't. I was there all night.

The ambassador's men arrived in the morning. Rajan and I greeted them outside the hotel. One was short and plump. The other was tall, with a narrow face, glasses, and long tufts of hair growing out of his ears. Rajan and I had given them names: Murga Sahib and Bakra Sahib. Master Chicken and Master Goat.

Murga extended a hand. It felt like a raw drumstick.

"We thank you," said Murga Sahib.

"India thanks you," said Bakra Sahib.

"For what?" I asked.

"For taking care of our boys. We have come to meet them."

"But first, we shall take some tea," announced Murga Sahib, holding up a finger to flag down an invisible waiter.

"The men are furious with you," I said. "The *New York Times* wants their story, but their own government is nowhere to be found."

"Not correct!" said Bakra Sahib, hurt. "Do you know what Ambassador Sa'ab said when he saw the news? 'Who will go?' Just like that: 'Who will go?' And we said, 'We will go.'" He put his hand on his heart.

"And we have come," said Murga Sahib. "On behalf of ambassador of India. Who is representing government of India."

"You've made your position clear to the press," I said. "'Greedy, illiterate Indians.' That's what you've decided without even meeting the men—that they are manufacturing their trafficking claims? Playing victim, gaming the system?"

Bakra Sahib considered my point, one hand twirling the hair from his earlobe.

"These are semiskilled workers. Uneducated. So when they complain, we call the companies to determine if they are lying."

"In that case, you cannot meet with them," Rajan barked.

"But we've come all the way!" Bakra Sahib protested.

"Go back to the ambassador," I said. "Tell him to come down here himself. With an open mind."

"This is deeply regrettable," Bakra Sahib said woefully.

"Before we go, at least tell us this," Murga Sahib said. I readied myself for the start of a real conversation.

"Is there a place you would recommend for dinner, which would fit into our per diem allowance of thirty-five dollars per head?"

"Go to Brennan's," I spat. It was the most overpriced spot in the city. "Order the étouffée."

THAT EVENING, IN a fit of powerlessness and anger, needing to strike out at someone, I decided to interrupt the ambassador's men at Brennan's. A waiter led me up to their table. Their faces brightened.

"Good of you to turn up, Soni!" said Bakra Sahib.

"Tell me this," said Murga Sahib. "What is gumbo?"

"A soup of bhindi," said Bakra Sahib.

"Then why not call it Ladyfinger Soup?" Murga Sahib said, plucking an imaginary harp with his fingers. "Gumbo! Why such a type of funny name?"

"*Gumbo* was the Geechie word for okra," I snapped. "Which was brought here by enslaved Africans to the Gullah islands. Do you even understand where you are?"

I was yelling. A young waiter stared at us.

"Our friend is taking too much tension," Bakra Sahib apologized.

"Tell me something," said Murga Sahib. "Étouffée. That is a type of shrimp curry?"

I left in disgust, feeling even worse than when I got there.

THAT NIGHT, MY first sleep in forty-eight hours was restless and fitful. Then my eyes popped open. I saw through the dark with a shining clarity. I knew what we must do. I squinted to check the time: 3 a.m. I reached for my phone.

Rajan answered, groggy.

"We're going to march," I said.

PART FOUR

TRUTH MARCH

1: Satyagraha

March 17–18, 2008
New Orleans, LA

AT 7 A.M., I was awake after three hours of sleep, wired on my late-night epiphany, and ravenous. All I had in the fridge was orange juice. I gulped it from the bottle. Rajan called.

"I had the craziest dream," he said. "You told me we were going to Washington, DC—on foot."

"Get the men together," I said. "You weren't dreaming."

EACH NEW DAY underground, the men had awoken increasingly restless. Today, when I arrived at the Canal Street Hotel, they barely took notice. They spilled in and out of the ballroom, buzzed with pent-up energy, veered toward altercations with each other. Rajan had recommitted to the chicken bribery sting operation and was prowling the room for victims. Those without cigarettes ganged up on those who had them. The mimicry artist was knocked off his stool before he could get a warble out.

"Our wait is over," I announced. "Or it can be."

That got their attention. They took their seats.

Their daring escape nine days ago, I said, had made global news. But despite the press, the Department of Justice hadn't yet contacted us. Nor had the FBI, after that initial call. The Indian ambassador had called us "greedy, illiterate Indians." But let's not be surprised. They were following the playbook of people in power: First they ignore you. Then they ridicule you. Then they attack you. Then you win.

How do we win? Not by sitting still, I said. How did Gandhi win? With a satyagraha, a truth march. And in this country, how had Southern freedom fighters won? They took a page from Gandhi, and *they* marched.

I proposed we march as well. From New Orleans to Washington, DC. Straight to the lawyers at the Department of Justice, to demand that they investigate. Whatever was holding them up, going right to their doorstep in DC would force their hand. When they began their investigation, it would trigger Continued Presence, which meant the men would have protection from deportation and work permits for the duration of the investigation. They could continue to pay down their debts and support their families. *You need to work, so we need to walk.* We would also take our appeal directly to the Indian ambassador, to demand that he help.

I admitted it was risky. The men had already come out as undocumented to their families. This would be coming out to the world. Lawyers advised undocumented people to stay hidden from view. But hiding wasn't working. Our march would be a traveling act of civil disobedience.

I studied their faces as they thought it over. What I didn't tell them was that there were no other good options. Now that the police were on their trail, they couldn't stay here. And I had nowhere else to put several hundred men.

Aby Raju rose. "I say we march."

Others cheered. The men leapt into motion. We couldn't take everyone, so the hundreds of men elected sixty leaders among them, a vanguard, to walk to Washington.

We sheltered the others in a network of safe houses spread out over Louisiana. We rented a bus, for emergencies, illness, and the tracts of highway you just can't walk.

I woke at the crack of dawn the next day to throw a few things in a backpack before we headed out. Only then did I finally register the papers that had been littering my tiny kitchen table for weeks.

A pang of anxiety punched through my excitement about the march. The papers were my own immigration application, to turn my current "conditional resident" status into permanent residency. It had been spread out on my kitchen table for months, but I had been too busy even to get started. Now it was due in a week, a nonnegotiable deadline.

I shoved the application into a folder and stuffed it into my backpack. I'd have to find a way to fill it out during the march.

Then we set out on foot for the nation's capital.

THE SIXTY MARCHERS gathered in Lafayette Square that morning in flannel half-sleeved shirts, baseball caps, and a mood of solemn preparation. But once they set off, something changed. A realization ran through them. *We're really doing this.* They walked tall, with purposeful strides, holding signs inspired by the 1968 Memphis sanitation workers' strike: DIGNITY. I AM A MAN.

"Who are you guys?" people asked on the street. The men pressed lengthy pamphlets into their hands. We got fist bumps, claps on the back, fists raised in solidarity, honks of support from drivers. A trombone player walking home gave us a few bars of "When the Saints Go Marching In."

All of that changed once we left the New Orleans city limits. Crossing into Chalmette, honks of support turned into angry blares. Drivers rolled down their windows to jeer and swear. In Baton Rouge, a beer bottle flew out of a car and hit Hemant in the Adam's apple. He couldn't speak above a whisper for an hour. Our bathroom breaks at gas stations became more cautious.

Much of the highway forced us to walk single file, which made conversation nearly impossible. By 8 p.m. each day, the men were starved for human connection and called India to wake up their families.

That was my favorite part of the day. Sixty men in one long line, phones pressed against their ears. Fathers trying to raise their kids via long-distance call, husbands negotiating with their wives, sons getting chewed out by their moms. Life. I'd move up and down the line, catching snatches of conversation. Lanky Hemant describing his heroics to Shruti. Stolid Jagpal Yadav being the man of the house. Stout Amar Singh doting on his daughter. Aby making gurgling noises to his son. Murugan describing the road trip to his mom.

But the voice I was most drawn to was the shyest one, speaking a language I didn't know. Saravanan was a Tamil welder, and at twenty-four, one of the youngest of the men. Amid the liquid sounds of his rushing Tamil, I'd hear the English words of our campaign—trafficking, DOJ, Continued Presence, Washington, T visa. It was different from the way most men talked to their families, giving brief "Updates." This was a deep back-and-forth discussion.

Afterward, Saravanan told me it was with his father. He was very supportive and wanted to know the ins and outs of the campaign. "He wants to read it like a book."

I said I was glad he had that kind relationship with his dad.

"That's new, brother," Saravanan said. He only ever called me *brother*.

"How new?" I asked, surprised.

"It just started."

When Saravanan was very young, he said, they were close. But when he was ten, his mother died and his father remarried. Saravanan was furious. He rejected his father's authority completely. At the first chance he got, he left home, bolted to Singapore, where a lot of Tamil migrants were working the shipyards, and learned to weld. Then he came to America.

But recently ("after your 'talk to your families' speech, brother") he called his dad out of the blue to tell him what he was about to do. He braced for the scolding, but to his surprise, his father was proud. Since then, they talked every day. At the moment they were furthest apart, they'd found a way to come together. I asked what kind of advice his father gave.

"He says it is like rock. Tamil rocks take a long time to form. He said inside myself there is something like that happening. It will take time. But it will make me strong."

2: Surveilled

March 21, 2008
Montgomery, AL

ON THE FOURTH day of the march, we arrived in Montgomery. Tired. Footsore. Hungry. But stronger for every step. We were in front of the black granite Civil Rights Memorial. The water running down its gleaming edifice seemed to wash away the curses that had been hurled at us, the shards of glass from bottles flung out of passing cars. The names on the tablet, I explained, belonged to forty civil rights workers who had died so we could march. We filed inside. In the memorial's cool darkness, our footfalls sounded like healing rain.

We emerged an hour later into the platinum light. Pausing again in front of the edifice, we felt that we ourselves were carved out of that dignified stone. Then one worker tapped my shoulder, pointed up to an adjoining building.

"That man on the roof," he said.

My eyes were still adjusting. "What's he holding?"

"A video camera. He's recording us."

I ran into the building. Hunted for the elevator. I guessed it was a white supremacist. I had dealt with them before. Chased them off of day labor corners when they posed as contractors to photograph workers. Faced off with them when they played cop for employers who didn't want to pay.

I raced out onto the roof. The cameraman was gone. From over the edge, I saw the workers below, peering up at the drama. "Into the bus!" I yelled down.

Then I spotted it: a van emblazoned with the logo of a construction company. It confirmed my suspicion. I ran down, rapped at the back door.

The door swung open. The man from the roof was inside. He was short, wiry, white, with a silver mustache.

"What do you want?"

"You were secretly recording a peaceful civil rights gathering," I said. "So the question is, what do you want?"

He offered a business card. I was surprised. Racist vigilantes didn't hand out cards. MICKEY PLEDGER, it said. ALABAMA DIRECTOR, IMMIGRATION AND CUSTOMS ENFORCEMENT.

I asked for his badge. He showed it.

"Why are we under ICE surveillance?"

"Above my pay grade."

"But you're the ICE director?"

"In Alabama. You've been under surveillance since you left New Orleans. You'll be surveilled till you reach DC."

Then he hid himself back in the van.

I WISHED MY WALK BACK to the bus could have been longer. I needed time to think. How would I explain what this was? Last summer, President George Bush's efforts to win an amnesty for the undocumented had been defeated by Southern Republicans. To appease the right wing of his own party, Bush had vastly expanded the immigration police force, a federal army that targeted immigrants. They had arrested over a thousand people without warrants and deported over three hundred thousand last year. Now we were in their crosshairs.

When I got on the bus, the workers applauded my bravura in the chase. *You showed him!* They were inspired. Entirely without fear—too much so. I found myself in the strange new position of needing to make them afraid.

I explained what this was. Not a lone vigilante, or Michael Pol's friends on the police force doing him a solid. It was a threat of a different magnitude. An interstate, government-sanctioned surveillance operation with us at the center.

The men absorbed the news.

"So what do we do now?" asked Rajan.

The truth was, I didn't know.

"We have three options," I said. "First, hide out here in Montgomery."

"We'd be sitting ducks," said Aby Raju. He was right.

"Second, abandon the march. Stay on the bus. Ride straight to DC."

On balance, that was the safest option. We'd be in DC in two days.

"And the third option?" asked Rajan. It was the most dangerous one.

"Keep marching," I said. Proceed on foot, with ICE on our tail, out of Montgomery, through unfriendly towns. To Atlanta. To North Carolina. To Virginia. Finally—if we were lucky—to DC.

"We'll march," they replied in a chorus. Their newfound boldness brought them to their feet and carried them past me out onto the street.

"Hang on," I said, catching up.

We started to walk, chanting the Mumbai call and response: "Awaaz do—Hum ek hain!" Past the surveillance lookout point. Past the first White House of the Confederate United States, where Jefferson Davis had his residence. Toward Atlanta, as the sky turned molten.

I imagined Mickey Pledger and his surveillance team in that white van, following us to the Tennessee border. Pulling up alongside their Georgia counterparts for the handoff. They'd roll down their windows. Talk logistics. They'd lose sight of us momentarily as night fell. But they'd know exactly where we were.

Because as we crossed over the Chattahoochee River, the men had broken out in song.

3: Greensboro, USA

March 25, 2008
Greensboro, NC

AS WE REACHED GREENSBORO, Saravanan was talking to his dad again, sounding brighter than ever. I was listening for English pebbles in the Tamil river.

"Montgomery . . . Alabama . . . ICE," he was saying. Then he pumped his fist. "Department *for Justice!*"

Saravanan was my bellwether of the men's mood, and tonight, he was too optimistic, which meant they all were. They hadn't fully absorbed what we were up against. They were clear that winning legal status would take a fight. But, for them, the march *was* the fight. The closer we got to Washington, the more confident they became. Arriving in DC was tantamount to winning, because they had faith in America's institutions—more than most Americans. In India, you bribe judges and buy the police. Here, the men believed, truth would prevail. It was right there in the name: the Department *for Justice.*

When we arrived at the Beloved Community Center at 2 a.m., Reverend Nelson Johnson was waiting there with the key. He had sheltered many people over the years in this warm brick building. Some had been on the run. But none of them had looked as happy to be there as the procession of Indian men who now streamed into the center. They thanked him as they entered, bowing slightly, shaking his hand and then touching their hearts. Inside, they unrolled their sleeping bags, tired, but with relish. It was the exhaustion of pilgrims, not refugees.

I WAS UP with the sun. So were the men. Some were outside already, talking to their families in India. The cell reception wavered, so they delivered news from the march loudly. *North Carolina today! Virginia tomorrow! After that, Washington, to the Department for Justice!* They looked up from their phones when they saw me and smiled brightly.

"Good morning, Saketji! Ready to march?"

"As soon as the pastor gets here," I said.

Reverend Johnson arrived at 9 a.m. "Good morning, brother," he said warmly. "What do you need?"

I thanked him profusely for the sanctuary he had provided. Before we got back on the road, I said, I needed these men to hear his story.

"Which one?" he said.

I explained our situation. During our Gandhian walk, we had learned we were at the center of a federal surveillance operation ordered by top immigration officials. We didn't know why. This worried me. But I was even more worried about how little the men seemed to understand what we were up against—American institutions designed to protect the status quo. They had no sense of our opposition.

He nodded. I assembled the men around him.

Reverend Johnson and his wife, Joyce, had once led a march, I told them. Its results were historic, and instructive. He wanted to tell them about it.

The men had been impatient to leave. But when Nelson started speaking, his brassy timbre drew them in.

It was the summer of '79. Nelson and Joyce, both North Carolina natives, were community organizers living in Greensboro. North Carolina was textile country, and Black workers there were trapped in a racial caste system. Nelson and his comrades, members of a Communist workers' group called Workers Viewpoint Organization, had been stirring Black millworkers to action in their plants, spurring them to fight for safe conditions and fair pay and trying to build an independent union. A breakthrough came at the Proximity Print Works plant, where almost one hundred mill workers unionized. Workers at other plants took notice and started streaming into the meetings Nelson held at the Cosmos Club, a Black-owned nightclub in Greensboro.

Unions had tried to win in the textile mills before. But this effort set out to be multiracial. That was new. When Nelson and others started inviting the white workers to join their efforts, it further energized the Black workers, who grasped that a biracial majority could change the rules of the whole textile industry.

Mill owners responded by stirring up the Ku Klux Klan. Once a force of terror in North Carolina, by the late 1970s, the Klan was a dragon's ghost. Membership was declining. But the new Black organizing gave the Klan a new reason for being. And the mill owners saw the Klan as a useful blunt instrument.

Nelson and other organizers decided to confront the Klan head-on. They learned it was planning a recruitment event in a nearby town called China Grove: a screening of *The Birth of a Nation*, a 1915 white-suprem-acist propaganda film that staged a lynching as a celebration. The town board and the mayor had approved the event. The Johnsons and their comrades showed up to protest, Blacks and whites side-by-side. The Klansmen came out in robes and hoods, shotguns in hand—with the town police at their side. Under a Confederate flag, the Klansmen took aim. The protestors stared into their deepest fear . . . and held on. The policemen whispered in the Klansmen's ears. The robed figures retreated inside.

The demonstrators broke out in song. They had never felt so strong. They pulled down the Confederate flag and burned it.

"After that, we decided to march," Nelson said. The Indian workers leaned in, faces alive with excitement, recognizing a daring like their own.

Workers Viewpoint planned a bold march through Greensboro for November 3, 1979. The name of the event was as fierce as the pride they felt at their progress: the Death to the Klan March. They invited workers from nearby plants up. The companies were against them, and the Klan was teaming up with the local Nazi party to shore up its ranks. But soli-darity was stronger than terror. In flyers and open letters, they defied the Klan to come out to the march if it dared, to face the public's judgment.

Nelson paused to scan the workers' faces.

"But there was something we didn't know," he said.

In retrospect, there had been signs. Whispers of warning. Encounters that didn't feel right. Maybe their guard was down after police in China Grove had turned the Klan back from violence rather than egging them on.

In the weeks running up to November 3, law enforcement officials were making moves against Workers Viewpoint behind the scenes. Both local police and federal officers were surveilling the organizers. And both had paid informants with the Klan and the American Nazi Party—which had teamed up in what they called the United Racist Front. Police knew the racists were coming out for a fight with Workers Viewpoint on November 3, and that they were coming armed.

Ominously, Greensboro police insisted that Nelson sign a pledge that the anti-Klan marchers would forfeit their constitutional right to bear arms at the event. Only when he did so was the march permitted—and then the police put the parade route right into the Klan's hands.

That morning, the Johnsons and their allies gathered at the Morningside housing development with dozens of joyful marchers, Black and white, from Greensboro and beyond, in hard hats and red berets. There were almost as many television cameras. But Nelson couldn't find the Greensboro policeman who had promised to meet him there. In fact, there were no police at all.

Instead, a nine-car caravan rolled up, filled with members of the United Racist Front. In the lead car, Nelson saw a man he recognized. *Y'all asked for us?* The man yelled. *Here we are.*

It happened in a blur: first a scuffle between the marchers and the racists alongside the caravan. Then the Klansmen threw open the trunk of one of their cars. It contained an arsenal.

For eighty-eight seconds, gunfire rained down on the marchers from forty Klan and Nazi shooters. When it was over, Nelson held his friend, fellow organizer Jim Waller, as he bled to death. Jim had been shot in the back—one of five marchers killed. Nelson was covered in Waller's blood, and his own. A Klansman had stabbed him with a butcher knife. He picked himself off the ground and screamed.

"This was a setup!"

The police wrestled him back down. A Black officer put his foot on Nelson's neck. Later, in the dead of night, a policeman and an FBI agent visited Nelson's jail cell to try to convince him to become an informant.

Your name's on the lips of every Klansman and Nazi in the state, they told him. *Your life's not worth a nickel. Your best chance to live is to work with us.*

NELSON LET THE STORY sink in. You could hear a pin drop.

"Leading up to our march," he said, "We didn't understand the threat we presented to the existing social order. We didn't understand our opposition. As you march, you will need to do that. As soon as possible. Because you will be tested, and when you are, you'll want to be ready."

I saw them struggle to process his advice.

"Your march," he said. "What did you call it?"

"A satyagraha," Aby said. "A truth march."

"Ours was a truth march as well. It didn't end on November 3. In a sense, that's when it started."

After the massacre, Nelson was isolated, his movement discredited. Even before the march, Greensboro's white leaders eschewed conflict in favor of "civility." Now Nelson was a public enemy to white liberals, who blamed the demonstrators for orchestrating "a shootout" with the Klan. In the Black community, Nelson and Joyce had been beloved figures. Now people were afraid of being seen with them. Meanwhile, the Black police officer who'd put his foot on Nelson's neck was promoted.

Nelson set out to win justice for his slain friends and some measure of dignity for their surviving relatives. But in each new forum, lies became the official record. Local papers called it "a confrontation between radical groups, a two-sided gun-toting exercise in which nobody was without blame." In a state trial, an all-white jury found Klan and Nazi gunmen not guilty, saying they'd acted in self-defense.

Later, there was a federal criminal trial, based on an investigation by the FBI—which itself had blood on its hands for failing to avert the violence it knew was coming. That trial also acquitted the Klan and Nazi defendants. The mayor of Greensboro insisted the acquittals were no reflection on race relations in the city.

The first small step toward justice came when survivors won a federal civil suit that targeted not only the shooters, but the officials who'd let them kill. The jury found two Klansmen, three Nazis, two Greensboro police officers, and a police informant guilty of wrongful death and civil rights violations.

But it was far from the full truth. That would take many more years. There was pressure for Nelson and Joyce to leave Greensboro, as most of their surviving comrades had. It was painful to stay in a city that had torn off its liberal facade and shown its true face. But Greensboro was home. The Johnsons knew now how broken it was. So they set about to fix it.

Nelson went to seminary and was converted to Dr. King's ideal of the beloved community: that a struggle for racial and economic justice could reconcile oppressors and oppressed if it was founded in truth-telling and nonviolence. The Johnsons built this place, the Beloved Community Center, to realize that principle in Greensboro.

Twenty-five years to the day of the massacre, on November 3, 2004, Nelson and Joyce marched through the city again with more than seven hundred others. They launched the Greensboro Truth and Reconciliation Commission, a process of public truth-telling modeled on the hearings in South Africa after apartheid. Archbishop Desmond Tutu, who had led the South African commission, advised and blessed their work. Over two hard years, the work of the Greensboro commissioners replaced decades of lies and evasions with a ground of truth on which to build the beloved community.

THE SUN HAD climbed the sky. Outside the brick building, saying their goodbyes, the workers embraced Reverend Nelson with a new sobriety.

I thanked him too, and asked his advice on recruiting the Congressional Black Caucus to get ICE to back off. The reverend promised to reach out to Mel Watt, the Congressman from this area, but asked me a question.

"What if that doesn't work?"

"You mean if the Black Caucus can't help?"

"No," said Nelson. "I mean if *you* can't help. What if you fail? Have you started preparing for that scenario?"

"Preparing the men?"

"Preparing your soul."

There was a warning in the question, derived from his own experience. Reverend Nelson had artfully compressed his story for the benefit of his audience, but I knew a little about his life after the Greensboro massacre. He had lost his job. No one would hire him. The FBI visited Joyce's supervisor, pressuring him to fire her as well. They lost their house, and most of their friends. No one would rent to them. To make a living, Nelson became a carpenter. He collected scrap wood from the furniture dumpsters in Highpoint and built anything for money. He built a house for Jim Waller's widow, Signe. And he spent most of his time wandering, scraping together money to feed the families of the dead and to keep the civil case alive. Nelson Johnson, a man who I experienced as dignity personified, spent a decade disillusioned and disgraced before he found a way to begin again.

I rushed past his parting question without a real answer. Walking on toward Washington, I knew why I had. I was scared of it.

Saravanan walked alongside me with the phone pressed to his ear and a look of new solemnity. It was his father calling from India. He asked where we had just been.

"Greensboro," Saravanan said. "Greensboro, USA."

4: Alarm

THE REVEREND HAD predicted we'd be tested. The test came the very next day.

We pulled into a Motel 8 in Virginia after busing through an unwalkable stretch of highway. Compared to the churches and gyms along our journey, it was luxurious—quite un-Gandhian. "Isn't there an unheated Catholic basement nearby?" Rajan had asked with a twinkle in his eye. But he knew we needed good sleep and showers. We had a big morning ahead preparing for Department of Justice interviews. We were due to hit DC the next day.

For weeks now, we had been pressing the DOJ for interview slots. They would only reply that they were still deliberating—and strangely, they refused to confirm that an investigation was underway. But I knew that the moment they did, things would move fast. They might pick witnesses at random. Any of these men had to be ready to withstand cross-examination, possibly at a day's notice.

At 9 a.m., I sat with one of the men in a matchbox-sized motel room for interview practice. There was no desk, so we perched on the edge of the bed. A few others listened in. I planned to do this in room after room, with five workers at a time, for as long as I could before it was time to walk on to Washington. I was playing the DOJ lawyer, breaking character every now and then to give notes.

We needed to tell a clear story about human trafficking. Many of the men hovered between generalities—"It is a case of cheating!"—and deadening details: "On my fifth visit to the banker, he agreed to grant half the loan." Other times they were heartbreaking: "I called my father from the man camp. He was in the hospital. I informed him, 'There is a problem with my green card. I cannot return from America. Do not wait for me. If the time has come, then die.'"

But to convince the Department of Justice that this fit the legal definition of trafficking, there were elements we had to drive home.

"How did each step ensnare you more, make you less free to leave?" I pressed. "The bank grants only half the loan. You turn to the usurer. He charges thirty percent. You have to work off your debt at Signal. You've barely put a dent in it when your visa expires. The promised green cards haven't come through. When your father falls sick, you can't visit. When he dies, you can't go to his funeral, because you're undocumented. All the while, you're afraid of being fired, because of your debt."

The men nodded. *Exactly.* Surely the government lawyers would understand.

"Only if you explain it," I insisted. "Government lawyers are paid to investigate things they haven't experienced. You can't just tell them. You have to teach them."

We were interrupted by the scream of a siren. I called the front desk, exasperated. A fire drill was the last thing we needed. It would eat up our time.

"It's not us," a hotel clerk said. "Someone pulled the alarm. Leave your room. Take the stairs."

Downstairs, outside, I stopped in my tracks. We didn't have to wait for the firefighters to arrive. They were already there—strangely, in no hurry to put out a fire. Instead, they were aiming cameras at us. With them were police officers, state troopers, men in plain clothes, many with cameras of their own. They recorded us in our strange, exposed position, in a grassy basin between two highways. As more men streamed out of their rooms, the cameras clicked and whirred.

We stared out, a dead fear seeping into the basin. These were immigration agents. It was one thing to catch a single agent on a rooftop who fled when spotted. These men *wanted* to be seen. The message couldn't be clearer: turn back, or we'll escalate.

I ran up the hillside, buttonholed the firefighters first. They said they were responding to the alarm.

"By arriving before the alarm went off, and recording us?" I said.

They shrugged and kept recording. The state troopers said they were assisting the firefighters. The men in plain clothes refused to say who they were. One claimed he was driving by and pulled up to watch the fire. But there was no fire, I said pointlessly.

Back in the grassy basin, I found the men agitated. A rumor was spreading that one of our own men had pulled the fire alarm. That would mean someone from the inside was working against the group. A collaborationist, who had perhaps cut his own deal with the agents. Papers for him, jail for the rest. Accusations rang out. The men were turning on each other. The basin was on the verge of going up like a tinderbox. I motioned to Rajan: *Get them on the bus, fast.*

We corralled them onto the bus. We'd have to pick up the pieces in DC.

BACK ON THE ROAD, I held an emergency call with allies in Washington—our supporters at the National Immigration Law Center and the labor coalition Jobs With Justice. I delivered an enraged report about the ICE surveillance in Montgomery and the undercover agents recording us in Virginia. Our goal in Washington was not only to convince the DOJ, I said. It was also to hold ICE accountable. And if ICE was interfering with the investigation, then we had to push them out of the way. The allies vowed to help. We planned an outraged letter to the ICE director, a round of calls to Democrats in Congress who oversaw the Department of Homeland Security.

Afterward, one of these allies called me back. She was an attorney who had given me advice on my own pending immigration application, and a close friend.

"Are you sure you want to take the men further into this fight?"

"They're insisting on it," I said. "I couldn't hold them back now if I tried."

"And you? Are you sure you want to fight ICE? They'll come at you and your organization with everything they've got. You want to be in their crosshairs?"

"No question," I said. I had asked these workers to risk everything by marching. How could I do anything less?

"Okay." There was something she was thinking over.

"What is it?"

"Did you get your application in?"

My heart dropped. I hadn't so much as glanced at it since we left New Orleans. She was forcing me to make the connection between my own tenuous immigration situation and the threat the workers were under. The longer I put off the application, the more vulnerable I was—and my vulnerability was the workers', too.

I'd have to fill it out in DC. We were half an hour away.

When the men were settled in their DC hotel rooms for the night, I gathered up a select few of them for one last order of business before we began the big fight tomorrow. Rajan, Hemant, Aby, Murugan, Saravanan, and a few others who had emerged as leaders: Jagpal Yadav from Haryana, Dhananjaya Kechuri from Andhra Pradesh, and Justin Poulouse from Kerala. They sat with me in a circle, intent. They were the most committed members of the campaign. The most strategic. The most farsighted. The ones I could trust completely.

Our fight was going to become more complex and challenging by the day, I told them. The campaign needed a core group that could follow the intricacies of the politics and the law as closely as I did. To be the first to know things, to discuss the most sensitive and confidential matters, to set the direction and lay out alternatives for the rest of the men. I was asking them to be that group. It was all the more important now, as our fight reached the national stage. We knew we were being surveilled, and the scare at the Motel 8 revealed the possibility of someone on the inside collaborating against the rest of us. We needed a core group that was bound by trust.

"It's the right thing to do," Aby said. "And I'm ready." The rest concurred.

It was one thing to announce a commitment, but I knew they would only *feel* it once they took their first collective decision—and I was lucky to have one ready for them. Signal had been suspiciously quiet since the day of the escape, apart from a few terse denials of wrongdoing in the press. I had suspected they must be maneuvering behind the scenes.

"As we arrived in DC," I told the men, "I heard from the lawyers supporting us at the Southern Poverty Law Center. They got a call about us." The call came from a consummate Washington operator and high-priced fixer. His newest client? Signal International. The fixer had called SPLC to assess our openness to an out-of-court settlement with Signal.

"This man solves DC problems," I said. "That means Signal thinks we're about to become their DC problem. They want to know if they can pay to make it go away. To make *us* go away."

I saw the sequence of reactions on the men's faces as they took this in: intrigued at first, then indignant, then emboldened. It was their first lesson in DC power games. A less canny group would have been flattered by the fixer's approach, lured into talks on a settlement.

"But their hiring this man is a sign of weakness," Rajan said.

"They want to settle because they're afraid to face us in public," said Aby.

"So that's exactly what we have to make them do," Murugan added with a grin.

The core group's first decision was a unanimous one. As Hemant put it: "Sure we'll settle. For justice. Nothing less."

Signal may have been the one paying the fixer, but that day, we were the ones he did the service.

5: Department for Justice

HIGH NOON IN THE NATION'S CAPITAL. We spilled out of the bus onto Pennsylvania Avenue and marched up to the Robert F. Kennedy Building, a million-square-foot colossus, the home of the Department of Justice. The men set up a beaten wooden podium with care. An inspiring lineup of allies from civil rights organizations and unions stepped up and pledged their support, to cheers. Then it was Aby's turn to speak. The other men looked on proudly as he told their story to a crowd of Washington reporters.

Behind those limestone walls was a young prosecutor from Northern Virginia who had just been assigned our case. His name was John Cotton Richmond. He had been in touch with our attorneys over email to introduce himself, and we'd sent over our complaint. I hoped he was reading it right now.

From online searches, I knew a little about him. Richmond worked in the DOJ's storied Civil Rights Division, which prosecuted hate crimes and police misconduct. He was only a year into his career at Justice, and hadn't yet tried a trafficking case, but he was fresh off two big wins. He'd successfully argued a cross-burning case to an all-white jury in Arkansas. Then he'd won convictions against ten corrections officers in Gulfport, Mississippi, who had abused inmates for years. In the horrific incident that sparked the investigation, a corrections officer had attacked an African American man named Jessie Lee Williams Jr. during booking, beaten him, pepper sprayed him through a hood, dropped him on his head, and waterboarded him in a restraining chair, while saying "I hope you don't drown." Williams died in the hospital two days later. The attack came amid a post-Katrina wave of police violence against African Americans. Richmond won a life sentence against Williams's killer.

Richmond was now part of the DOJ's Human Trafficking Prosecution Unit, created to bring violators of the Trafficking Victims Protection Act to justice. I imagined him sitting with his section chief, charting the path to indictments against Signal International, Malvern Burnett, Michael Pol, and Sachin Dewan. Richmond would be paired with an investigator either from the FBI or ICE. For obvious reasons, we preferred the FBI, so it had been a relief when they had called us just days after we submitted our complaint. It was safe to assume that Richmond was paired up with an FBI investigator for the duration. They would be working hand in glove throughout, starting with victim interviews. In many cases, victims are scared to speak, in spite of the "Victim-centered" approach the DOJ promises. In this instance, the victims had been readily available for weeks, and were eager to testify. The victim-centered approach here would be to grant them Continued Presence. In three weeks, Richmond hadn't delivered this. But now, we were literally standing outside his front door. That would have to speed up whatever sign-off Richmond needed.

Outside, Aby finished his testimony.

"We'll wait," he thundered from the podium, loud enough for Richmond to hear him. "If they don't come out to interview us today, we'll be back tomorrow. And then the day after that!"

6: The Diplomat and the Coolies

March 27, 2008
Washington, DC

OUR NEXT STOP that day was with Ambassador Ronen Sen. We approached the limestone mansion that housed the Indian Embassy, a regal residence from 1901 on Washington's old Millionaire's Row. A statue of Mahatma Gandhi—determined, midstride, in a peasant's loincloth and shawl—stood in stark contrast across the street.

I announced our presence to a guard. He slammed the heavy door shut and disappeared inside. From the foot of the stairs, I peered through thick glass. The guard came back out with a harried official who surveyed the crowd and fixed his eyes on me.

"India welcomes you," he said.

"And we thank India," I said.

"How many people will come inside?"

"Sixty."

"I request you to select ten. Sorry to inform: room can accommodate ten only." A low rumble from the men.

"Sorry to inform: we're all coming in."

The men behind me cheered.

"Who has the chit?" he said.

"Excuse me?"

"The appointment chit."

"The chit! Of course."

Rajan fished out a folded, creased printout, damp with sweat, and handed it over. The official's eyes narrowed. It was the *Times of India* article from the week before, with the headline, SEN CANCELS TRAVEL PLANS TO MEET WITH INDIAN WORKERS.

"Please ask India to find a bigger room," I said.

He looked back with a hard stare. Then he blinked. The guard swung open the doors.

WE STEPPED INSIDE. The murmuring and footfalls of dozens of men filled the great hall. Stony-faced officials in suits stared at the men's jeans and coveralls.

"Welcome to India," I whispered to Rajan.

"India welcomes you," he whispered back.

Adjacent to us was a magnificent, winding staircase. Our gazes followed it up to the slight, elegant man in a gray suit and blue tie. He paused at the top of the stairs and struck a Roman senator's pose, one hand on the balustrade, the other behind his back. This had the intended effect: a hush fell over the men, the awe of supplicants.

I knew exactly why he'd pulled this maneuver. We were threatening the biggest deal of his life.

SEN WAS THE DIPLOMAT who'd only made one mistake. His first thirty-nine years in the service had been flawless—in Mexico City, Moscow, Bonn, Berlin, and London. In 2004, India's newly elected prime minister, Manmohan Singh, sent Sen to Washington to work on India's top global priority: a nuclear deal with the Americans. Since India's independence, the country had wanted both nuclear energy and nuclear weapons, but the rules set by the US and the Europeans said that only five countries were allowed that privilege, and India wasn't one of them. India developed both anyway. As a result, it was barred from nuclear commerce with the rest of the world.

President George W. Bush was now willing to reverse that, giving India access to US nuclear fuel and technology. In return, India would submit to inspections. The deal would mark India's arrival as a great power: the only country in the world that enjoyed nuclear weapons and power without signing the Non-Proliferation Treaty, and without facing sanctions for it.

Sen got to work crafting India's "Message" in Washington. Then, on his way to his crowning achievement, Sen made his first-ever error.

On a hot day in August 2007, he took a call from a journalist. The momentum toward signing a bilateral deal had been interrupted by an uproar—not in Washington, but in New Delhi. India's right-wing opposition party, the BJP, was trying to torpedo the deal. The Communists followed suit. They said that India had given up too much, that the deal would undercut India's sovereignty. The India press was having a field day, feasting on the dysfunction.

Sen was "amazed" at the drama, he told the reporter. This was a done deal, approved by the leaders of two great democracies. "So why," he asked, "Do you have all this running around like headless chicken, looking for a comment here or comment there, and these little storms in a teacup?"

Politicians looking to take offense in New Delhi seized on the quote. An infuriated BJP leader said Sen's comments were "Demeaning to the self-respect of members" of Parliament. The Communist party chief accused Sen of being a foreign agent—not India's ambassador, but Bush's. "If the government has any self-respect, it should immediately recall him." Not used to being on the defensive, Sen typed up a clarification at once. The foreign minister read it to Parliament. Sen had been having a casual chat, off the record, he said. And by headless chickens he meant *journalists*, not parliamentarians.

The uproar redoubled. Prime Minister Singh was now deploying bureaucrats to suppress journalists? Parliament shut down.

Sen's crisis deepened when his full comments from the "Headless chicken" interview were published. In them, he lamented the immaturity that held India back: "I am really bothered that sixty years after independence, they are so insecure—that we have not grown up, this lack of confidence and lack of self-respect." Opponents of the deal with America weren't just wrong. They were colonized.

Many in Sen's circle abandoned him. The deal teetered on the edge of collapse. In October, Prime Minister Singh called Bush with a painful admission: "certain difficulties" would prevent India from moving forward with the agreement.

Anyone else in Sen's place might have resigned. But instead he flew to Delhi to face the monsoon Parliament. He deployed humility and humor. Apologized unconditionally. Put his comments in perspective. He explained that he often called his own wife a "Headless chicken" when she ran around attending to guests at his parties. This drew guffaws from members of Sen's own party and endeared him again. The Prime Minister extended Sen's contract, and he returned to Washington to pick up the pieces. He had survived. Now, he had to revive the deal.

Sen set about focusing American minds on the "Right" Indians. He rallied a legion of wealthy, professional-class Indian Americans—professors, entrepreneurs, doctors, lawyers, hoteliers—to blitz Washington with briefings and calls in support of the nuclear deal. Observers noted their sophistication as lobbyists. They wanted results. Here was a classic American story: an aspirational class of immigrants having its coming-out moment.

Then on March 9, we knocked the nuclear deal off the front pages with a very different kind of Indian immigrant story: oil-rig builders who had escaped American labor camps to battle human trafficking. We followed up with a letter to Sen asking for help.

A *Times of India* reporter revealed the attitude toward us inside the embassy: "Although they would not say it on the record," he wrote, embassy officials appeared "Irritated that they are often left holding the can for the stupidity of greedy or semi-literate workers who give up their life savings to recruiters for a placement abroad."

Instead of responding directly, Sen dispatched Murga Sahib and Bakra Sahib to New Orleans—a tactical error. We'd since learned their first stop had been Signal International, where they'd apparently taken the company's word as gospel. We were furious. We announced we'd walk from New Orleans to Washington to meet with Sen directly.

Suddenly, a problem below Sen's pay grade was a wildfire running right up to his doorstep. The wrong kind of Indians at exactly the wrong time. He had to try to contain it. Which is why, seven days into our march, he finally replied in a letter:

"My doors are always open to any of my fellow citizens of India."

HE DESCENDED THE STAIRCASE with imperial cool.

He'd literally taken the wind out of the men. I had to reset the balance fast.

"Awaaz do!" I shouted. The ambassador paused on the steps.

A hundred men shouted back: "Hum ek hain!"

The chanting grew louder as the ambassador approached. He stepped off the stairs into a sea of discontent. He raised his hands for calm, a perfect half inch of cuffed white linen gleaming from under each jacket sleeve.

"You are all part of the family," he said.

"Mr. Sen," I began, "allow me to introduce India's pride: builders of rigs, refineries, nuclear power plants. Not the 'greedy, semi-literate people' your officials described."

Sen denied, strenuously, that any embassy official had ever said any such thing. But, he said, "If inadvertently your feelings are hurt, I apologize." It was the smart move: sound sincere, disarm instead of defend.

We weren't concerned with hurt feelings, I said, but with the integrity of a criminal investigation. The embassy's assessment, repeated to me by the officials Sen sent to New Orleans, was that the workers themselves were to blame. Sen's emissaries had met with Signal's officials, but not with the workers. In my mind, this broke with every accepted norm in a trafficking investigation. Now we were reading in the Indian press that those emissaries were "Finalizing a detailed report." Was this true?

A flicker of discomfort crossed Sen's face, then vanished.

"Let there not be any mutual suspicion," he said. "There is nothing in the report except facts." The evasion sent outrage through the crowd.

"This report," I said, "Is based entirely on the company's point of view. You prepared an assessment of human trafficking claims by your own citizens without talking to a single victim?"

One worker spoke up, demanding Sen show us the report. A chorus followed: *Yes or no! Yes or no!*

"Internal consultations are not shared with anybody," he said, defensive. But his expression showed he'd been knocked back on his heels. "It is an interim report," he said.

A small concession, but an important one. It meant the report could not be complete without hearing the workers' side.

This brought us to our next demand: a criminal investigation of the Indian labor broker, Sachin Dewan. Sachin wasn't just any labor broker. Dewan Consultants was a talent agency to Fortune 500 companies, the glossy face of the manpower industry. Sachin's father Jagdish was a leader in the brokers' national trade association. An investigation would send a message: that the industry had to clean up. Would Sen push for a Central Bureau of Investigation probe? *Yes or no?*

A silence hung from the high ceiling as Sen pondered. Then he fixed his gaze on the worker who had spoken before me.

"I will do what is in the best interest for the citizens of India," he said carefully. Then he made an unexpected move. He softened.

"We don't need interlocutors or interpreters," he said. I realized he was referring to me. "All of you Indian workers can approach me directly."

His voice took on a new intimacy. The workers strained to listen. They stepped in and, finding themselves closer to Sen, switched from rancor to pleading.

"He threatened to tear up my passport if I didn't pay," one worker said.

"He threatened to burn mine!" another called.

Sen nodded with sympathy. It brought more exclamations.

"He will threaten my family if I continue with this case!"

The tone had changed. The workers were no longer substantiating a demand—they were pouring their hearts out. I was momentarily bewildered. Sen was soaking it up, encouraging them like a benevolent father.

"And the moneylenders—they are also threatening."

"Please, sir!"

Behind the courage of their march to Washington, the men were riven with worry for their families. Now their helplessness was revealed, and stories flowed: crippling loans, notes come due, usurers in towns and still-feudal villages, circling their parents, their wives. I had lived on these stories for eighteen months. But losing ourselves in them now meant losing our power in the meeting. We didn't walk 1,500 miles to touch the ambassador's heart. We were here for action, not empathy. We needed to press him to use his authority in clear ways. With each new story, our advantage bled out.

But it was too late to try to wrest the meeting back. If I did, I'd be seen as the one out of touch with the men. They had spent most of their lives working abroad, but never talked about the indignities they suffered. Back home on furlough, they never shared how it feels to be fighting over moldy mattresses in Saudi work camps, or to be brown and bleeding in the Azerbaijani winter after your first racist attack. This American experience was not the first injustice in their lives. But it was the crowning one. And they were fed up. They had come all this way, and they were now arm's length from the most powerful figure they might ever meet. So, by God, they were going to tell him. How could I interrupt?

Sen played it perfectly for the press corps: patient, kindly, quiet. For a full hour, I watched the ambassador listen to the men, head tilted empathically, having to promise them nothing.

Afterward, we stood across the street, gathered around the Mahatma Gandhi statue. I wanted to collapse on the lawn. For the first time since we'd started our journey, I felt spent. I tried to remind myself what a mentor had taught me long ago: not to "Live or die by a single meeting." Ronen Sen certainly planned to move on after our battle. We must as well.

I asked Rajan how he thought it went. To my surprise, he was smiling. "Better than I expected."

"Why? He didn't give us anything."

"He was never going to," Rajan said. "We're just coolies to him."

The word *coolie* initially referred to indentured Indian (and Chinese) workers that the British Empire exported to its plantations in other colonies. In modern times, it's used colloquially as a demeaning label for low-wage workers in India, and a racial slur for Indian workers abroad.

Rajan's saying it made me understand: I didn't feel depleted. I felt demeaned. The land enclosed by the embassy's four walls, legally speaking, was Indian territory. That afternoon, we had traveled all the way to India. But not our India. Ronen Sen's India. The limestone mansion, the guarded door framed with inlaid marble, men in suits and wide ties inside, educating us on what the government could or couldn't do.

And yet, Rajan was smiling. In my head I played back the end of the meeting. The men had laid their armor at Sen's feet, shown him all their scars, hidden until then as a matter of honor. It was cathartic for them. Then they'd looked expectantly at Sen, awaiting a promise commensurate with their pain. But he stayed silent. A sense of futility quickly filled the void. A young unmarried welder spoke up, exasperated. Now that he knew their troubles, would the ambassador insist on the investigation of Sachin Dewan?

"I will convey your request," Sen had said.

The men understood. He would use none of his capital for them. Their bodies, which had bent to the posture of a plea while they had told their stories, straightened now. Their armor was back on.

With a sweeping, ambassadorial gesture, Sen invited the men to lunch. In a room off to the side, a table was laid with a feast fit for dignitaries. The men stared at it: russet-hued samosas, three kinds of chicken, perfectly cubed shahi paneer, and gulab jamuns that looked like carnelian gemstones against the snow-white tablecloth.

The men assumed their full height. With the press corps watching, they walked right past the food and out through the doors of the mansion. Right out of Ronen Sen's India.

Outside in America, under the Gandhi statue, they possessed nothing. No homes, no family, no papers, no prospects. But they had their self-respect. I watched them with admiration. They were standing tall.

"We have an hour till our rally in front of the White House," I said.

Rajan grinned. "Do we have time to eat? I'm starving."

7: A Conditional Resident

Early April 2008
Washington, DC

A WEEK LATER, we mounted a full-court press in Congress. The Department of Justice was still a black box. No word yet from John Cotton Richmond on Continued Presence, or even confirmation that an investigation was open. To press for an answer, we reached out to congressional Democrats, and some Republicans who were sponsors of the Trafficking Victims Protection Act, lobbying them to sign a congressional letter to the Attorney General.

I was elated when we set a meeting with George Miller, a California Democrat who had recently become the chair of the House Committee on Education and Labor. After Hurricane Katrina, the Bush Administration had suspended the laws that protected Gulf Coast workers' wage rates. Miller had been a key proponent in reinstituting them. And he was a friend to immigrants. If he met the workers, he was sure to become a champion.

But on the morning of our meeting, his staffer called with an apology. Miller was needed on the House floor for a vote, but the staffer could meet with us instead. I agreed. Then, at the last minute, the staffer called again. Now he was held up too. But we could brief his intern. At a Starbucks.

"He looks like a starving child," Rajan muttered to me in Hindi. The intern was as thin as a fireman's pole in a suit. He had a legal notepad, a brass tie pin, and baby-smooth skin. We commenced our "briefing." Rajan showed pictures of his wife, Shamitha, and his old mother. He described how he'd paid Signal International's recruiters $20,000 after selling ancestral land, his wife's jewelry, and taking out high-interest loans.

"Hang on," the staffer said. "That's my order."

The intern returned with a salad. We asked if his office would help organize a congressional briefing for other Capitol Hill staff. He wasn't sure. Staffers were swimming in invitations from lobbyists. But these weren't lobbyists, I said. They were immigrant workers. Trafficked from India. Who escaped from a labor camp. And walked 1,500 miles. Lawmakers were debating immigration reform as we spoke. Wouldn't they be a draw?

"Indian workers, I don't know," he said. Then his eyes brightened. "Now if you had Indian *food*—I'd go to that briefing!"

A desultory start. But then a dozen unions and civil rights groups called Miller's office for us. Meanwhile, other lawmakers in the Labor committee vouched for us. A week later, we had a meeting set with Congressman Miller himself. Rajan and I high-fived.

ON THE MORNING of the meeting I realized with a chill what I'd managed to ignore until then: my immigration application was due. I hadn't touched it since we'd arrived in DC. Today was the last possible day I could send it in. And it would take hours.

I prepared Rajan and the others for the meeting and walked them over to Miller's office. Outside, I broke it to Rajan that I wouldn't be attending. There were a number of other advocates who would join our delegation, far more seasoned in Washington than me. Just as Miller's door opened, I slipped away, leaving Rajan dumbfounded and furious.

I raced to the offices of Jobs With Justice, the DC labor coalition that was lending me a desk. I pulled the crumpled application out of my backpack. I should have sent it in weeks ago. Months ago. Back in New Orleans, I had thought I would finish it on a tranquil Sunday, after a stroll through City Park among enchanted oaks. I'd clear my head to revisit the part of my life that I kept locked away even from myself most of the time, the part that was at the center of my immigration dilemma: my first great love, my subsequent marriage, and its ending. But there would be no tranquility today.

My phone rang: Rajan. I put the phone on silent and pulled up the website of the United States Citizenship and Immigration Services (USCIS), the part of the federal government that issues all visas. Scanned through instructions on how to fill out the form. I heard them in a warning, gravelly tone, an immigration adjudicator played by Tommy Lee Jones:

> Your permanent resident status is conditional if it is based on a marriage that was less than two years old on the day you became a permanent resident. Your status is conditional *until you prove that you did not enter the marriage to circumvent the immigration laws of the United States.*

I hunched over the eleven-page application.
Marital status.
Married.
Place of marriage.
Chicago, Illinois.
Have you resided at any other address since you became a permanent resident?
Yes.
Provide a list of all the addresses and the dates.
I stopped in my tracks and confronted my dilemma. An adjudicator would decide, based solely on my answers, whether my marriage—to a woman I hadn't lived with for more than a year—was a real one. Since 9/11, immigration officials read marriage-based green card applications through a microscope, looking for fictitious marriages made for the sake of gaining legal status. If you applied, you were assumed to be guilty of fraud until proven innocent. And my application would raise huge red flags. Just three months after I was married, I moved across the country to New Orleans while my wife remained in Chicago, where I had no plans to return. This fact could sink me—without context, it looked like a textbook green-card marriage. Explaining it with a simple lie might be convincing: I took a job out of state, but visited often; my out-of-state assignment had been extended unexpectedly. But I couldn't

lie. I needed the adjudicator to know the full truth and base the decision on that.

If you need extra space to provide additional information, use the space below.

I stared into the white box on the form, drew a breath, and dove in.

Dear Adjudicator: Thank you for this opportunity to provide additional information. Here's what you need to understand.

HER NAME WAS TUYET. We met at a conference for professional advocates. She was all of five feet tall, and very pretty. She crackled with sarcasm. Laughed musically at her own jokes. She walked with a sway from a disability, in small shoes fitted with braces to support her legs. The cane she carried only made her more commanding.

I was smitten as soon as I saw her, and I thought, *she's out of my league.* I was twenty-six. After two years undocumented, I'd regained status through a temporary work visa. I was working for an immigrant rights coalition—my first job as a professional activist after several years juggling volunteer positions and low-wage service jobs. Tuyet was already a superstar. At thirty-three, she was the executive director of a civil rights group for Asian Americans. So I was surprised when, one day in April, she invited me to dinner. I arrived early and excited. But this wasn't a date. It was her organization's annual fundraiser, and she was the keynote speaker. I took my place deep in the packed banquet hall, and Tuyet told me (and five hundred others) the story of her life.

Her family left Vietnam on the day Saigon fell to the North Vietnamese, in April 1975. Her uncle, a navy captain, negotiated a place for the family on a fishing trawler in exchange for his navigation skills. "The original deal he was offered didn't include us," Tuyet recalled, "but he refused to leave his seven siblings and their families behind." After days on the open sea, a Taiwanese schooner pulled up with orders to pick up only refugees of Chinese descent. There were two of those on the trawler, a father and daughter. "But they refused to be rescued unless their fellow passengers could come"—all two hundred Vietnamese. The Taiwanese relented, and took the whole group to the Philippines, where they were processed as refugees. Two days later, they were on their way to the United States. "And here I am," Tuyet said, offering her life as proof of generosity's dividends. The room erupted. A server came by to clear the plates. I hadn't touched my dinner.

Afterward, we walked together in the warm April night. She leaned on my right arm for ease. In case I got any ideas, she pointed out that the sidewalks in Chicago tilt toward the street: leaning on me helped her with balance. Still, I was thrilled. She was still buzzing after her performance, the first time she had told this story to anyone. I launched into a glowing appraisal of her speech. Her eyes glazed over.

"Do you like TV?" she said.

"No," I said, "I don't."

"I love TV." I kicked myself. But she went on. "Do you want to watch TV with me?"

She had deep bonds with TV characters, celebrated their wins, mourned their losses, laughed loud enough to drown out the laugh track. When our first kiss came a few weeks later, it was on her grown-up couch with the embroidered slip covers, soft and slow, in the glow of the TV.

AT THAT POINT I shared a one-bedroom apartment with a roommate. She had the bedroom; I slept on a mattress in a stairwell with my clothes in a duffel bag—a habit from my undocumented years. I started bringing the duffel bag to Tuyet's house. One evening, she told me to unpack it.

She met my parents over a long-distance call to Delhi. I went to visit hers in Milwaukee, where they had been resettled by a church. Tuyet's father invited me to play chess. She eyed us nervously, and was astonished when, midgame, he started telling stories of their journey to America, sharing things she had never heard. The following year, Tuyet's family decided to mark an anniversary of their arrival in the US with a picnic. They invited the Lutherans who had taken them in years before. I suggested we write a play for the occasion: a version of her father's recollections to introduce the kids to the family lore. Tuyet wasn't sure, but came around. After juicy bratwursts and bahn-mi sandwiches heaped with cucumbers and paté, the children performed the family odyssey in their shady backyard. A six-year-old niece played a composite of all the children. She had only one line, which she delivered in a voice like a wind chime: "Where are we going? Does it snow there?" She said it when she was woken up in Saigon and rushed onto a boat, and when she docked in the Philippines, and when she rolled out of a bunk bed in Arkansas and fell into a box of shoes. In the final scene, she arrived in Milwaukee just in time for the snow. *Curtain.* When it ended, the fireflies were out, and Tuyet and I were in love.

That's when I started to worry. As our feelings deepened, so did my dread of being separated from her by the end of my temporary work visa.

On the couch one evening, nearly two years into our relationship, I blurted out my news. "My third visa is about to expire, and they won't renew it, and no one else will hire me, because it's too much of a hassle to apply for the visa, and another one would only last ten months." Tuyet listened quietly, then asked what my options were. I laid them out. I could become undocumented and stay in Chicago. I'd be out of work, but we could stay together. Or I could return to India and look for another US company to sponsor my return.

"Those are the only options?" she asked.

I hesitated. There was another. I hadn't wanted to consider it.

"We could get married," I finally said.

"Let's do that."

In a taxi to a work meeting the next morning, I called my parents for advice. My father said that he had always been impressed by "The Vietnamese national character." My mother asked if I would be able to bear being separated from Tuyet. No, I said, we belonged together. The taxi driver chimed in as he let me out. "Sounds like you should marry her."

Weeks later, newly married, Tuyet and I arrived at the USCIS office in the Chicago Loop. We had protested outside this hideous slab many times, but never stepped past its X-rays. We laid the bona fides of our relationship out on an agent's desk. The marriage certificate. Pictures of us dressed up at the courthouse. Pictures of us at home afterward, munching egg rolls with friends.

"Where are your parents?" the agent asked.

"India and Milwaukee. We'll have receptions there eventually."

"Who are these?"

"Friends."

"What are these?"

"Egg rolls."

The agent was satisfied. Our marriage was certified. I became a conditional resident of the United States. Back outside, Tuyet leaned against my arm. We started down the steps and into the rest of our lives. That night we splurged on Trader Joe's green tea mochi and ate it while we watched TV.

ON THE OUT-BREATH that came after our marriage, I relaxed into love. Suddenly everything was newly charged: the pressure of her hand on my arm when I walked her to work, how we talked about TV characters like they were her friends visiting, our trips to the Swedish bakery around the corner. In our talks, we revealed more to each other than either of us ever had to anyone. Each time I thought we couldn't get any closer, we did.

But Tuyet started to understand something about me that I hadn't yet understood myself. I was obsessed by a quest for a purpose I hadn't yet found, a desire to do something meaningful on a different scale, and she saw the signs it would pull me away from her. In my job as a community organizer, I would work fourteen- or sixteen-hour days knocking on the doors of low-income renters on the North Side. These were Black and brown people hanging on to their homes by the skin of their teeth in rapidly gentrifying neighborhoods. When I got home, all I wanted to talk about was the tenants' heartbreaks and my own frustration at how little I could offer them. My supervisors wanted me to focus on "Winnable issues"—broken doorbells, stop signs, and absentee landlords—while the tenants were up against global finance and neoliberalism. *It's like organizing on the Titanic*, I'd pound at the dining table.

My rants were the last thing Tuyet needed after her own long days. She was fighting Mayor Daley to keep Asian Americans in affirmative action, and fending off Republican attempts to erase them from congressional districts. She just wanted to connect over a quiet dinner. As I railed on, she tried to watch TV.

But she was deeply attuned to my restlessness. Where she wanted to see signs of stability, she saw my thrashing search for something dramatically different. One night in bed, I described my latest dream: to organize the taxi drivers I'd been meeting in Rogers Park, mostly low-income Indians and Pakistanis, into a union. If I woke up at 4:30 a.m., I could get to O'Hare Airport by 6 a.m. with fliers from Kinko's. In the evenings I could continue conversations with drivers in their homes. I thought I could pull one thousand people together in a year. What did she think?

"That sounds hard," she said quietly. "You're not a morning person. But if you really want to do it, then you should." She turned out the lights. Then, almost to herself, she asked, "Who's going to walk me to work?"

I was sad and ashamed at the question. Before we met, she had been fiercely self-reliant. Over our two years together, she had allowed herself to rely on me. I became part of her machinery, helping her get in cabs, carrying laundry down, taking out the trash. And that was trivial compared to the way she'd let down her emotional guard. The more signs she saw that I might pull away, the harder she clung.

That August of 2005, Tuyet and I watched the TV coverage of Hurricane Katrina. New Orleans residents, most of them Black, waiting to be rescued from rooftops. We reeled between sadness and anger but couldn't look away.

In my organizing meetings with tenants now, many of them African American, all we talked about was Katrina. Most of their families had come North during the Great Migration, seeking opportunity while fleeing lynchings and racial terror. What they saw on their screens in New Orleans now was not an aberration of American history, but a continuation of it. The more I listened to them, the more I realized: I had to go.

In December I told Tuyet I was going to New Orleans—just for a week, as a relief volunteer. I arrived early in the morning on Christmas Eve and spent Christmas Day in City Park. The place had turned into a sprawling, muddy encampment for residents who had lost their homes, and for migrant workers who had arrived to pick up rebuilding work. They were living in tents and cars. They were Black, white, Native American, Latino, Asian American, documented and undocumented. I'd heard veterans of the 1960s voter registration campaigns in Mississippi talk about learning to see America through "Mississippi eyes." I was learning to see through New Orleans eyes.

On New Year's Day, I went to a much-loved coffee shop on Frenchmen Street that had just reopened, and found myself among a dozen veteran activists. I told one I had been phone banking, calling New Orleans residents who had evacuated as far as Oakland and Denver.

"When you call, don't say, 'Do you have a way back to New Orleans,'" he advised. "Ask if they have a way back *home*. Then get them to start telling some stories." He turned out to be John O'Neal, a civil rights hero of mine. He'd moved south from Illinois himself in the 1960s to work with the Student Nonviolent Coordinating Committee, ran Ella Baker's first Citizenship School, and stayed on to start a theater company called the Free Southern Theater. I had studied his work for years, first as a theater director and then as an organizer.

The man next to John offered to join me on calls. This was Hollis Watkins, the Mississippi sit-in organizer who helped put together Freedom Summer. The tiny coffee shop was crowded with giants.

"What time do you get started tomorrow?" Hollis asked. "Or are you leaving?"

"Oh, he ain't leavin' nowhere," John laughed. He was right. I'd been in search of something. This was it: the purpose I'd been looking for.

Later that night, I called Tuyet.

"When do you get back?" she said.

FOR MONTHS I HID from Tuyet that my move was permanent and that our marriage was over. I told my parents about the move during a family visit in New Delhi the following April, but even then, I held back the worst part.

"Will Tuyet be moving with you?" my mother asked.

"Probably," I said. "Not right away. We'll visit each other."

My soul creaked from the lies. I was desperate to tell the full truth to someone, anyone, if only to relieve the pressure and be able to lie some more after that. Before my flight out of Delhi, I found a therapist for a last-minute appointment. She was young, and pregnant past the point where she was seeing clients, but she agreed to see me because a mutual friend told her I was desperate. Most importantly, I'd never have to face her again.

I sat across a desk from her, took a breath, and launched into self-condemnation. Tuyet and I were deeply in love. And when I'd needed her, she was there for me. She did this incredible thing: she married me. I agreed to it because our love was real. I would never have used her. But now I was leaving. Abandoning her when she'd come to count on me. When I finally told her, she'd think our love was a lie. Maybe it was. I fell silent and waited for judgment.

"No," the therapist said. "You are experiencing confusion. Naturally, people in love want to be together. But love doesn't mean you'll be together forever. Your love can be real, and you can still leave." She set her notebook down. "Now, love does mean this: you owe her the truth as soon as you know it. If you have made a decision—and it sounds like you have—you must tell her."

When I returned from India, Tuyet and I separated. We could never unlove each other, but our relationship was over.

NOT ALL OF this fit into the space provided on the application. But I put down the heart of it and looked at the time. Fifteen minutes till the post office closed.

If you do not apply to remove the conditions in time, you could lose your conditional permanent resident status, and potentially be removed from the country.

I tore down the street and mailed it in the nick of time.

Then I called Rajan.

"Where the hell did you go?" he asked.

"I'm sorry. How are you doing?"

"I'm furious. And starving."

AN HOUR LATER, Rajan glared at me over a platter of vivid meats at an Ethiopian restaurant in Adams Morgan. I demonstrated how to tear apart a spongy, pale injera. He pointed a spindly finger at me and spoke above the dining room hum.

"You'd better have a very good explanation of where you've been."

I came clean. Rajan listened and chewed without a word. When I was done, his glare had become a puzzled squint.

"You live together two years. Then you get married. Then you move away and *change your mind*. And not for another woman. For some sort of great *cause*."

"I suppose," I said.

"And what about Tuyet?"

"We're still friends, but our relationship is over."

"And your parents haven't disowned you?"

"Well, they don't play a role in my relationships, other than wanting the best for me," I said. Rajan washed down a morsel with honey wine.

"Just one more question. Are you actually an Indian?"

I laughed. I was finally relaxed enough to dig into the food.

"Well," Rajan said, "I'm glad you got the application in. Good luck. And I appreciate you letting me know. But when it comes to the rest of the men . . ."

"Don't tell them?"

"Not a word."

The rest of the workers were in a good place right now. Their debts were piling up, but they had confidence in the campaign—because they had confidence in me. That hadn't been easy to earn. They had started out believing only "an American attorney" could help them. If they got wind that my own future in the United States was precarious—that I was anything other than invulnerable—they could come apart at the seams.

"So," I said, "are you going to keep me in suspense all night? What happened in George Miller's office?"

Rajan broke into his familiar grin for the first time that evening.

"Order us some more honey wine." He flashed his eyebrows. "We got him."

8: Food of Wanderers

April–May 2008
Washington, DC

WITH REPRESENTATIVE MILLER'S SUPPORT, our campaign built up steam. Now the staff of other members of Congress were asking *us* for meetings. I ran out to buy an iron. In the evenings the men pressed their shirts for the next day's outreach. Each morning they picked themselves off the church basement floor, laced up their work boots, and clopped through Washington's maze of power. They crammed lawmakers' offices to make the case for Continued Presence, and Democrats piled on with pledges to help.

But at the end of two weeks we hit a wall. I started hearing a troublesome whisper, first from congressional offices, and then from our allies. On one particular day I heard it three times, like a deadening drumbeat—the grimmest kind of DC message discipline. I must have looked shaken, because that night, while the others were ironing, Rajan took me aside.

"Something wrong?"

"We've got a problem," I admitted. Rajan's eyes narrowed.

"What kind of problem?"

"I'll get the groceries," I said.

BY THEN, RAJAN and I had a tradition. Serious problems required serious meals. We'd meet for late-night strategy sessions over dinner after the other men were asleep—food trucks for logistics gnarls, Ethiopian for big dilemmas. Tonight, we faced an existential threat, so Rajan was cooking a feast. We were in the tiny kitchen of my borrowed basement apartment in Adams Morgan. He was bent over a drum-sized pot with a towel draped over his shoulder, frying chopped green chilis. With one hand, he beckoned the steam toward his nostrils; with the other, he motioned me over with his spatula, a happy orchestra conductor. I unloaded groceries right into the pot. Cumin, garlic, tomatoes, carrots, turmeric, cinnamon, green cardamom, black cardamom, white pepper, black pepper, a dozen other things. Then, chicken stock, and plump chicken thighs with the skin on. He plucked a single clove from a bottle.

"You found them!" he said. "Good man. Wars were fought over cloves."

The clove went in. The lid went on. The orchestra played.

"So," Rajan said, "What's the problem?"

I explained. I had been talking to a staffer at George Miller's office, trying to understand why the DOJ still hadn't responded to his letter. After an awkward pause, the staffer said he probably shouldn't be telling me this, but that the DOJ official had said, "We've looked into this. It's not that strong of a case." I was instantly furious. The staffer insisted that wasn't the position of Miller's office. Later that day, I was meeting with a staffer at the House Judiciary Committee, which has jurisdiction over the DOJ. This staffer told me, more authoritatively than Miller's, "It feels like it's not that strong of a case." And then that evening, our contact at the AFL-CIO called. He'd run into Bush's top global anti-trafficking czar, a distinguished foreign policy expert in the State Department. Our contact asked if he was following this investigation. As if on cue: "I've looked at it. Not that strong of a case."

"Whatever investigation may or may not be moving," I told Rajan, "We know where we stand now. In Washington, when people from both sides of the aisle repeat the same phrase, it means—"

"We're losing," he said. He rubbed his chin. I started to chop cilantro stems for garnish. A sweet, spicy scent filled the kitchen.

"How are the men feeling? What's their mood?"

"The pot's simmering," Rajan said. "The pressure's building. It's about to boil over. Some are beginning to wonder if they were wrong to escape from Signal."

"At Signal, they'd still be undocumented," I reminded him.

"And working. And wiring money home every Friday, however little. Paying off their debts. These men need to work."

Back in India, the loan sharks were circling. They expected payments weekly, and the men had now gone thirty-two days without work.

"Debts aren't the only pressure," Rajan continued. "There's also the doubts."

The men's families knew nothing about the complex and bizarre American immigration system. How could they? They were buoyed initially by the news of the march, proud of their husbands and sons. But when it yielded nothing but more waiting, some started to wonder what their men were hiding. The wife of one of the men asked him, point blank, if there was an American woman in the picture. The father of another man told him no matter what crime he'd committed, all would be forgiven. The men's nightly phone calls with their families were increasingly tense.

Rajan lifted the lid. A thick column of steam rose up. He spooned the juicy chicken thighs out, moved them to a hot pan. The chicken skin sizzled and popped. He poured rice into the pot. The lid went back on.

"What about your family?" I asked Rajan. "How's your wife holding up? And your mother?"

"Don't worry about me. I have no children. You know who you should worry about? The new dads. Like Aby. People gossip at home. Neighbors are starting to call them deadbeats. Deserters."

I pulled out the plastic card table propped behind the door. Unfolding it became a struggle. When did it get to be this damn heavy? Rajan laid two plates down, flashed his eyebrows. *Cheer up.*

"I present our dinner! Al Kabsa in Washington."

On each plate was a brick-red mound of rice the size of a small hill in Kerala, with a crispy chicken thigh placed on top. I scooped up the rice. It burned my fingertips, but I couldn't wait. I pressed the rice into a ball in the palm of my hand and pushed it into my mouth with my thumb. I tried to make sense of what I was eating. Silky tomato. Smoky clove. Surprising raisin. Each grain of rice was perfect. The sweet steam fogged my glasses. I found the chicken thigh. Underneath its crackling skin, the meat was moist.

"My God," I finally managed to moan, "Where did you learn to make this?"

"Al Kabsa is a Bedouin dish. The food of wanderers. I used to work in Saudi Arabia. The cook in our labor camp was Jordanian. What a man. King of the one-pot meal."

"Well, now that title's yours," I said.

We chewed in silence as the spices overwhelmed our synapses.

"If only that title came with a work permit," he said several minutes later.

I laughed.

"So," Rajan said, "With a problem like this, what's the system in America?"

"What do you mean?"

"In India, first you file a case. Then you protest. Then you march. Then you lay a tree across a railway line. Then you burn down parliament. And so on and so forth. What's the system in America?"

With no good answer, I spooned a green mango pickle out of its jar and switched tracks.

"What was the breaking point for you?" I asked. "At Signal. What turned you against the company?"

"Oh, let me tell you," he said with vengeful relish, sucking on a clove.

He had been in the Mississippi man camp for a month. He was assigned to solder a stairway at the top of a new oil rig. Usually he liked the cold morning air: it reminded him of working in Baku. But in the lift to the top of the ten-story scaffold he didn't feel like himself. He was hungry, nauseated, drowsy. Breakfast had been old bread and rancid butter. And no tea. As the day wore on, he felt weaker. Just before lunch, he slumped over with his finger still on the torch trigger. He came to in horror. His torch was lying precariously close to the edge of the scaffold. If it had fallen from that height, it could have killed someone. *He* could have killed someone.

Head pounding, legs dangling over the scaffold, he pried open his tiffin. Lunch was plain rice, like every day. But today it was frozen. Sucking on the ricicles, Rajan grew angry. He flipped his torch back on and finished the stairwell job in a blue fury. When he got back to the camp, he marched straight to the cafeteria. He grabbed a cook by the collar, yanked him off the serving line, and started beating him. "Just enough that he got the point." It was when Rajan leapt over the service counter and lunged for the second cook that the guards rushed in. A melee ensued as the men's frustration with weeks of inedible food boiled over.

Camp manager Darrell Snyder stood up the next morning to condemn "The food riot." Rajan remembered him calling those who joined in "animals." The cooks all wanted to quit, scared for their safety. So Signal made a concession. They let Rajan cook. He scoured through the kitchen. To his amazement, it contained real food. A bag of canary yellow lentils. Another of rajma, deep red kidney beans. Rajan cooked the daal soupy, with salt, and served it in cups. For the first time in a month, he slept sated. The following week Signal let him buy minimal groceries—out of his own paycheck. He cooked chicken and red onions with rice. And this time, real daal. Eating the thick puree, fragrant with fried mustard seeds and garlic, he and the others felt human again.

I had tomato sauce dripping from my fingers as Rajan concluded his story. He was scooping up his next mound of rice, but he froze with a thought when it was halfway to his mouth. I had the same one. Our eyes met.

Food was power.

"Rajan—I think I know the solution."

He said it before I did: "A hunger strike."

9: Hunger

ON A RAINY May evening a week later, I gathered the coordinators and we considered our options. Since my dinner with Rajan, the whisper on us in Washington ("not that strong of a case") had hardened into a consensus and stopped all of our momentum. Even Congressman George Miller's staff were walking back their support, nervously asking if we had drawn them into a battle that was less righteous than we had initially let on. If our claims were shaky, they wanted to protect their boss from any fallout.

Meanwhile, our negotiations with DOJ prosecutor John Cotton Richmond had taken an ominous turn. He was finally ready to interview victims. But his offer had warning signs written all over it. For one thing, more than two months after we sent him the initial complaint, there was still no sign of Continued Presence. For another, he was insisting that we bring our chosen witnesses to *Gulfport, Mississippi.*

This was absurd. We were right there in Washington, blocks away from his office. But it was also troubling. Gulfport was a stone's throw from the Signal yard in Pascagoula where the men had escaped. The DOJ touted its "Victim-centered approach." But Richmond was asking the men to go back to the place where they'd had the most terrifying experience of their lives. Even more worrisome was his proposed location for the interviews: the Gulfport ICE office, so that a Mississippi ICE agent named Alvin Ladner could be present. Why on earth was Richmond, based in DC himself, asking half a dozen witnesses, their interpreters in three languages, and their attorneys to fly to Mississippi to accommodate a single ICE agent? We pushed back. Why not DC? Where was the Continued Presence? Who was this Ladner, and what was his role? Where was the FBI, which was supposed to be heading the investigation? Richmond's silence compounded our worry.

We had to win back the faith of Washington's lionhearted liberals— Miller, Ted Kennedy, Bob Menendez. But we were stuck in the minds of their congressional staffers as another "Interest group." We needed them to see us differently. It would require a demonstration that we were undeniably, uncompromisingly, driven by the truth.

The men were in favor of a hunger strike, but from the way they were out-declaring each other, I could tell they were scared. They were right to be. It was risky at many levels. They wanted to see the math. By what percentage point would a hunger strike increase their odds? I wanted them to confront the physical danger, the long-term impacts on their bodies even if the hunger strike succeeded. So I introduced our guest that evening: a doctor. He was an Indian American man in his midthirties, elegantly dressed in a tie that matched his green-checkered socks. Just above the air conditioner's mournful thrum, he described the day-by-day impacts of a water-only hunger strike, and the process known as ketosis.

"To keep the brain alive, you need food," he said. "When you don't eat, the body turns to its own stores of fat. That's what it consumes first, and when those are exhausted, it turns to feeding on muscle. And after muscle—" He paused.

The men were listening intently. Some pulled their chairs closer.

"The body eats the internal organs," he said.

The men smiled. They nodded to encourage the nervous doctor. *Go on. You're doing so well.*

"If you starve long enough, crashing levels of potassium, thiamine, and other nutrients can lead to physical and cognitive injury. This damage can be . . . permanent."

The men clapped politely. Then they walked him out, holding an umbrella over him as he laced his shoes, offering encouragement like they were his dissertation committee.

"First-class presentation!"

"Well put-together."

"And so are you! Dressed very smartly."

"India's pride. America's future!"

"My daughter shall marry a doctor just like you!"

His presentation, intended to dissuade, had the opposite impact. The men had been swirling around political considerations and hypotheticals; the doctor's speech pulled them all back into their own bodies.

When he had driven away, nonplussed, Rajan made a motion to vote. All hands were raised in favor of a hunger strike. Hugs were traded. The beefiest men were the happiest—their ample reserves of fat would be put to noble use. They teased Saravanan, the scrawniest of the bunch, whom they'd all outlast. And everyone laughed at the only unhappy men in the room, the ones with diabetes. The doctor had forbidden them from fasting. They were relegated to supporting roles.

"You'll be like Indian politicians! On camera, while we suffer," Aby said, to laughter. I shook my head, mostly in admiration. Some might be frightened on the eve of a hunger strike. Others grim. These men were newly at ease. Their decision had unlocked a reserve of power.

The hunger strike was a superlative action of Indian freedom fighters against the British Empire. It was sacred and strategic—duty and weapon at once. The man most associated with it, of course, was Mahatma Gandhi. He preferred the term *fast*, connoting Hindu religious practice, and harnessed the experience for purification and penance. And though Gandhi grew increasingly mystical over the course of his seventeen hunger strikes, he was quite clear that the action was a tool for power. One of his earliest fasts was on behalf of workers on strike for wage increases at a Gujarat textile mill. Four days later, the mill owners blinked: the workers won raises and formed Gujarat's first labor union. "Suffering even unto death," Gandhi wrote, "and therefore even through a perpetual fast, is the last weapon of the *Satyagrahi*"—the truth-seeker.

On May 14, our own battalion of truth seekers woke up with the sun, prayed, and took proud strides over to the park in front of the White House. Five leaders had been chosen to launch the hunger strike.

Murugan was one of them. As cameras clicked, he explained their simple demand to the crowd of allies and reporters: that the DOJ open an investigation into human trafficking and treat them as witnesses, allowing them to stay and work in the United States until it was concluded.

"It's already DOJ policy," he explained confidently. "It's known as Continued Presence."

"And if the DOJ finds no evidence of trafficking?" one reporter asked. Murugan didn't bat an eye.

"Then we'll honor the DOJ's decision and turn ourselves in to be deported."

The men linked arms. Supporters cheered. Pastors prayed. Saravanan, appointed the Chief Logistics Officer, spread out a blanket, and the fasters sat down cross-legged with a vigorous thump.

ON DAY 5, I asked Murugan how he was really doing, beyond the brave face he was keeping up for reporters. "My body cries like a baby," he said. "'Give me rice. Give me sambhar.' So I scold my body. 'Sambhar or victory? Your choice.' A few hours later, the baby cries again." But this internal struggle was hidden from view. Liberal allies expected an encampment of the dejected. Instead they found men steeled by their belief in the righteousness of their cause. A dozen times a day, they patiently explained American anti-trafficking policy to passing tourists, and pulled family photographs out of their wallets to show whose future was at stake. At sunset they folded up their blanket and retreated to the "Hunger strike house."

This was one of two houses we had rented, a row house nestled on a narrow elm-lined street for the hunger strikers. The other was the "supporter's house," for everyone else: the reserve army of other men preparing to join the fast relay-style, the logistics team, the diabetics, the supporters. The hunger strike house contained mattresses, cartons of bottled water, and little else. Most crucially, not as much as a grain of rice or a salt shaker. NO FOOD, read a sign on the fridge. NO DISCUSSION ABOUT FOOD, read another. The only theoretically ingestible substance allowed was toothpaste. When the hunger strikers returned each evening, they proudly submitted themselves to pat-downs for hidden candy bars, exultant when they were cleared. Other Indian men arrived at night to entertain the fasters with stories, songs, and dramatic readings of the day's press clippings. They were patted down as well. Men who smelled of dinner were turned away, instructed to shower and return in fresh shirts and cologne.

On Day 7, I rushed over to the hunger strike house.

"Pat me down fast," I said, fumbling off my shoes. I leapt over the rows of other shoes and sandals on the steps. The laughter and singing in the living room came to a halt so I could share the news: at a supporter's rally, Representative George Miller himself—not a staffer—had just vowed to press the DOJ for an answer, and to recruit other top Democrats. The hunger strike was working. Our champion was back. A smile crossed Murugan's ashen face, though he was too weak to clap.

The interim victory let him and three other fasters agree to be taken to the George Washington University Hospital, where nurses filled their bodies with nourishing fluids. They passed the baton to the next wave of hunger strikers, who vowed to press ahead for Continued Presence.

But one man from the original group kept going. His name was Paul Konar, and while others were experiencing blood pressure drops and crippling abdominal cramps, he hadn't seemed to miss a beat. This was all the more astonishing because he was the oldest hunger striker: on his fifteenth day without food, Paul turned fifty-four. In a church basement festooned with balloons, he blew out a candle atop a bright green sippy cup full of water. He beamed as we read him birthday messages the campaign had received from around the world for "The Hunger Strike Strongman." One of them came from my mother, who signed hers "In Solidarity."

The party was the perfect occasion to break the fast. Paul wouldn't hear of it. "I'm stronger than ever," he said. To look at him, it seemed true. The next day, I convinced him to go to the hospital for a routine checkup, sure that the doctors would order him off the hunger strike. But Paul's blood tests came back normal. The doctors couldn't explain it, but Paul could.

"It's God's gift."

Then we had our next breakthrough. Two influential members of Congress had joined George Miller in demanding an answer from the DOJ. One was Zoe Lofgren, Miller's colleague from California. The other was John Conyers Jr., the Michigan civil rights icon, a founder of the Congressional Black Caucus, and importantly for us, the ranking Democrat on the Judiciary Committee, which oversees the DOJ. The DOJ finally blinked: officials confirmed for the first time that they had opened an anti-trafficking investigation.

The men were ecstatic. I rushed to Paul's bedside. By now, he was visibly weaker.

"You did this," I said. "And now you can stop."

But he still refused. He'd stop when the men had work permits in their hands.

I took Rajan aside. We needed to gather the others, I said. If we all came to Paul together, hands folded, we might prevail.

"Why stop him?" Rajan said. "He's doing great."

"He's not doing great," I said, indignant. It was the first sign of the hairline fracture running through our committee. Rajan was one of a small group that believed Paul should persevere until we saw results—regardless of the risks.

"Paul's suffering is our leverage," he said.

DAY 22. A windless June evening. I arrived at the hunger strikers' house in secret. The elms stood perfectly still, like sentinels. I hid behind one of them and watched a mailman pass. A woman with a dog. I scanned the row house porch. No sandals, no shoes. The others were all at the supporters' house. Paul was alone. I was there to get him to stop, and I could only do that on my own.

The rift among the coordinators had deepened. Our previous decisions had all been by consensus, but the men were deadlocked over Paul's hunger strike—the first impasse of its kind. The DOJ still hadn't yet granted Continued Presence, and a small faction led by Rajan insisted on Paul's "Right" to remain hungry. They cheered him on to bolster his resolve, even as his health took a sharp dive. He was slurring his speech. A clump of his hair had fallen out. So I needed to overrule the deliberative process. Paul's life couldn't be in the hands of a committee. Especially since the committee wasn't privy to the terrible new information I had.

After the DOJ announces an investigation, especially one as visible as this one, law enforcement agents spring into action. In this case, no FBI agents were dispatched. And when the men's attorneys reached the DOJ official in charge of the investigation to ask about Continued Presence, he said only that he would check with ICE. Asked when witness interviews would take place, he said he'd get back to us—after checking with ICE. I started to suspect something too grim to contemplate. A few days later, a Washington ally confirmed it. The law enforcement agency in charge of the DOJ investigation wasn't the FBI. It was ICE.

Things that had seemed strange up until that point suddenly made sense: why the Mississippi FBI had vanished from the scene after calling us at the very start of the campaign; why victim interviews hadn't been scheduled for months. There was a struggle within government over this investigation. ("Inter-agency distress," ICE would later call it.) ICE, it seemed, had wrested control. I didn't know why. But one thing was clear: as long as they were in charge, there wouldn't be Continued Presence or work permits for these workers. ICE wasn't in the business of helping undocumented people stay in the United States.

With ICE in control, Paul's fast would win us nothing more, no matter how long he kept going. But I couldn't share the news that ICE was in control—not yet. If I did, panic would rip through the committee, the men would scatter, and the campaign would fall apart. The right way to tell them was with great care, once Paul was off his strike and stabilized. I would explain our new reality, and we would find a new way forward.

THE HOUSE WAS eerily quiet apart from the thrum of the air conditioner. Empty water bottles lined the hallway like trophies. Printed news stories from hometown papers dangled from walls.

Paul was in the living room. His face crunched with exertion as he tried to sit up on the mattress, then fell back on his pillow. I extended my hand. Even with the weight he had lost, it took all my strength to pull him up.

"What can I offer you?" he whispered.

"Just water, please." Our running joke. I laughed on cue—but today, he didn't. His face was gray. He looked straight ahead. Worried, I tried our other joke.

"Good haircut, Paul."

His hair, once thick as rope down to his collar, had started falling out five days ago. Each day I complimented his new hairdo. Each day he had a new comeback. He was saving money on barbers. He was offering his scalp as a mirror for shaving—but not free of charge!

This time he said nothing. Scared, I decided to cut to the chase.

"Listen, Paul," I said. "It's time. You need to come off the hunger strike."

He turned his gaze on me. Spoke with a voice that scraped gravel:

"Not today."

"You haven't eaten in twenty-two days."

"Has DOJ granted Continued Presence?" He knew the answer but made me say it.

"No."

"Until victory," he said, making a weak fist.

I tried to explain it simply. In slow-moving Washington, the DOJ investigation itself was a victory. It wasn't Continued Presence—yet. But the fifteen members of Congress pushing for it weren't minor players. I ran through their names.

His eyes narrowed. "Who was the one who gave me water to drink, called me Junior Gandhi?"

"Representative Kucinich," I said.

"Can he get us to victory?" he asked.

We had won as much as we were going to in this phase of our campaign, I said. Any day now, a major *New York Times* article would be coming out about the hunger strike. The world was watching. He could come off the hunger strike a hero. *Times* story in hand, we'd start a new phase, go to more congressional offices.

He took a deep breath. His broad chest expanded. Strength returning, he sat up on his own. We were now at eye level. He was fully awake.

"*No*," he growled. "Not today."

"Paul," I said, "Think of your family."

He had three daughters. Before they were born, he worked the Middle East oil fields. He paid for his sister's wedding with that money, then his cousin's, and then his own. When his wife had their first daughter, Pinky, he moved back home. Then came Tina. Then Priyanka. To build them a proper house, he left for the oil fields again. At the height of his career, he was working for United Arab Emirates' National Drilling Company. He supervised crews of Indian laborers in four languages. It was good money. But he was fifty-two. The company aged out its workforce at fifty-four. What then? His daughters were growing. Soon, he'd have more weddings to pay for. That's when he saw the ad in UAE papers. PERMANENT LIFETIME SETTLEMENT IN USA, FOR SELF AND FAMILY. A godsend! So he paid, and flew to Mississippi.

"How are your daughters?" I asked.

His baritone revived: "They always wanted me with shorter hair. They always warned me that they'd make me get a haircut for their weddings."

A week ago, on his birthday, his wife had called and asked him how he was celebrating. *Would there be a cake?* No, he said. He was on a hunger strike. A fight so they could join him in America. *How long?* He didn't know. *No—how long since you've eaten?* She was distressed beyond words at the answer.

Paul smiled, softening at the thought of her. "She's always saying, 'Paul, stop this. Please, stop this.'"

"She loves you, Paul. A lot of people do." I felt my voice catch. "I love you."

"You're like my son."

"And I want you to be well."

His smile radiated warmth.

"I worry about you," he said. "Always working, never resting."

"You're right. I must change my habits. But listen, Paul, I'm here to talk about you. You don't look well at all."

"I'm strong," he said, with great affront. "Feel these. You know how I got them? Boxing. With the Egyptians in Abu Dhabi." Admittedly, his biceps felt like lead.

"And this," he said, pointing to his heart. "Just as strong. Do you know why? Because a hundred nuns are praying for me." He talked about these nuns all the time. They were his constant solace through the hunger strike. He said their church, near Pala in Kerala, had been built in 1030 CE. The three nuns leading the prayers were family members of his. Their names were Christi, Crucifix, and Virgin Mary. Their *legal* names.

"You deserve every prayer," I told him.

"The point is, I'm not dying," he said. "But if it happens, it's my contribution."

I felt a chill on my neck. "What do you mean?"

"If others receive Continued Presence because of my death, it will have been worth it."

"My God, Paul," I said, burying my face in my hands.

His commitment to help the other Indian men was all the more incredible because he had never actually worked alongside them. Back in India, he'd caught the tail end of the recruitment process. He was still in India on March 9, 2007, when Signal's guards locked up Jacob Joseph and attempted to deport him. After the workers' uprising to defend Jacob, Signal officials called Sachin Dewan. *No more Indians.* But Sachin and Malvern Burnett still had a few men in the queue, and they apparently wanted to extract all the money from them they could. In April 2007, Paul Konar arrived at Sachin's office with the last installment, close to $7,000. Sachin took the money, gave Paul his passport with a worthless visa in it, and sent him to America.

In Mississippi, Paul was greeted at Signal's gates by John Sanders. "We're not taking any more Indians," he said, then dumped him at a hotel. An hour later, someone knocked. It was a friend of Paul's from Kerala who'd snuck out of the labor camp to rescue him. Signal had called the police, he said. They would be here any moment to deport him. The man told him to run, and Paul did.

He was homeless and destitute. He could have blamed his plight on the workers inside the labor camp, whose uprising had left him stranded while they continued to work. But he heard about our movement and found me. The first time I met him, I asked him if he needed anything. "To be of use," he said.

Facing him now, I didn't know what else to tell him. The others were my contemporaries. Under pressure, there were ways I could override them. Not Paul. He was my elder.

"Paul, I'm sorry," I said. "This is my fault."

We had been right to carry out the hunger strike, I said. But I had been naive. There were so many things I didn't know. How much time things take in Washington. I should never have set the expectation that we'd unlock Continued Presence from DOJ in a matter of weeks. I should never have allowed Paul to keep fasting past his birthday. Now he was talking about dying for the cause.

"That's not the way," I said. "And the truth is, even if you did, it might not help us. That's not what this fight is about. Killing yourself will not get us what we need."

Paul thought for a second. Then he said, "I understand."

I exhaled. Finally I'd gotten through.

"You've run out of money," he said.

"What?"

"I can carry on. It's you who can't. The campaign is broke. I run a household too. I get it."

"No, that's not it!" He wasn't wrong. The campaign *was* broke. But that wasn't the reason I wanted him to end his hunger strike. Paul pressed on.

"I don't need this rental house. I'll sleep on the street. Beg from blessed people. But I'm not stopping." Then the surge of strength went out of him. His face went ashen again.

I started to plead. Our civil rights allies were activating the Congressional Black Caucus. We were reaching out to Republicans who had led on the Trafficking Victims Protection Act . . .

"Paul?"

His eyes were closing. I took his hand. His eyelids fluttered open, then shut tight. His jaw rested on his broad chest like the hull of a great ship. He was asleep.

I held his hand. Watched his belly rise and fall. His soft snoring blended with the sound of the air conditioner. I searched my mind for a new way to make my case when he woke up. I found nothing.

PAUL'S HAND PRESSED mine. His eyes were still closed.

"How long did I sleep?" he said.

"Not long. How are you feeling?"

He sighed. I stayed quiet.

"The Gandhi statue," he said softly.

"What?"

"Take me out to the Gandhi statue tomorrow morning. Spread out a blanket for me. There, I'll announce an end to my hunger strike. I'll thank my supporters. Including that one—who called me Junior Gandhi."

"Kucinich."

"I'll thank them all. Then you'll call an ambulance."

"Yes. We'll arrange that, Paul."

A tear left the corner of his eye and made its way down to the pillow.

"I'll leave you to rest," I said.

"No," he said, and patted my hand. "Stay."

WHO HAD VISITED Paul in his sleep? Was it Pinky, Tina, and Priyanka, prevailing on their father as only daughters can? Or Christi, Crucifix, and Virgin Mary, with the hundred nuns of Pala arrayed behind in their veils and rosaries? What had let him change his mind? Love, prayer, or both?

10: Breakdown

June 11, 2008
Washington, DC

WE WERE STANDING in the shadow of the Gandhi statue in front of the Indian Embassy, cheering on the world's most joyful starving man. After twenty-three days, Paul Konar was ending his hunger strike. He sat up on his blanket, head held high, and beamed with his last ounce of energy. The crowd burst into applause. Medics put him on a stretcher. He waved like a king from a palanquin. Then the doors of the ambulance shut and it drove off.

Rajan whistled behind me.

"Bravo," he said, his voice laced with contempt. "We may not get Continued Presence, but you'll get that job in Washington."

I turned around.

"Rajan," I said. "We need to talk."

"*Now* you want to talk! You violated our process. Went behind our backs. Paul would have lasted three more days!"

"There's something I knew that you didn't—I've been waiting to tell you," I said. "Listen. *ICE* is running the DOJ investigation. The same ICE that surveilled us. It's why we haven't won Continued Presence. It's why we have to leave Washington."

He registered my news like a blow and shot back. "And you didn't think to tell us?" All he heard was more betrayal.

"This was life and death. I'm telling you *now*. First I needed to get Paul off his fast—without debate and controversy. Now that he's safe, we sit and talk it through. Then, tonight, gather the men to plan, so they don't—"

Rajan stormed off. I chased after him, grabbed his arm. When he turned around, his eyes were pure fury. He stabbed the air with his finger. "You're lying!"

"Rajan, *brother*," I implored, "We're facing a serious threat."

"No, *we* are facing a threat. *You* are moving on. I get it. You got your *New York Times* story. The media's crested. Now you go scouting for your next poor immigrant to trot out on stage. That's it, isn't it? That's how you make your money?"

"Money?"

"Well," he said, "go to hell. We'll run our own campaign without you. But all the cash you collected, from all the goras who cried at our plight—you need to turn that over to us. We'll divide it equally among the hunger strikers, to send to our families."

"What are you talking about? Rajan, the satyagraha alone cost us $75,000. I'm on the verge of laying off a third of my staff!"

"Lies on top of lies," he cried, and escalated. In his version of events, "all the union money" that came into the campaign went into raises and hefty bonuses for me and my staff. I was leaving for New Orleans, he charged, to live high on the hog. I became indignant. There wasn't any union money. The only significant donation, $20,000 from the aid organization Oxfam, was long spent. My staff and I earned $35,000 a year each, less than a welder's salary. He chortled in disbelief and challenged me to prove it. He wanted to gather the coordinators for a "Money meeting," where I would open my books. As flabbergasted as I was, I agreed. My finance director in New Orleans would walk them through the budget. But there was no getting through to him. When I suggested we meet later after a cooling-off period and assess the campaign, he thundered that he'd report me to the Attorney General for misuse of "The people's money." Then he did the unthinkable. He spat at me.

"That's what I think of your campaign, *brother*."

I stood there stunned and watched him walk away.

I met the remaining coordinators at the hunger strike house, where their shoes lined the front steps like open-mouthed faces.

When I'd asked them to gather for a committee meeting after the rally with Paul, they guessed something was wrong. Rajan's disappearance from the scene only added to the ominousness. Even mild-mannered Saravanan, with his always-pleasant eyes, looked haunted. Whoever had last swept the living room, he said, had left the broom and dustpan out. When I confessed it was me, the men shook their heads; the Hindus among them folded their hands. Apparently, coming home and seeing a broom out carried a curse. We sat silently for an awful minute. Then there was nothing to do but level with them.

I told them what I'd tried to tell Rajan. ICE was running the DOJ investigation. Very likely, ICE had been blocking Continued Presence from the start of our march. The DOJ investigation was still open but as long as ICE was in charge of it, there was no real chance of Continued Presence, no legal protections, no work permits. That road was closed.

Our hopes were now pinned to T visas, the humanitarian visas designed for trafficking victims, granted by USCIS. A battery of pro bono attorneys was getting ready to conduct hundreds of hours of interviews for T visa applications, a process that would take months. In the meantime, the men were all undocumented.

And they were desperate to work, I knew. Their debts in India were piling up. Ever since they escaped from Signal's Pascagoula yard, labor brokers and contractors had been circling them, offering work at major companies across the country. A Chevron plant in Mississippi. A power plant in Kentucky. A shipyard in Rhode Island. I knew they needed to take those offers.

Our days in DC were at an end—at least for now. But as the men prepared to fan out across the country, there were things they needed to keep in mind. If they decided to work without papers, I told them, they needed to take great care. Phalanxes of ICE agents had been conducting workplace raids across the country. With the approach of the US presidential election, these raids would likely intensify.

"Avoid counties where sheriff's departments turn undocumented immigrants over to ICE," I warned. Some of the men had been offered a job at a North Carolina power plant, for example. They should refuse: the most routine interaction with a local cop in that state—even a traffic infraction—could land them in ICE custody. "Avoid Mississippi." They were still blacklisted there. "Avoid Southeastern states entirely if you can. And shipyards are out." Any shipyard could have US government contracts, and since 9/11, workers on federal maritime projects had to submit to background checks. When undocumented workers walked into Southern shipyards to apply, ICE was called on the spot.

Beyond that, they needed to keep their numbers small in any particular place to avoid attention. These men loved traveling together like a tribe. But in most power plant towns in America, the sudden appearance of dozens of brown men was a big event. In places like Southern Illinois or Kentucky, people would talk. Locals might feel threatened. Police would ask questions. An uneasy neighbor might call ICE. I warned them to stay in small clusters, twenty-five at most.

But what was most important was that we maintain our network. Wherever there was a cluster of men, there should be a coordinator. That would let me stay in touch with the whole group, keep them informed, detect dangers, and help in a crisis.

In the meantime, I said, I was heading back to New Orleans to start working on the next phase of the campaign. We'd continue to push the DOJ to bring an indictment while we raced to submit T visas. Not to worry: we weren't retreating, and wouldn't relent. Feeling my voice quaver, I told them that representing them was the greatest honor of my life. I'd keep going till the end.

We cleaned and packed up the apartment. Saravanan warned me not to hit anyone's foot while I swept—a double curse. Murugan came up and told me that a crew of about twenty men had been offered jobs on a big ethanol plant. He was one of them. The plant was in place called Fargo.

"Wow," I said. "That's far away. And cold. Well, congratulations."

"I'm not going," he said. "I'm thinking I'll come with you to New Orleans instead. You'll need help."

"Thank you, brother," I said. "I will." He took the broom from me.

"I'll finish up here," he said.

THE MEN LEFT for Galveston, and Baytown, and Corpus Christi, and Louisville, and Fargo, and boomtowns across America where plant managers needed welders and pipefitters on the cheap. As the last car pulled away, I was overcome by the senselessness of their journeys. I had imagined such a different future for them, and it had seemed within reach. Why ICE had worked so hard to close that future off was beyond me. If the DOJ seemed intransigent, ICE was a black box. All I had was a name. The agent that Richmond referred to in his emails, who we now knew had been running the DOJ's investigation from the beginning.

Alvin Ladner.

PART FIVE

HUNTED

1: The Hunter

1719–2007
Mississippi Gulf Coast

ALVIN LADNER CAME from a long line of hunters—though the family line began with a fugitive.

Christian Ladner of Lucerne was a tobacco smuggler when French police captured him in 1719. His sentence was a seat aboard *Le Marie*, a limited artillery ship carrying deportees to America. He was twenty years old. During the voyage, he fell in love with another passenger, a married woman named Mary Ann. Christian threw Mary Ann's husband overboard. When *Le Marie* docked in Mississippi, Christian and Mary Ann fled to the forest and hid there until they were sure her husband hadn't swum ashore. (At least, that's how Alvin heard it, chuckling whenever the tale was told.) They married and had three sons. Alvin Ladner was descended from their oldest, Jean Baptiste.

After Christian, it was hunters all the way down. Ladner men scoped out land, stalked deer, hunted Native Americans, chased runaway slaves, laid ambush for jayhawkers come to steal their cattle. And the Ladners were relentless. Alvin's great-great-great-grandfather, Victor Jr., was fighting in the 3rd Mississippi Infantry when Union soldiers captured him at the siege of Vicksburg. He won his release by vowing never to fight again—then he got his rifle back and went right on fighting. After the war he walked two hundred miles to get home to Lakeshore, Mississippi, stopping only to marry a local girl he met on the way.

Alvin Ladner was born right down the road from Victor Jr.'s gravestone. He grew up with a passion for catching things. As a boy, he made a trap out of his mother's laundry basket and hid out of sight to capture birds who took the bait. When he was eleven, he was out riding his little motorcycle down back roads when he caught an unmistakable scent. He waited till dark, then came back to sniff out the source deep in the woods. He found a group of men around a fifty-five-gallon barrel—a moonshiner's whiskey still. Soon he'd found others. He told his father, who then warned him to stay away. The next thing Alvin knew, explosions were shaking the woods. *His tip* had led tax police to the illegal stills, and now they were being dynamited into splinters.

While still in high school, he talked his way into a dispatching job at the sheriff's department. After college at Southern Miss, he joined the department as an investigator. He quickly came to focus on drugs. Bank robbers you could only catch after their crime—Alvin's passion was catching criminals in the act. Not just the street peddlers, but the smugglers. Most Americans associated dramatic narcotics raids with the Drug Enforcement Agency. But in the late 1980s, as Alvin learned, 80 percent of the cocaine seized in the United States was confiscated by US Customs. So Alvin took the test to join them, and passed.

His first cocaine bust, a trap laid in the dark New Orleans harbor, was the greatest thrill of his life. When he got hot on the bad guys in New Orleans, they ran to South Florida. When he caught up with them in Miami, they shot out to Mississippi. Alvin stayed in pursuit, volunteering for twenty-four-hour-long shifts once a week, crisscrossing state lines behind kingpins, surveilling their crews in condo buildings, marinas, harbors, malls.

He knew it wasn't enough to be faster than the drug traffickers; he had to be smarter than them. So he studied their patterns. Noted when they shifted from fishing boats to freighters. That meant they'd need nautical charts. Where would they get them? Ladner house-called every map store in five states, looking for South or Central Americans in the market for nautical charts. After months, he got a name that cracked a case.

He had his dream job. A family with three kids. He couldn't imagine a better life.

Then 9/11 blew up his dream.

The Bush Administration shifted from fighting drug lords to fighting terrorists. US Customs got swallowed up by the newly created Department of Homeland Security and was forced to merge with the Immigration and Naturalization Service to form a new agency: Immigration and Customs Enforcement.

At Customs, Ladner had chased South American mobsters on speedboats, spied on heroin parties in South Florida. Now he was sent after Central American roofers or Mexican dishwashers. Targets who cowered in apartment buildings, cried as they piled into ICE vans. What he did now, you couldn't even call it a hunt. Ladner spent more time processing detainees in the office than he did locating them.

His discouragement dragged his home life down. After twenty years, his marriage came apart. Just over a year later, Hurricane Katrina bore down on Mississippi. After making sure his son and his ex-wife were safe, Ladner fled from Waveland to Gulfport—in time to see the hurricane land in the city he'd just left.

He returned the next day. The city was flattened. His house was flooded, everything in it destroyed. He found his seventeen-foot Boston Whaler in the woods, stuck between two trees, filled with swamp mud.

He was assigned to a midnight patrol shift in support of local law enforcement. He prowled the streets in a government Chrysler with orders to stop anything that moved. But police were the only thing moving, apart from beavers and raccoons.

Ladner ached to be on a real hunt again. The kind that had always gotten his blood pumping. A case with real fugitives who were committing a crime in real time. Worthy opponents. Men with a strategy, who didn't just elude law enforcement, but baited them, the way his old nemeses at Customs had. Opponents who arrived undetected from some faraway country, to carry out an audacious operation on American shores. If only ICE pursued cases like that. If only he were the one assigned to the hunt.

That's when the Signal case landed on his desk.

2: Notice To Appear

October 2008
New Orleans, LA

AFTER MONTHS of waiting, John Cotton Richmond of the Department of Justice wrote saying he was ready to interview witnesses. But there were conditions.

Richmond would come to New Orleans to take statements, but from only four workers. We had to choose which four, from the hundreds of men, would present "Exemplary" testimony. On the basis of this, the DOJ would draw conclusions about the entire group's trafficking claims. The pressure was enormous.

Worse, the interviews could only proceed once ICE had processed the witnesses as unauthorized aliens and issued them Notices to Appear before an immigration judge. In other words, as a condition for giving their testimony about human trafficking, the men would have to be formally arrested and entered into deportation proceedings. After the interviews, ICE could as easily disappear the men into a deportation center as release them on their own recognizance.

Why this condition? Alvin Ladner, the ICE agent, was insisting on it.

The witnesses would be taking a serious risk. But the interviews were the only possible way to make progress toward an indictment. I told the coordinators. Promised that we would do everything in our power to protect them. They considered for a long, pregnant moment. Then Murugan said he'd be the first.

MURUGAN NOW TOOK a deep breath. He was seconds away from one of his life's greatest tests. There were two campaign lawyers at his sides in the elevator. One of them squeezed his shoulder. "You're good," the lawyer said. "We're going to be with you every step of the way." The elevator bell sounded the countdown.

His anxious mind raced back to the last time an American official had interviewed him, that disastrous day in Chennai when the US visa officer rejected him and his world went dark. *Ten thousand dollars, lost.* Only by making himself indispensable to the recruiters had he won a second chance.

Now Murugan was once again carrying the hopes of hundreds of men, but the stakes were even higher.

He steeled himself. The other coordinators trusted him to play this part. And who better to do it? As the rest of the men scattered to different cities to work without papers, Murugan had made the freedom struggle his whole life. He was living in New Orleans in a shelter for victims of trafficking. He had been working to improve his English so he could translate for the other Tamil men. All while his own debts loomed.

He just needed to stay focused. Remember that he wasn't alone.

The last bell sounded. In the silver doors he saw himself: a fatherless boy, far from home. But who had that boy chosen as his new role model after his father died? At a wedding soon after, where the other kids fixated on the groom on his white horse, Murugan watched the sambhar server who went from table to table, bowing slightly, pouring sustenance into the plates of guests who didn't notice.

Service is its own reward, Murugan reminded himself.

"You've got this, Murugan," one of his lawyers said.

"We're right here with you," said the other.

The doors opened.

What happened next was a blur. Immigration agents loomed over him, huge men in dark blue with weapons strapped to their belts. Somehow they got between him and his lawyers. The lawyers shouted in protest, but the agents seemed to be made out of granite. The next thing Murugan knew, he was being pushed into a small, windowless room. The door clapped shut behind him.

Alone inside, he paced in terror for what could have been ten minutes or two hours. He tried to make out his lawyers' voices in the commotion outside. Finally the door opened. An immigration agent came in. A burly man, dressed for combat.

He asked for Murugan's name. Nationality. Proof of permission to be in the United States. He explained that Murugan was being arrested. He was being issued a Notice to Appear and was now in deportation proceedings. He would be released today only if he promised to present himself in court. The agent was holding something out toward him. A pen. Murugan signed a document. The room swayed and tilted like a bamboo canoe.

He somehow wound up in another room, this time with a man in a suit at a conference table, a government lawyer.

"John Cotton Richmond," the man said, hand out. "Thanks for coming in. Good morning so far?"

Murugan was still clutching the pen. *Arrested. Deportation. Present yourself in court.* He hadn't imagined it like this.

He strained to focus. On the conference table, a glass of water caught the window's light, October blue with gypsum clouds. A fly settled on its rim. The government lawyer's questions seemed to reach him from another world:

"How did you learn about the Signal job opportunity?"

"How much did you pay?"

"Who did you pay?"

"How much did you have to borrow?"

"How many people did you share a room with in the labor camp?"

"What made you stay at Signal in those terrible conditions?"

He was barely aware of having answered when he realized the government lawyer was standing, hand extended again.

"Thank you," he said, and ushered Murugan out.

"Thank you," Murugan repeated, his voice faltering.

HE FOUND HIS LAWYERS pacing in the hallway, red-faced with outrage and humiliation. It wasn't supposed to go like that—ICE had deliberately made it as terrifying as possible. Between apologies, they asked him for details of the interview, while insisting he must have done brilliantly. All Murugan could feel was the rising blade of fear as he approached the windowless room, bracing himself to be cuffed and shackled before he had a chance to escape.

That night, over rice and sambhar, I tried to restore Murugan's faith in our campaign. I had limited success, perhaps because my own confidence was shaken.

The only winner that day was Alvin Ladner. Murugan and the others had prepared for this interview for months. When the day came, ICE sideswiped them, leaving them to blunder through their testimony in a daze. And as far as I knew, Ladner had managed this without even being there. Neither I, nor any of the lawyers, had ever laid eyes on him.

The futures of these men were in his hands, and he was completely hidden from view.

3: Damage

ABY AND I were three hours into our meeting, and nerves were fraying.

"Okay, Aby," I said, wiping my brow. "Let's try to get through this."

With the DOJ interviews past—and nothing to do on that front but wait—we turned to preparing the men for the long-term prize, the biggest they could win: T visas. These visas, granted by US Citizenship and Immigration Services to victims of human trafficking, were the men's only real path to what Signal's recruiters had promised and charged a king's ransom for, but never meant to deliver: "Permanent lifetime settlement in US for self and family."

I was helping Aby prepare his "Victim statement"—his description, in his own words, of why the US government should deem him a victim of human trafficking. If they did, his T visa would let him bring his family to the US and put him on a path to citizenship.

Aby's prep wasn't the only thing on my mind. I had just gotten a call from a congressional staffer in Washington—about my friend Rajan. After our bitter argument at the end of the hunger strike, he had refused to regroup in New Orleans, opting to stay in DC with a splinter group of men to continue to visit congressional offices with volunteer interpreters. I had called him dozens of times, but he never picked up. The congressional staffer who called was confused and worried, warning that Rajan was now arriving at their offices unannounced and lashing out at them for being unable to move the DOJ.

It was a mess, but I tried to put it out of my mind to focus on the matter at hand.

"Ok, Aby," I said. "Let's talk about March 9, 2007. That's the most important day to focus on: the day Signal locked up Jacob Joseph and the rest to deport them. Why did the raid terrify you? What conclusion did you draw from it, and how did that leave you deeper in the company's control? That's the thing the government most needs to know."

"No, Saketji," Aby said. "Let's talk about June thirtieth. The day Bobby was born in India. And the fact that on that day, I was on top of an oil rig in Texas. That's what the government needs to understand!"

Aby never failed to move me, but this afternoon, he was grating on my nerves. Today wasn't for the poetry of exile. My job, as much as I hated it, was to fit him into the mold that the US government had set for victims of trafficking. Aby kept breaking out of it.

"We'll get to Bobby being born. But first, March 9. The terror. The knowledge that they control you completely. You've described all this to me before. Now let's tell the government."

"What they need to hear is how I felt on June thirtieth when I got the call. You know I broke all the safety rules to answer? I was twenty feet in the air, holding a welding gun. But it was Bincy, calling from the operating table in Meenadom. She told me was about to have her C-section—then a nurse snatched her phone! Can you imagine?"

"I know, Aby."

"I broke in two! Do they get that?"

"But that doesn't, by itself, convince them you should get a T visa," I said.

"Okay, then imagine how it feels when my mother calls an hour later. 'You're a father.' What kind of father? Ten thousand miles away! Write that down, Saket-ji." He tapped on my yellow pad, as if my scribbling held special powers.

"Aby, I know all this. I can't even imagine going through it. But we should only include what's relevant to your trafficking claims."

"Fathers hold their newborn sons and look them in the eyes. I opened an email account and looked at his face on a screen! Three days old. Beautiful."

"That doesn't get you a T visa!" I said, my exasperation rising.

"Isn't that what all this is for? To reunite me with Bincy? To let me hold my boy?"

"Aby!" I erupted, surprising myself. "The pain of separation is terrible. But there is no sorrow visa. There is a *trafficking* visa. To get it, you have to be *trafficked*. By *their* definition, not ours. You came to America because of fraud and force. In America you were subjected to . . . what?"

"Involuntary servitude," Aby muttered.

I hammered on. "Exactly. Not heartache! Not lonely nights! *You weren't free to leave.* That's what gets you the visa. But you have to prove it, and they're going to be skeptical. They'll say: 'But Aby, you're not the one who was kidnapped on March 9, that was Jacob Joseph. Why do you deserve a T visa?' And you say?"

"What happened to Jacob was a message to all of us. I was terrified."

"Why? The raid on March 9 happened in Mississippi. To quell a worker uprising that happened in the Pascagoula camp. You worked in Orange, Texas. So what does that have to do with you? *If* you make them see that, then you get to hold your son."

Aby looked inconsolable. He stared out as if Bincy and Bobby might materialize in front of him. Then he looked at me.

"She had a plan," he said. "Bincy. She had a way to get here. Not all the way to America. But to Canada. And I told her no."

Aby revealed to me that even before the campaign had begun, when he was trapped at Signal with dwindling hope of a green card and no clear way out, Bincy had taken matters into her own hands. She was a nurse, and billboards all over Kerala were screaming about the nursing shortage in Canada. She applied for a Canadian nursing visa. If she could find a job somewhere near the US border, at least Aby could spend some time with her and Bobby. Not an ideal solution, but a border between them was better than several oceans.

Then we launched our campaign. Aby was on a high, convinced that victory—including the ability to bring his family to him—was just around the corner. So he told Bincy to rescind her application. She resisted. But Aby was adamant. It was a matter of his masculine pride: it was *his* responsibility to find a solution, his responsibility to make things right, and that's what he was doing. He put his foot down. Reluctantly, she agreed.

"And now it's been a year and a half. And that's not all. My parents are going to lose the house. I've failed them," he said. I searched for a way to console him. I couldn't come up with one.

He took a deep breath to settle, reached out, and tapped my legal pad.

"We can start again."

HOURS LATER, AROUND SUNSET, I hugged Aby goodbye. In the months since the hunger strike, we had become close friends. As tough as our conversation had been, I felt closer to him. I hoped he felt the same.

"You'll see Bobby," I promised.

Then Aby drove away. I couldn't move, weighed down by guilt and failure. I still had hope for Aby and the rest, but in the meantime, damage was being done every day.

Aby's attorney sent his T visa application in shortly after. His victim statement focused mostly on March 9. But the most important event of his life—Bobby's birth—did earn a mention:

My son was born on June 30, 2007. I asked the camp manager if I could possibly go to India for a short while and return to the United States. He refused to allow me to go.

And so did his marriage:

I have also had marital problems as a result of this. My wife tells me often that she believes that I have lied and cheated her because when I left for America, I promised her that we would be together again in nine months. She constantly asks me why I married her. I crave to see my child, but there is nothing I can do because of my need to support my family.

4: Fargo

November 2008–
March 2009
Fargo, ND

FOUR WEEKS LATER, my greatest fear for the men came to life.

When the men dispersed around the country seeking work after the hunger strike, twenty-three of them had wound up on a construction project in North Dakota. They set about building the nation's seventh-largest ethanol plant. Production had been stalled because of a lack of local welders and pipefitters. Then these men came to town to build miles of interlocking pipe right off blueprints while their foremen looked on, astonished. When they raised it all from the shop floor to the sky— ahead of schedule—everything fit perfectly. Supervisors got bonuses, slapped the workers' backs and promised beer.

Then one morning, at the regular safety meeting before the shift, a supervisor asked the Indians to get back in their cars and drive out to the main office. *Now?* the workers asked, puzzled. The supervisor shrugged. The men drove over and found the main office empty, eerily quiet. They sat in rows at the long tables, trying to decipher the papers placed neatly in front of each seat. Then the doors opened, and they heard a shuffle of boots. Immigration agents. Faster than a jolt of fear, all twenty-three of them were forced to the floor. They were cuffed, shackled, and incarcerated.

It was what I'd always dreaded. From the first warnings at the company gates on the day the campaign launched, to the increasingly aggressive ICE surveillance during our march, to the spike of nerves I felt any time a worker called me unexpectedly, there had always been the threat that ICE would smash the men's fragile foothold in America. Now it was happening.

The US Attorney prosecuting the case was a strapping conservative, a fourth-generation North Dakotan named Drew Wrigley. To him, the men were illegals trying to cut in on the state's green jobs boom. He charged them with felonies that carried twenty-five-year sentences.

When I went to visit the men in the jail, they were twisting with terror and shame. One of them emerged from his cell covered in bruises. The previous night he'd balled up his fists and started to beat his own face in, until his cellmate woke to restrain him.

I knew only one person who might be able to bring them back from that kind of despair. I called Murugan to ask for his help. He had every right to hang up on me.

Instead, two days later, he met me at the arrivals terminal of Minneapolis airport on a minus-ten-degree day. He emerged in a spotless collared shirt, carrying a simple duffel bag. I hugged him with a mixture of gratitude and horror.

"You didn't bring a jacket?"

He refused to put on my winter coat. After some jostling, we came to an impractical compromise: I held his bag while he held my coat, both of us freezing until we dove into a taxi.

"Can you take us all the way to Fargo?" I asked. "Cass County Jail."

The driver, an old Somali man, perked up.

"You here to help those illegals from India? It was on the radio."

The men had become the talk of the town. They'd even been given a name: the Cass 23.

Murugan had agreed to help in any way he could. But I could feel his guardedness as we sped along the frost-rimmed highway. His hurt and confusion from being arrested at his DOJ interview ran deep.

"Will the men be deported?" he asked me.

"Not if we can help it."

He looked straight at me. "Is this the end? The beginning of the end?"

"No," I said. "When we get to the jail, our message to the men is: We're pushing forward. We'll get you free."

"Why should they believe that?" he asked. The unspoken question was all too clear: *Why should I?*

"They might not believe it coming from me," I said. "But they will believe it coming from you."

That's why I had asked him to come. The twenty-three men in jail knew and respected Murugan. He had been made a foreman at Signal because of his skill and English ability (though without a foreman's salary), and these men were among those he had supervised. He had later helped convince them to escape Signal. And now, after his own arrest at the DOJ interview, he had a new kind of authority.

"Use your own example," I said. "Tell them you were arrested as well. And you're still here. If you still have reason to hope, so do they."

"But I'm going to be deported! Isn't it just a matter of time?"

"A new president is on the way," I reminded him. Barack Obama had been elected only weeks before. "Things in Washington will change."

"Your Obama will help us?" To the men, he was always *my* Obama.

"A new administration means change of leadership in ICE, at DHS, at the DOJ. That's our opening. We need to hang on till it happens."

Murugan stared out at the white expanse for a long moment.

"Promise me something," he said.

"Anything."

"The day all hope is lost, you will tell me."

His eyes searched mine.

"I promise," I said.

The taxi pulled to a stop.

"Cass County Jail," the driver said. My frozen fingers counted out the fare and a tip. His leathery face pinched in gratitude. "Good luck."

Outside, the air hit our faces like a handful of broken glass.

MURUGAN RALLIED THE MEN in the jail, managing to deliver the hope that even he no longer had. He offered his own body, arrested but free to roam, as proof that we could get them out.

Then we set out to do it. It was an uphill battle. With the help of a faith-based community organizing collective called ISAIAH, we recruited local pastors, including US Attorney Drew Wrigley's own pastor, Reverend Jeff Sandgren. Rev. Sandgren considered Wrigley a friend, but led a prayer for the men at a Sunday service while Wrigley sat in his pews. Then he braved a snowstorm to lead a public prayer vigil out in front of the federal building where Wrigley worked. The men watched the coverage of it on the TV news from the rec room at Cass County Jail, astonished to hear their names on the lips of God's own emissaries in Fargo.

We followed this up with a short story in *The New York Times*, where we asserted that the men were victims of trafficking who deserved protection from the DOJ as witnesses in their own investigation.

Wrigley shot back, telling local press that he was prosecuting our men "With the full knowledge of the Department of Justice."

That could only mean one thing. Wrigley would have reached out to the DOJ to verify our claims. Whatever he heard didn't tell him to back off based on credible trafficking claims from the workers. It emboldened him to treat them as criminals.

The men did plan to plead guilty to using fraudulent social security cards. But they also wanted to use their hearing to explain why. It had been a year and a half since they had come forward to report trafficking. The special status due to them had never been granted. With their debts in India, they'd grown desperate.

The men got their day in court, but never had the chance to make their case. The courtroom was a shoebox in the basement of an office park. The men were led in shackles to a row of card tables. The judge refused them individual hearings. Instead, he rushed through their pleas seven men at a time, as if on an assembly line, then adjourned the court. A government attorney told one of our lawyers that "Everyone knows this isn't a real trafficking case. It's a trafficking case made up by attorneys."

Murugan and I met with Congressman Keith Ellison, just returned from a pilgrimage to Mecca. He had followed our hunger strike months before and asked how he could help. Now at our request, he announced a twenty-four-hour fast in support of the men. This won them wider public support, but not freedom. Christmas passed, then New Year's Eve. In January 2009, they watched President Obama's inauguration from the detention center.

Finally one day in late January, facing another round of press and protests, the immigration judge handed the men a compromise. Their deportations would be postponed until the government decided on their T visas. In the meantime they could be released—as long as they paid an absurdly high bond of $20,000 each and agreed to stay in Fargo. Donations poured into a bond fund from the national audience they had won.

On the night their four-month imprisonment finally ended, the workers called me from Fargo, elated. One of them asked me to deliver a message to the White House: if his T visa was granted, letting him work again, he'd spend a portion of his remittances erecting a statue of the new American president in his hometown in Tamil Nadu.

"Tell your Obama!" he cried.

BY THE END of March, the ground beneath the men's feet unfroze, and the Red River swelled and crested. Fargo residents prepared for disastrous floods. Unable to work legally and forbidden to leave, the men put their bodies to use. They became a roving, voluntary disaster preparation corps, laying sandbags to shore up Fargo and surrounding cities against the coming flood. By Easter the next month, they were clearing ice jams, and still with no word on their T visas—or anyone else's.

The Obama Administration was in place, but apparently, ICE was steadfast. We testified in Congress. A new Department of Justice had our files. Democrats had the House and Senate. But nothing seemed to make a difference.

I found it harder and harder to take the men's calls.

"Any updates, Saketji?" they'd asked after ritual pleasantries, desperate and often drunk. I projected hope, dispensed political context, dignified their limbo by giving it an opponent. But it all felt hollow.

Then, a letter showed up from USCIS, and I opened it to discover that my own immigration problems were resolved: my application for permanent residency had been approved. Instead of relief I was flooded with guilt.

The hardest calls to take were the ones from my parents. They were still basking in my apparent successes from the previous year, when the campaign had been on the front page of the Indian papers for weeks. When Obama was elected, they took special pride in their son being a community organizer. But my mother came to sense something was wrong. When she asked, "Are you eating well, betoo?" the question hung on the low end of her lilt.

I wasn't eating at all. I wasn't hungry. I didn't think I could feel worse. Then came my reunion with Rajan.

5: Death of a Friendship

April 2009
Trimble County, KY

HE TURNED UP in Kentucky. It had been almost a year since I'd seen him last—since the day he stormed off in fury at the end of Paul Konar's hunger strike.

I was in Trimble County, on one of my periodic trips to wherever workers were clustered, to put out fires and try to keep up morale. More than a hundred of the men were there building a 600-megawatt coal power plant. I had warned them that so many in one place would attract a dangerous level of attention. That's exactly what happened: a local Indian American convenience store owner got nervous at their frequent visits. He assumed they were undocumented and didn't want them to cause trouble for him. When he attempted to ban them from his store and there were words, he threatened to call ICE.

I flew out to ease tensions, intervening with him as the workers' "American friend." Afterward I offered updates at an afternoon meeting. Standing in the parking lot when it was done, I heard a voice I knew.

"We need to talk."

Rajan was in the driver's seat of a red Ford pickup, smoking, eyes hard. Ever since our rupture in DC, I had wondered what I would feel at the moment I saw him again. I hadn't expected to be afraid.

"We can talk right here," I said.

"Get in."

He was changed. No clever joke. No crooked grin. Just a dead stare and a barked order.

I got in. My lock clicked shut.

"Leave it unlocked, please," I said. Instead, he reversed out of the parking lot.

"You're safe," he said, pulling onto the road. "There's a gun in the glove compartment."

"You can't be serious? Rajan, stop the car."

"Don't worry," he said. "I won't be using it today."

We were on the highway, racing I knew not where.

"Rajan, please," I said. "Help me understand the last year. What's happened to you?"

"Since your photo op in Washington? Fending for myself as best I can."

I had recently heard the strangest thing about him. A worker called me from Houston. He said Rajan had just been there, trying to position himself as a labor broker. Apparently, he was collecting cash from the workers, promising to lease them out to a contractor, who in turn would lease them out to a shipyard. But Rajan just disappeared with their money. *Rajan.*

As we sped down the road, I pried carefully.

"Say, there's this rumor I heard, that you switched careers. Went into the manpower supply business." Even hearing myself say it was strange.

"No," he said, almost cheerily. I felt a flash of relief. "That didn't work out. The contractor disappeared."

My heart sank.

"But you tried it? My God, Rajan, what's happened to you?"

"You're surprised?" he barked. "*You* did this." He stabbed at the air.

My own exasperation boiled over. "Right. It's *my* fault. I confess. *I'm* the racketeer who trafficked five hundred men from India. Call the DOJ."

"Ending the hunger strike! Retreating from Washington! *That* was you. Where did it get us? *Kentucky*, motherfucker."

"For God's sake, Rajan," I said. "Keep your eyes on the road!"

His voice rose over my alarm. "You made your name. I tried to make some money on the side."

"Made my name? In the crosshairs of immigration cops, while my own immigration status was insecure?"

I regretted the words as soon as they were out. Rajan smelled my embarrassment and went in for the kill. He lifted his hands off the steering wheel and applauded.

"India's Hero in America, starring Saket Soni!" he cried in English, clapping. "First-class picture!"

"*Rajan!*"

He gripped the wheel again and chortled.

"I don't believe this," I said. "All the work we did to build this campaign. And you use it to make yourself a two-bit contractor?"

"We used each other, *brother*. You use us for publicity. We use you for green cards. You were just a convenient instrument."

"There was a bond between us. We were fighting for each other."

"It was useful for a time. Then you failed us. We moved on."

"The campaign's not over," I said.

"Then *tell me how we win*," he yelled, swerving across the double yellow line.

A police siren sounded behind us. The cop car closed the distance in a flash.

"Pull over," I said. "Keep your hands on the wheel."

He did, and stopped the car.

"Is there really a gun in there?" I asked.

Rajan was muttering something. I strained to hear. He was praying.

We rolled down the windows. The officer sized us up.

"Speak English?"

"Yes, sir," I said.

"Where y'all headed?"

"We going Milton, Kentucky," Rajan said.

"Headed to Milton, officer," I repeated in my best American twang.

He peered into the cabin. We sat frozen. I imagined the worst. A deep blue streak of immigration agents racing up the highway. Picking up Rajan. Asking where he worked. Surrounding the power plant. Raiding it with the force of a SWAT team. Rounding up the other Indian men.

I did everything I could to avoid looking at the glove compartment. If there really was a gun in there, Rajan would be lucky just to be deported.

The officer's radio crackled on his shoulder. He took a step back from the car and said something into it. It squawked back.

Without another word, he headed back to the patrol car. We watched him in the rear-view mirror until he got in. His siren turned back on. Then he sped past us like we had never existed.

We sat silent, shaken—Rajan by what had almost happened, I by what had not. A long minute later, Rajan unclenched the steering wheel and turned the ignition. The Ford revved and rumbled. We crawled back onto the open road. Cars shot by.

"Rajan," I said softly, "What happens now?"

"I'm going back," he said.

"To DC?"

"To India."

I came to. "What? Wait. Hang on."

He looked dead ahead. "I've made my decision."

"But why? You've done so much. Don't leave now. We can still win."

"It's Shamitha."

His wife. Rajan never talked about his family. I'd often ask how they were doing back home. He always deflected. *Spare your concern for the men who left children behind,* he'd say. *Luckily, I have none.*

With no other information to go on, Rajan's home life was fixed in my mind as idyllic, because of a photograph he had once shown me. He and Shamitha stood atop a lush, low mountain. She was smiling. He was at ease, like I had never seen him. It was taken just after he returned from a two-year stint in Azerbaijan, cash in hand to buy a small patch of land and dig a well in it. With the money left over, they took their only vacation. Three November days in Kodachadri. At the last minute, Rajan brought along an entourage of cousins, nephews, and friends. Shamitha was exasperated. What to do? He was popular! He promised her a getaway one day, just the two of them, to a place even more enchanted: the Niagara Falls. Two months later, he came to America.

"Rajan, listen to me," I said. "You need to hang on. I promise you, one day, you'll be able to bring Shamitha here. You'll take her on that vacation."

If Rajan returned to India, the door to the US would shut. By law, trafficking victims have to wait for their legal status in America. If they go home, the case is closed. Whatever chance there was of winning a visa, Rajan would be giving it up if he left. Why not wait a few more months?

"Unless—" I said. "Is Shamitha sick?"

"No one's sick. Just me. I'm fed up."

"Rajan, I know. Living without papers, lying, hiding. Dodging bullets like we just did. It's a war of attrition, and you're worn down. That's their strategy: they want you to give up and leave. But you've lasted this long. If anyone can bring this to the finish line, it's us. Not in years. In months!"

"It's not about that anymore," he said. "It's about children."

In the months before he came to America, he said, he and Shamitha had tried to conceive. Something was wrong. They saw dozens of doctors, took a battery of tests, tried again, failed again, went back to the doctors. It was a mystery. They were healthy. Then the clock ran out—it was time to fly to Mississippi. They decided they'd try again in America.

This was not agreeable to Rajan's mother. No conception, no America, she said. Rajan begged for a reprieve. In just nine months, Shamitha would be able to join him. Or a year, at most, according to the recruiters. His mother gave in. But now it had been three years, and she felt cheated. On a recent call, she demanded that he break off his marriage. Start over. He'd switched countries. He could switch girls. Rajan forbade it. Throw Shamitha out on the street? She'd be disgraced. Her own family would refuse to take her back. Besides, he loved her. *Fine*, his mother said. *I won't throw her out. But if she leaves on her own, there's nothing to do.*

Rajan's mother was about to carry out her own war of attrition, against Shamitha. Only he could stop her. And he was continents away, in Kentucky.

I sat for a minute, absorbing all this. Our families were so different.

"Brother," I said, "I'm so sorry."

He took an exit off the highway. On the way down, over the turn signal, I tried a different appeal. For most of the workers, this was a fight for their own legal status so they could be reunited with their families. Rajan wanted that too, of course, but his prize was so much bigger.

"You remember that first dinner we had, Rajan? When you cooked that Kerala dry-fry and we talked about a new world?"

"The world as it can be," he remembered.

"Family is important," I said. "But people like you have an even greater responsibility. There's a world you can imagine."

Rajan pulled into the lot of a Super 8 hotel, parked, undid his seat belt. He turned to look at me.

"You know, all that freedom stuff—I know it's real for you. Not for me." He spoke gently, warmly. "You have those ideals. I don't."

"I don't believe that, Rajan."

"We don't live in the same world. Your life is a cause. You're a general. Your army's full of angels. I'm just a mercenary. Perfectly willing to be bought and sold, as long as I get the money I need. There is nothing lofty in it for me. No world to win."

"I don't see you that way," I said, fighting to stem my sadness. "We went together to those lofty places. Those were your dreams too."

"You misunderstood. You were fooled. I was using you. We all were."

"I didn't feel used by you at all," I insisted.

"You just said that I used the campaign to make myself a two-bit labor broker."

"At your lowest point. We all scrape bottom. I'm not judging you."

"You're hurt that I'd get into the people-leasing business," he said. "You make sense of it by thinking that it happened once, after a long, desperate struggle. But there's something you need to understand."

Right from the beginning, Rajan said, workers were playing all sides. Many schemed with labor brokers. The smarter ones schemed to *be* labor brokers. How far back? Even before they escaped from Signal's labor camps.

It started at the same time that I was holding those early, clandestine gatherings in Mississippi and Texas. Workers were starting to see, with my help, that Signal had no intention of providing them green cards. The false promises were a method of control. I channeled their anger and indignity. Offered a vision equal to their desperation. It gained momentum, and each evening, workers burst into freedom songs.

But every night, back in the labor camps, the euphoria would congeal into practicality. The men were shopping for a way out, comparing my offer of freedom to any other option they could find. If I couldn't deliver what I was promising, what then? Where would the money come from?

One man announced he had a better offer than I did. This was a worker I knew, one at the very heart of the campaign. While I was out of earshot, he described the opportunity to Rajan and the others. He had found a hotel owner who was willing to put up the money to buy the men a "Release agreement" from Signal. The hotel owner would approach Signal and pay them to "Release" the workers—to him. Then he'd lease them out to other companies he had already lined up. The workers would kick money back to the hotel owner each month.

The workers wanted in. Over a hundred paid up, $80 apiece, including Rajan and many others who were central to the campaign. It seemed a safer bet than what I was offering them.

But the deal was a nonstarter. "Release agreements" sounded plausible to the workers, since in the Middle East, oil companies "Released" guest workers to each other all the time. But in the US, the terms of the workers' visas barred Signal from "Releasing" them anywhere. Besides, the Indian men were Signal's most valuable asset. Why would it relinquish them?

The workers demanded their money back. *Nonrefundable! This is America*, the schemer snapped. He had already wired it all, nearly $10,000, to his family in India.

"And that, dear brother, is why you got your beautiful freedom movement."

Rajan smiled triumphantly. I tried to mask my shock.

"Okay," I said. "So workers hedged their bets. So what? They did escape from Signal. They marched to Washington. So did you. No matter what got you on this path, you did walk it."

"Yes, but not for principles. We'll do anything to survive. Lease ourselves out. Lease others out. Cut deals with Signal. With immigration agents, if it will get us status. In fact, that's what I did."

"What do you mean?" I said, growing numb.

Six months ago, Rajan had gotten an offer via an Indian consular official in Houston. Immigration police were investigating "certain people" who, allegedly, were manufacturing false Social Security cards and supplying them to the Indian workers.

"He meant you," Rajan said. "He asked if I knew you. If I would be a witness against you, I could get a special kind of visa."

I knew which visa he meant: the so-called S visa for undocumented witnesses, with the *S* standing for "snitch."

Rajan knew the allegation was an outright lie. And if he took the offer, I knew I'd be fighting false felony charges for years.

The blood ran from my face.

"What did you say?" I stammered.

"I said yes. In a heartbeat."

"I don't understand," I said.

"*Exactly*. You don't understand me. Or us. Our lives. Our pressures. Tell me this: How many rupees to a dollar?"

"What does that have to do with—"

"How many?"

I searched my head for the exchange rate. There was a time I knew it painfully well. When I first came to America, I did the conversion every time I spent a reluctant dollar. Each time I gulped down a Snapple peach iced tea, my favorite indulgence, I would stare at the empty bottle afterward, awash with guilt at the hundreds of rupees that had run down my gullet, thinking about the vegetables my mother could have bought with that money. Somewhere along the way, I stopped doing the math. I hadn't done it in years.

"You see," he said, "You don't have a foot in India anymore. And so you don't understand my life. In my world, I have to be willing to do things you can't imagine." I reeled from the body blow of the betrayal. A chasm opened between us. Rajan sighed into it.

"Lucky for you, my wife called about my mother. And since I was going home anyway, it was no longer useful for me to destroy you. So I backed out of the deal. But others will not. That is why I came to meet you today. So you can look after yourself. Be safe. And grow up."

It was suddenly clear to me that this was the last time we would ever see each other.

Rajan nodded at the glove compartment. "Open it."

As different as the tone was now, I still felt a tremor as I did. There was no gun. Just a Tupperware box.

Early in the campaign, when the travel was intense, Rajan and I had started a tradition of cooking for each other and exchanging "Tiffin boxes," like Indians take on railway journeys.

"It's daal. For you."

A simple workman's meal. A world away from Al Kabsah. He probably made himself a big pot of it on Sunday nights to feed himself all week on the tightest budget possible. It was what he'd cooked for himself and other Signal workers after the "Food riot" back in the man camp in the winter of 2007. The first time he'd taken his fate into his hands in America. The first proper taste of home.

I didn't want to let him go. "Rajan," I said, "Let's start over."

"I'll drive you to the airport," he said.

BACK IN NEW ORLEANS, I told myself it was time to face reality. I invited Murugan over to my apartment for dinner. He was living nearby, in a Catholic Charities housing unit for trafficking survivors. He insisted on cooking.

I could barely register his small talk as he breezed through my meager kitchen, tending pots and pans on four burners at once for sambhar with rice.

When we were seated across the table from each other, I couldn't put it off any longer.

"Murugan," I said. "I have to keep my promise."

He knew what I meant without my saying another word. I was telling him all hope was lost. I fought back tears.

"You tried your level best," Murugan said.

"If there was anything left to do, we would do it."

We were both quiet for a long time.

"There is something you can do," he finally said.

"What?"

"When are you going to India?"

"No plans."

"You should go. Visit my village," he said. "Spend some time with my mother. Because I can't."

6: India

May 2009
Newark, Kerala,
Tamil Nadu, New Delhi

I FLEW TO INDIA two weeks later. Strapped in a middle seat for take-off in Newark, I twisted with apprehension at the prospect of seeing the men's families. I'd hoped that Murugan would keep the news of my travel to himself. But the very day I spoke with him, others started calling. They took the news of my trip as an admission. Over the years, each time they called for "Updates," our pleasantries would swirl around my family and theirs, then they would ritually ask when I was going to India. *I'll go when we win*, I'd always reply. So the fact that I was going now meant something. I was conceding.

"If you are going to India," they said now, voices quavering, "Then you will come to my home?" Each invitation stabbed me, and there were dozens.

The airplane climbed the blank sky. I wondered what I'd say to the families. I shared a bond of love with the men themselves—but at bottom it was because of my promise to chart their course back into the arms of their wives, children, parents. How would I explain to those loved ones that it wasn't going to happen? To Murugan's mother, who marked time by counting the Tamil festivals her son had missed—nineteen so far? To Aby's wife, and Paul's daughters, and Hemant's mother, and Shawkat's wife, and to all the rest—what would I say?

They'd all heard of me. When they'd called their men with escalating worry and fear, the men would respond not with their confidence, but with mine. "I've just spoken to Saket Soni." When Murugan's mother wept into the phone, he soothed her with my name. "There's a man named Saket Soni helping us." When money lenders circled her at the temple, he told her to stay strong. "I'm in Washington with Saket Soni." Months later, she pleaded on his wife's behalf that he come back. Neighbors were whispering that he'd taken an American woman. He said he needed to stay and wait for his visa, "but I'm sending Saket Soni to meet you."

Now it turned out I was no different than Sachin Dewan. He had promised American riches and lured them away from India. I had promised American freedom and lured them away from the only sure thing they had: work in Signal's man camps. Without me, however subjugated they were, they would have paid off their debts by now. Instead, their families faced penury. If their men ever did return to India, their families would find them damaged, prematurely aged, hands unsteady from drinking, sleep insecure from the constant fear of immigration agents storming through their doors.

As the engine thrummed in my chest, I realized that all I had to offer the families was my shame. They were preparing to receive a dignitary, but I would arrive as a penitent. I was the reason they had lost their men. I'd bend down in apology, hoping not for pardon but for condemnation. The harsher, the better. *I'm Saket Soni*, I'd say to Murugan's mother. *You've heard of me. I'm the reason you might never see your son again.*

I touched down in Dubai and dragged myself to my connecting flight. At the gate, I fantasized about skipping it. But once I was in my seat, forgotten, familiar things started to shift my mood. The cheery Hindi on-board announcement. The odd Air India motto: "Proud to handle." The sweet, nutty smell of mass-produced butter chicken. The flight attendant's boredom and contempt as he carted it around. The Indian men ringing bells for free scotch. Hindi movies flashing from monitors. When the plane began its descent, I tilted from ease into excitement.

In the airport, moving through the swirl of a thousand arrivals, watching reunited relatives hug, I exhaled, letting go of a breath I'd forgotten I was holding.

MURUGAN'S BROTHER WAS waiting off the Thanjore highway to lead me to the first stop on my apology tour. He waved down my car and dove in. He gave me a thumbs-up sign and flashed the big grin that ran in the family.

"Your journey—okay?"

"Yes-yes."

"My brother—okay?"

"Yes-yes."

I braced to make my apology as he directed my driver down an ochre road, around tea carts, past perfect gardens dotted with rosy temples. We pulled up to a low, sprawling complex. Was their home somewhere inside it? No, this was the Neyveli Lignite Corporation's coal power plant. Murugan's mother prepared food for the employees. We were meeting her at work.

My heart sank. What I had come to do would have been painful in the darkest cavern in the remotest place on Earth. Couldn't it at least have been in the privacy of her home? Here, there were hundreds of people, a chattering lunchtime crowd that would gather in an instant for public theater in the courtyard: a stranger on his knees, an old lady excoriating him.

We stepped out of the car. The heat could split a rock. I scanned the place desperately for a tree whose shade might offer a semiprivate enclave for my confession.

We came up to a red carpet. Chilies drying in the sun. A woman bent over them. She was crushing them into dry, sandy heaps with a handheld machine that required great strength.

She looked up from her work, then stood. She was small and wiry, with a shock of white in her glossy black hair.

"Vannakem," I said, with folded hands.

She wiped the chili dust from her hands against a corner of her sky blue sari.

"Vannakem, vannakem," she said. Her bangled hand gave the slightest wave: a blessing. Should I come out with it now, here, without another word? Tell her why I deserved not a blessing, but a curse?

She tilted her head toward her son to confer in Tamil. I waited for him to translate, my hands still folded, frozen through the excruciating delay.

"She is saying that: come, take tea."

I unfolded my hands. I would have only as long as her tea break.

In an adjoining cafeteria, waiting for the end of these awful preliminaries, I scrolled through the pictures of Murugan I felt obliged to show her.

"Here he is marching in Mississippi," I said. She seemed only to stare at the distance between them. Had thirty years of chili-crushing dimmed her vision? I pointed him out: the one with his fist in the sky.

"Here he is with a congressman." Keith Ellison. "A member of parliament in America." I searched her face for a reaction. She hummed. Ignoring Ellison, she pointed to Murugan and murmured something.

Murugan's brother interpreted: "She is asking that: he is not eating in Am-may-rica?"

This was my opening. I took a deep breath.

"I am sorry for the delay in Murugan's visa," I started gravely.

A server arrived with tea, and I paused. Murugan's mother said something. The server's eyes widened. He disappeared, then came back with a tray full of biscuits and sweets. He bowed. She smiled. She noticed I hadn't touched my tea and pushed it toward me. I took a sip: it was syrupy and sweet. She was halfway through hers already.

"I'm so sorry for what Murugan's going through," I said. "You can blame me. You should."

Murugan's mother looked at me directly for the first time. Her soft eyes scanned me. Again, the tilted head, the murmur. The awful delay before her son interpreted.

"She is saying that: Is there one picture with both of you?"

"Oh. Yes."

I scrolled to a picture of Murugan and me, that freezing day in Fargo outside the jail. He held my winter coat. I held his bag. We smiled, shivering.

She shook her head in consternation.

"No, he is not eating in Am-may-rica. He is never cooking."

"Actually," I said, "He is cooking quite well. He makes an excellent sambhar."

"You are eating his sambhar?"

"Yes. He cooked for me."

"In his home?"

"Actually, in mine. He insists it's nothing like yours. But it was delicious."

"He is cooking sambhar," she said, impressed.

More tea appeared. She piled a heap of biscuits in front of me. She asked if Murugan's beard was a permanent fixture. (Yes.) Did he still obsess over reading? (Yes.) Did he still insist on serving everyone else twice before he ate his own sambhar? (Yes.)

Bit by bit, I understood what she wanted from me. Not details on her son's immigration trials. Not an apology. I'd been close with Murugan during the time that she hadn't, and that was all she wanted in the world. *Give me some of that*, she was saying, smiling, murmuring. Thanking me each time I did. Thanking *me*.

A merciful breeze blew through the palms, and her sky-blue sari billowed out. Then her tea break was over. Another graceful tilt and murmur.

"And you. You must also be cooking in Am-may-rica."

ABY'S WIFE, BINCY, shook her head angrily.

"He was supposed to be here," she said.

She meant for the birth of their son, Bobby, who was two now, stomping and laughing in the next room. We were sitting in the front room of Aby's family's home in Meenadom, which would soon be sold.

If the others had shown their sadness at the disappearance of their men, Bincy did nothing to disguise her anger—and it brought my shame surging back. I remembered that Bincy had made her own plan to reunite them by moving to Canada as a migrant nurse. But because of our campaign, Aby had made her abandon it. Instead, Bincy had thrown herself into supporting the campaign from here in India, gathering other family members into delegations, petitioning Indian ministers, waiting weeks, months, a year and more.

Now Bobby was two, and thought his father lived in a picture frame above the door.

"Bincy," I said, "He's fighting every day to be reunited with you." I told of his courage in protests outside the Department of Justice, and even as we testified in the US Congress together.

"Oh, he is a great narrator, I know," Bincy said, her voice rising. "He calls each time. Tells me all about what he is doing for us. But I need him *here*."

I didn't know what to say. I sat silent, receiving her anger on his behalf.

Bobby stepped out of the kitchen, moved toward his mother in small sideways steps, keeping his eyes trained on me. He hid behind her, then popped out a little hand. It held a single golden plantain chip.

"You can give it to uncle yourself," Bincy said. "Go."

He stepped out slowly, placed it in my open palm, and ran back to his mother.

I thanked him, an unexpected joy bubbling up in me. I was exhilarated from watching him, with Aby's eyes.

"Listen, Bincy," I said, "The thing you need to know is, the night Bobby was born, Aby wanted to leap over an ocean. He broke every rule in that labor camp to throw a party like you'd never believe."

Bincy looked up. A party?

I told her how over the fence that kept him in the man camp, he had called out to the cook in the kitchen and shouted his son's arrival. Inspired him to make a Texas Chicken 65. Aby had burst into the places where Indians weren't allowed, to distribute food, to share his joy. He'd done everything he would have done at home, but in a labor camp, where it should have been impossible.

The corners of Bincy's pursed lips curled into the slightest smile. She shook her head. *That man.*

I FOLLOWED MR. NARAYANASAMY, the father of Saravanan, into the grassy grounds behind his house.

"Your lunch. Did you enjoy?" he asked.

"Sir, I more than enjoyed it. It was my greatest honor." I was still hurting from having eaten too much pongal, rice served on bright banana leaf mats on his table, with cousins, aunts, and uncles gathered around, laughter flowing like water from a cool clay jug. We'd talked about Tamil rock formations and Tamil grammar. Mr. Narayanasamy was a teacher, and he loved to share all he knew about the world's oldest language and the land that had given it shape. And we talked about Saravanan, the eternal optimist who broke into every room like a ray of light. The old man's silver handlebar mustache rose with his own memories of his son.

"You know," he said, "I harvested that rice from my paddy field. Like my father. Like we were supposed to. But not Saravanan. From the moment he could walk, he wanted to run away."

He was telling me I had nothing to apologize for. But I still felt the need to say it.

"I'm sorry. Truly. I thought I could help him. He trusted me. He followed me. I failed him, and you."

He turned to me. The corners of his eyes crinkled into mahogany-colored crow's feet.

"It is a great responsibility to bear others' burdens. Not everyone would try. Sometimes, we fail. That's part of it, isn't it? So, thank you for your apology. I accept it."

We paused in the shade of a teak tree.

"You see," he said, "Everyone did exactly what they were supposed to do. Rice is supposed to grow. My son was supposed to get sick of harvesting it. He was supposed to travel out to work, come into hardship, and meet you. You were supposed to try for him. And when you failed, you were supposed to come here to apologize. And I was supposed to serve you my rice and forgive you. Everything according to the plan."

"But aren't you upset at the situation Saravanan is in?"

"Tamil boys and girls have always gone away to work," he said. "Especially from this area. Often, they haven't come back." For generations, from his town and others nearby, young workers had been recruited, defrauded, sometimes kidnapped outright to be indentured in the British Empire's plantations.

"It shouldn't be that way," I said.

"That is true. But so is this: as a result, there is no place in the world without a Tamil. Isn't it?"

I followed his slow strides around the lush perimeter of his grounds.

"Everywhere they are going, Tamils plant a garden. Always a garden. Even in your New Orleans now, there is a Tamil. Isn't it?"

"Your son."

"And over there, he will plant a garden. Under the soil, roots will grow, search for other roots. Over time, they will come together, roots clasped end to end. And so, after many, many years, these gardens will all join together. Isn't it?"

I nodded.

"At such time when all the gardens join," he said, "Then all of the Tamils will have their reunion. We will have pongal together in the garden, as we are supposed to. Maybe after I die. Maybe after one thousand years. But surely it will happen, according to the plan."

We had walked to the garden's edge, where grass ran into forest. Beyond the borderline, it was too dense to see. I turned to him. He was gazing at the young grass just in front of his sandaled feet.

"Come," he said. "Let us take coffee."

SARAVANAN'S FATHER AND the rest built me a bridge of connection; I crossed it back to my own family. Landing in New Delhi, I fished out my phone to call my parents. It was dead. My eyes darted out into the waiting crowd. The moment I saw them, joy flooded in, and I realized how much I had missed them.

At home, I laid gifts out on the dining table, from the men's families to mine. Cashews, pistachios, nutmegs, cinnamon bark, filter coffee. Setting down tea, my mother asked about the smooth, white pebbles strewn among the presents. Mementoes from one of my stops in India. The children of a worker named Christopher Glory had taught me how to skip them on a pond.

"**DID YOU KNOW** when I met your mother, she used to write poems?"

I sat with my father in the sunny living room of my parents' tiny flat, surprised at his newfound openness. My childhood relationship with him was shaped by silences so long and heavy that any stray remark would fill my chest with relief. He hated small talk like I hated boiled turnips; it's just how he was made. When he did talk, he used as few words as possible, and never about himself. I could sometimes prod him into discussions about books or international affairs. When I exhausted my topics, he would lapse back into the concentrated quiet that was dinner time's center of gravity.

Now he shared stories about his life I'd never heard. Over the morning paper. During walks. At dinner as he munched raw green chilis, his version of salad. And as the conversation ranged over his childhood, I came to understand the silence that had shaped his own early years.

When he was twelve, he told me, my grandfather's civil service job sent him from Delhi out to a yearlong stint in faraway Shimla. My father went along. My grandmother, a public-school teacher, stayed behind with their younger son. I had imagined that year in Shimla as an enchantment on the Himalayan foothills, but what my father recalled most vividly was my grandfather's silence. In that year, they barely exchanged a word. They lived in silence, ate in silence, walked an hour out to my father's school in silence. Once, my father asked why he couldn't just go to the school right next to where they lived. The unspoken answer said it all. They were too poor. But for my father, his family's silence was more scarring than their poverty. When he met my mother, he let her into a club of one—the only person with access to his stories.

I realized that the silence that marked my childhood was a shadow of the silence that had marked his. He had traveled a very long way to give me what he could of connection and conversation. Years later, he was still traveling. In this new stage he and I were finding fluency together. Now, my mother and I were together, in a club of two.

My father asked about my romantic life. I told him about Marielena, the woman I was dating. He asked where she was from. Her parents had emigrated to Rhode Island from Colombia, I said, when she was three.

"Well, that should work out very well," he said. "India imports all its bulletproof vests from Colombia—the ones our politicians use. India and Colombia have an excellent relationship."

AFTER MY FATHER retired to bed, I sat with my mother as she drank a nightcap, dunking biscuits in deep, gingery tea. She asked me how I was doing. Great, I mumbled. She asked how the workers were doing. How was Paul Konar? How had my visits been to their families?

I skipped over all of the tender visits to share with her the one that had haunted me the most, to Paul's family. His house was kept like a mausoleum to him, with garlanded portraits on every wall. His wife and his daughter Pinky were inconsolable, and as I was leaving, Pinky asked me whether Paul was even in America. The strongman's daughter was being bullied at school by kids who didn't believe it. I assured her he was—in America, fighting to be reunited with them. I wasn't sure she believed me. Her desolate goodbye had stayed with me since.

Barely realizing it, I launched into a self-lacerating account of the campaign. My mother listened patiently, dunking another biscuit until I took a breath.

"So, tell me something," she said, handing me the biscuit. "As you're working on this, do you find time to eat?"

It was the first of a train of questions that slowed me down. She didn't need an account of my successes and failures. She gently steered me to what she did want to hear: what I was eating, how I was living, who was by my side. If I was safe, and well, and happy. As for my frenetic accounting, here at home I could let the balance sheet go.

We drank tea together. Rummaged through old photographs. Charted out family trees. And went to buy vegetables—on the condition that I keep my mouth shut.

My mother was a bargaining shark. If I said a word, the vendors would gleefully mark her as the mother of an American, and for the next six months, she'd be charged double for onions and potatoes.

We returned to the kitchen with bags of fresh produce. She taught me to make baingan ka bharta, a dish I loved and only ever got to eat at home. Under her instruction, I roasted an eggplant on the stovetop, pulled away its blackened peel, spooned out its velvety flesh, and mixed it with studious care into a just-made tomato puree full of roasted cumin and golden onions. "Wait till the tomato bits dissolve," she said. "Round tomatoes are better. Ovals take too long." She stirred in cilantro. "There, right at the end."

My mother held up a teaspoon of the bharta. It was impossibly bright and smoky at once.

"Good?" she said.

The phone rang in the living room. My father answered.

"It's Sonali," he called. My sister. I set the spatula down and ran up to answer. She was working in a hotel in Dubai but was flying out to see me. We'd be spending my last few days together, our first time seeing each other in three years. I told her I couldn't wait. She was just as excited to see me and gave me a little preview of the big life problem she needed my help on. "I have two boyfriends right now." I laughed and took her flight information. When we hung up, the phone immediately rang again.

"Sonali?" I said.

"Saketji?" It wasn't her. It was a man's voice I recognized instantly.

"Aby!" I said.

"How's the family?"

I had promised to be in touch after I met Bincy and his son. "I'm sorry I haven't called," I began.

"That's okay—have you heard the news?"

"No, my phone's been off."

"*T visa approved*, Saketji!"

He and the others had been checking the Homeland Security website obsessively between shifts. Last night, suddenly, Aby had found his status updated to "approved."

I sat down to absorb what he was telling me. There were nineteen other applications we'd submitted with his, and if he'd been approved, the rest were bound to follow. Which meant hundreds more could, too.

"When can you meet?" he asked, elated.

"I'll be back next week," I said. "We'll pull our committee together."

"Saketji, we've got to celebrate."

"We will," I said. "I'm going to cook."

"You cook now?" he asked.

My mother's voice came from the kitchen:

"Dinner!"

PART SIX

FAITH

1: Revoked

June 2009
New Orleans, LA

ANTICIPATING HIS VISA, Aby entered a frenzy of preparation for Bincy and Bobby's arrival. He left his isolated spot in Texarkana and found a job building a power plant in Macon, Georgia, where he thought they might like to live. After work each night, he scanned apartment listings, darted out to furniture stores and car dealerships—the places immigrants go to peer into freedom when their foothold in America starts to feel secure. When I called him soon after I'd returned from India, he was in the toy section of Walmart.

"Saketji!" he cried. "Welcome back! Bulldozer or firetruck for Bobby? Or *both*?"

"Listen, Aby," I said. "We need to talk—there's been a new development."

Less than a month after their announcement that Aby's visa had been approved, US Customs and Immigration officials had unexpectedly issued him an RFE, or "Request for evidence."

"So they want more evidence," Aby said. "We send it over, right? There's plenty!" He took it as just another hurdle to leap over as he blazed toward the finish line.

"Aby, it's not a routine request. It's a much bigger problem."

"What do you mean?" he said, halting.

"We need to talk."

There was a fraught pause on the line.

"I can be home in thirty minutes."

"No—not on the phone," I said. "How soon can you get to New Orleans?"

"Saketji, now you're scaring me."

"Can you make it by Friday night?"

"Crack of dawn Saturday."

"Good. And call the other coordinators. Murugan and everyone else. We need the rest of the committee to meet in person. We'll put them all up."

"That bad?"

"Aby, please," I said. "The coordinators only. Other than that, *tell no one*."

WE HAD KNOWN that Bush's ICE officials had been blocking the T visas, and we had counted on Obama's arrival in Washington to dislodge them. When officials finally granted the first twenty T visas, we exhaled, vindicated, and waited for the rest.

Then, suddenly, Aby and the rest of the twenty men received these new "Requests for evidence." I couldn't believe it. It was one thing to request evidence before a decision. But to approve the visas, and then turn around and request new evidence before issuing them—that was unheard of. ICE was still at work behind the scenes.

I made dozens of calls, deep into Washington. Contacts who were now insiders, or knew insiders, confirmed my instinct. The RFEs meant that the visas had, in effect, been rescinded. But why, if the adjudicators agreed with the men's claims?

Swearing me to secrecy, my sources told me what they knew. It knocked me back into my chair.

I SERVED BISCUITS and tea, and took a breath. It was Saturday morning. A dozen men had driven all night from around the country. Murugan from Port Arthur, Texas. Hemant from Houston. Saravanan from Shreveport. Aby from Georgia. They sensed they were here for bad news. Still, they had greeted me with new intimacy. Now I knew their families. Now I *was* family. But as the rest of them had hugged and laughed at seeing each other, Aby had been silent, grim. Now he was seated behind the others, in the back of the room, arms folded, face leaden. I began.

"As we feared, the twenty T visas that were granted have been revoked. By ICE. And the rest aren't coming. But that's not all."

Hemant spoke up, gesturing with his eternal Styrofoam cup.

"Revoked by ICE—how? Visas are granted by USCIS. It's a whole different part of DHS than ICE. What happened to the line between them?"

He'd come a long way. A year ago, Hemant had believed the "Department for Justice" would welcome them into Washington, visas in hand. Now, he knew more about federal agencies than most Americans.

"ICE punched through the line," I said, "Yanked back the visas. But listen, there's more."

Others interrupted with their own questions, precise and increasingly outraged, as if they were conducting a congressional inquiry. Weren't Obama's officials in place at DHS by now? And what did this mean for the DOJ investigation? Wasn't that still open?

Only Aby stayed silent. He sensed there was something else coming. His glare burned a hole in the conference room wall.

I finally revealed the worst of what my sources had told me.

"The DOJ investigation is still open," I said. "ICE is still running it. But here's what we've learned that's new. They're not investigating Signal. They're investigating you."

"Us?" cried Saravanan.

"For visa fraud."

They understood. In line at the US Embassy in New Delhi, or at the US Consulate in Chennai, American officials had asked if they had paid any money for their Signal visas. They had said no—a lie.

"But they've known that," said Murugan. "We admitted it in our T visa applications. We understood from the recruiters that it was the only way to get to America."

"Yes," I said, "but now ICE is using your admission as grounds to move against you. They're not coming for Signal, or Malvern, or Sachin. They're coming for you." At any moment ICE agents could haul them in on charges of defrauding the US government.

They sat with the news.

"Brothers," I said, "I need you to keep this to yourselves for now. Before we tell the others, we've to get clear on our plan."

"And what is our plan?" asked Hemant. His abandoned clove biscuit had turned to mush in his tea.

I looked at Aby for help. At the lowest moments of the campaign, I had relied on his strength. He kept the others strong. But now he stared past me.

I cleared my throat. "That's the next part of our meeting. Let's take a break. Get some air, stretch. We'll come back in ten minutes."

A few men nodded. But no one moved.

Then Aby stood, walked down the hallway, and slammed the door on his way out.

2: Belief

June–July 2009
New Orleans, LA

IT WAS EVENING, hours later. On the street outside my office, the band of exiles said quiet, grim goodbyes, as if leaving each other's last rites. They got into their beaten cars. Saravanan rolled down his window.

"Have faith, brothers!" he called out.

I waved back, touched, as the tattered caravan pulled away. Faith was all we had. The rest of our meeting had yielded no concrete plans, just a promise to keep our terrible knowledge a secret for now. Two hours of summer light remained. I went to City Park for quiet and clarity among the centuries-old banyan trees.

Our journey had started with a human trafficking complaint from as emblematic a place as possible: a labor camp in Mississippi. We triggered a DOJ investigation into Signal International and its network of recruiters. But ICE had wrested control of it. In their hands, it was a gun trained at the workers. ICE's endgame wasn't simply denying the T visas—they intended to blast the workers into oblivion.

In taking over the investigation, ICE seemed to have cowed the very people in government we were counting on to help us: the prosecutor, John Cotton Richmond and his boss, Robert Moossy Jr. Without them, we couldn't win. ICE had knocked them out cold. We needed to revive them. Then we needed to remove ICE from the field of battle entirely. The question was how.

I circled back to my contacts in Washington. It was clear that ICE had muddied the waters. Allies who had been outraged now said, *You know, it's not a clear-cut case. Turns out, the Indians lied at the embassy.*

That lie was coerced! I shot back. Besides, we had long since owned up to it, publicly and in government testimony. *Well*, the allies said, *you can't expect a one-sided investigation.*

But a one-sided investigation is just what we had: an ICE investigation of the workers.

A few weeks later, we managed to pry loose a small concession. John Cotton Richmond would fly back down to New Orleans to interview one additional witness of our choosing. But we were warned that this interview would be different. Murugan had been arrested while walking into his DOJ interview—but after that, Richmond had conducted the interview alone. This time, Richmond would be sandwiched between a murderers' row of ICE agents, with their own questions and their own agenda. "Big boys with big toys," one ally called them.

In that threatening atmosphere, our new witness would have to find a way to get through to Richmond person-to-person, shock him back into action. In my frustration, I'd come to regard Richmond and his DOJ with contempt. I called them *the trafficking bureaucrats*. But I knew that no one ends up at the DOJ's Human Trafficking Prosecution Unit accidentally. Someone like Richmond could have worked anywhere. He'd taken that job because deep down it was his calling. We needed to remind him of it. We needed to reach the John Cotton Richmond who had taken down the cross burners, who had brought dirty cops to justice, the way very few could, for killing a man in custody.

But who could get through to him like that? Not just recite the details of a collective story we'd already told, or check off boxes from an anti-trafficking handbook. The worker who went in would have to reconnect Richmond with his sense of purpose—even restore Richmond's own dignity. Someone who could send the lawyer back to Washington saying, *If we can't help these men, what the hell are we doing here at all?*

I had a man in mind. It was Shawkat Ali Sheikh, the welder from Bihar. I hadn't seen him in over a year, since I'd tracked him down and he'd handed over his wad of receipts as evidence. I wasn't sure of the state of his soul. When I had last called him, to wish him well on Eid, the Muslim holiday, he'd sounded in a bad way. But he was the best chance we had.

SHAWKAT ALI SHEIKH headed down a hallway in the ICE building
for his interview, like a broken soldier returning for one last battle. He
clutched a manila folder with both hands, holding it over his heart like a
feeble shield. Only a task this grave could have brought him out of hiding. He wasn't sure he was the right man to wrest the investigation back
from ICE. But he knew full well why he needed to try.

The other men might have been able to tolerate the lie they told at the
American embassy three years ago. Shawkat's faith made the deception
an open wound. It had separated him from his family and from God.
It had made him a fugitive—from the law and from himself. When his
phone flashed and he heard the request to serve as the campaign's final
witness, he understood what it was. A chance to tell the truth.

Shawkat took his seat in the conference room. Across the gleaming
table sat a dozen men, most of them hulks. Their vests read ICE and FBI
and DHS. Among them, in a dark suit, was a lone attorney from the
DOJ's anti-trafficking unit, a man in his late thirties with mild blue eyes.
He introduced himself as John Cotton Richmond. He looked like a lamb
among lions.

An ICE agent opened the interview, bearing down hard. Shawkat
took a long breath while he waited for his interpreter to speak.

"About the labor camp. You say there were twenty-four beds in each
trailer. But we talked to Signal. They said it was only four."

Shawkat squinted, tilted his head. He was here to come face-to-face
with his great lie. Could they really be asking about the trailers?

"How many guys to a trailer?" the ICE agent asked again. "Four or
twenty-four?"

"Twenty-four doesn't make sense," another jumped in. "The math
doesn't add up."

Petty questions, meant to paint him as a liar—but about a triviality, and one he'd never lied about! For forty minutes they piled on with
questions like that. Shawkat answered with slumped shoulders. When
his voice shook, they smirked. They might as well have slapped each other's backs.

Then an FBI man spoke up.

"Let's talk about your visit to the US Embassy in New Delhi when you were seeking a visa. You said you paid no money for the visa. Just plane fare."

Shawkat lifted his head. His eyes flickered to life. Now they were coming to the main thing. The reason he was here.

"I did say that," he said.

"Was that a lie?"

Shawkat leaned forward. He felt God listening. God was always listening.

"Yes," he said.

The interrogators looked at him, waiting for the inevitable evasion, caveat, context. Instead Shawkat laid his hands out on the table, palms up.

"I lied. I wish I hadn't. But I did." His voice cracked at the admission.

The DOJ attorney, who had been slouched over his legal pad, sat up now, looked at Shawkat more closely.

"Why?" the FBI man asked. "You could have told the embassy that the recruiters made you pay, had them call the police, made the recruiters give your money back."

"In what India?" Shawkat asked, incredulous. He had paid $15,267 before he even got in line at the embassy, he said. Sachin Dewan had warned it was nonrefundable. If Shawkat went to the police, whom would they believe? A Muslim welder from Bihar, or the son of a Mumbai recruiting dynasty? And when the embassy workers swallowed Shawkat's lie, they stamped the Signal visa into his passport and returned it not to him but to *Sachin*. Then Sachin upped his price by another $400 just to give Shawkat his passport back. He wouldn't let Shawkat fly until he promised to return the receipts Sachin had given him for his payments.

Explaining all this, Shawkat worked himself into an agitated tremor—then he caught himself. He was wavering from his purpose. He wasn't here to cast blame. Sachin would have to do his own accounting with whatever god he had. Shawkat had no god but God. And He only permitted lies in defense of someone else's safety—not one's own selfishness.

Shawkat recentered. He started again.

He made his full confession with force. Told how his initial lie had spawned calamity after calamity. His journey started in sacrilege. He departed on the holy night of Eid, a time for Muslims to return to family. This haunted him all the way to America. When he reached the man camp in Mississippi, his only comfort was his daily call home. But his lies invaded even that narrow refuge. When his wife, Mazda, warned that the Hindu moneylenders were circling, Shawkat didn't divulge that Signal was deducting $245 a week from his paycheck for rent. He only advised her, each day for months, to duck the usurers till his green card was approved. Almost a year later, pressed up against the end of his visa, he understood that no green card was coming—and he hid that from her too. Suicide wasn't an option. Mazda would only inherit his debts.

On the day his visa expired, he signed up for a company trip to Walmart. Deep in the maze, he eluded the watchful chaperone and escaped into the parking lot. He spent whole nights on a bench outside, then ran away to Louisiana. He hid there for nearly a year, working in a shipyard without papers. Then one day, he learned that hundreds of workers were planning to escape from Signal and come forward with the truth. He leapt at the chance to live in truth again. He presented the organizers with a trove of evidence: every receipt from every payment Sachin Dewan had demanded for the visa. The receipts he'd saved and promised to send Sachin but never had.

But soon after the campaign hit the headlines in India, his wife called, scared. She said Sachin had telephoned the house. *Tell Shawkat to be quiet*, he'd said—*or else*.

Shawkat told her to leave in the night, like a thief. To take the children with her. Somewhere Sachin couldn't find her—Lucknow, where her brother lived. That night, his wife and their children became fugitives like him. Shawkat's ignominy before God was complete. All that was left was for him to disconnect their home phone line in India, the one that had taken his father, the local prophet, years to acquire. His lie had delivered its final result. His home was no longer his home.

The ICE agents chewed their gum, their jaws rippling all the way up to their crew cuts. Their eyes were blank, like sharks' eyes. Only Richmond had a different look.

"What was that number?" he asked. It was his first question, four hours in. His pen was poised over his legal pad.

"Excuse me?"

"The home phone you had disconnected—what was the number?"

Shawkat recited it.

The other interrogators, annoyed at the distraction, swarmed back for questions about Shawkat's life without papers. Even while he answered, from the corner of his eye, he saw Richmond fish out his Blackberry and dial. It was strange. The American seemed quite adept at dialing India. Shawkat could just make out the woman's voice on the automated answer: *the number you have dialed has been disconnected.*

Richmond looked at Shawkat with a look of recognition, like he'd heard a shibboleth. There was something in his eyes Shawkat had ceased even to hope for: belief.

The ICE agents stood up, pulled at the crotches of their pants. The interview was over. The burly investigators stretched and chatted as if Shawkat had never been there at all.

Shawkat sank back in his chair, spent. He barely noticed Richmond—who had a glow to him—striding around the table. Suddenly he was towering over him. Shawkat sprang up, casting his eyes around the room. Where was the interpreter? But Richmond just opened his arms and pulled Shawkat into a hug. Shawkat's shoulders stiffened, his arms hanging by his sides. The burlier men blinked at the two of them. But Richmond's frank embrace continued. He said something for which Shawkat needed no interpreter:

"Thank you."

It was the voice of a man who'd been saved.

When Shawkat reported the strange embrace, I was as mystified as he was. Only much later did we learn the strange journey that had led to it.

ON THE FLIGHT back to Washington, John Cotton Richmond knew what he had to do to get the Signal case back on track. He'd walk into his boss Moossy's office as soon as he could get time with him, likely first thing in the morning. He'd brief his boss straight off his legal pad. He'd outline a strategy to prosecute the case. The traffickers' defense attorneys would want to use the workers' lie to the embassy to discredit them as witnesses. But Richmond would beat them to the punch. He'd bring it up himself. Shawkat had shown him how the lie at the embassy was *evidence of the coercion*. Shawkat could explain his reasons to the jury. His virtue would disarm the defense.

The excitement Richmond had felt when he was first assigned the case came rushing back. Why could he dial Indian numbers like a native? Because his anti-trafficking work had begun, of all places, in India. Just four years out of law school, Richmond was offered a job with a faith-based anti-trafficking NGO called International Justice Mission, to run their Chennai office. Friends told him he was crazy even to consider it: he didn't know the field or the country. But he and his wife, Linda, felt a compulsion to go that they couldn't explain. So Richmond quit his prestigious job, and Linda put her master's program on hold.

They moved to Chennai in 2003, with their fifteen-month-old daughter and a second child on the way. At first, it wasn't easy. Richmond struggled to get IJM's local work off the ground. Then Linda nearly died during childbirth. The doctors pulled Richmond aside and told him she wasn't going to live through the night. Richmond stalked the halls of the Chennai hospital, arguing with God. If anyone deserved to live, wasn't it his loving wife, a teacher who had followed him halfway across the world at the drop of a hat? Weren't they here to do His work, bringing justice to the oppressed? Isn't that what God commanded? How could this be their reward? The answer came to him with startling clarity: *It's not about you. Obedience is not a game that earns you blessings. I want people to be free because I made them and I love them. If I can use you for that, I will.*

Linda recovered. Richmond spent the next three years working to free forced laborers from farms and brick kilns in Tamil Nadu. In the evenings, the heat brought the Richmonds to the roof of their apartment building, where they formed bonds with their neighbors. Richmond felt ready to spend the rest of his life in Chennai.

Then in 2006, the DOJ called. Richmond took the job, but packed his bags with a sense of loss. He was leaving Chennai just as his staff of crusaders in the Chennai IJM office was coalescing. What he loved most was building a team around a common mission. He wasn't sure he'd ever get to do that again. His Indian friends asked if he was happy to be "going home." But Chennai was home.

He and Linda found a little townhouse in Northern Virginia. Finding community was another story. He enjoyed his colleagues, but they all lived in different area codes. He never saw his neighbors—they'd drive from work right into their garages. Starved for connection, Richmond took to waiting in his car near the shared mailbox of their enclave of townhouses just to catch a neighbor for a chat. Home life was tough too. Linda was finishing up her master's program, so he barely saw her. And when she was home, he didn't want to talk much about work. He spent his days reducing sex trafficking victims to names and details in spreadsheets or watching CCTV footage of police officers carrying out torture. He didn't want to bring work home. But the isolation began to take a toll on him, and his marriage.

Then he got pulled into the chief's office with a new assignment: the Signal case. It was labor trafficking. It was India. Many of the workers were Tamil, some even from Chennai. He remembered it as the most exciting day of his career. All the pieces of his life were coming together.

But things hadn't gone as he'd hoped. After fifteen months of investigation, he still wasn't close to an indictment. Nowhere near. His clear moral imperative was shrouded in gloom.

Until Shawkat's honesty blasted it clear. One man of faith had found another.

3: The Smoking Gun

December 2009
New Orleans, LA

WHAT WAS I *missing?*

It had been nearly six months since Shawkat got that hug from John Cotton Richmond, and still no word on possible indictments against Signal—or on the T visas. Aby and the other nineteen men who'd had their visas granted, then revoked, had sent in a pile of new evidence to USCIS—with no response. The T visa applications for the larger group had been frozen by new "Requests for evidence" as well. Everyone was still undocumented and in limbo. Alvin Ladner was still in control of the investigation, holding the threat of prosecution over everyone's heads.

There had to be a way to break through. But what?

There was something I wasn't seeing. Each day I woke up with a tingling feeling: it had something to do with the day that Signal tried to deport Jacob Joseph, and shocked the rest of the workers into realizing they were not free to leave.

Late one night in the weeks before Christmas, I hung three yards of blank butcher paper on a wall in my office. On one end I wrote, in large red letters: *March 9, 2007.*

I started to fill the butcher paper with every forensic detail about that day. I paced the length of the canvas. I called worker after worker and asked them to relive that traumatic day moment by moment. Over dozens of hours, phone pressed to my ear, I learned new details.

One particular story caught my attention. Aby told me about a coworker of his in the Orange, Texas, camp, an experienced pipefitter and a father of two. He was so outraged by Signal's treatment that he escaped the labor camp on his own one night in search of a union. He'd been a trade unionist in India, paid dues all his life. Somehow, this man found the metal trades union hall in Beaumont, Texas. He waited at the door all night, and in the morning, presented his bona fides to the union officers. He asked if he could sign up as a member, and if there was work for him. The union officers looked at each other, and then at him. *Sure,* they said. *Come back tomorrow, same time, and we'll take care of you.* The man left, gratified. *That's solidarity.* When he returned the next day, a Mississippi ICE agent was waiting for him. He brought the pipefitter in, charged him with an immigration offense—and then brought him back to the Signal facility and handed him over to a security guard. Signal managers warned him not to leave the camp again, except for mandatory check-ins with his deportation judge. Eventually, he asked the judge to deport him.

In my years as an organizer, I had never heard of such a thing: a federal immigration agent hunting down runaway workers at a private company's behest.

Another worker remembered being astonished that the events of March 9 had drawn a top Signal executive out of the C-suite. Until then, senior management was literally fenced off from the workers, and dealt with them only through camp managers like John Sanders and Darrell Snyder. But after the uprising, a suited Signal executive had arrived in the man camp. The worker remembered his name, Ron Schnoor, and his chilling words of caution to the workers against challenging the company: *I want you to think very, very carefully . . . We have lawyers too, very good lawyers.*

I called on our own very good lawyer, an attorney named JJ Rosenbaum. I had met JJ soon after I arrived in New Orleans. She was working for the Southern Poverty Law Center, suing big contractors who were stealing the wages of immigrant workers in the post-Katrina cleanup. I had partnered with her on the Signal case soon after I met the workers. Behind the scenes, she was an architect of the civil suit against Signal, and was coordinating our legal strategy. Soon after the hunger strike, JJ joined my staff.

I asked her to comb through the thousands of pages of depositions from the civil suit, which had been crawling along in federal court for eighteen months now, handled mostly by a New York law firm working pro bono.

One night, deep in December, JJ handed me a sheaf of documents. They were pages from the second day of the deposition of Signal Senior Vice President Ronald Schnoor, taken just the previous week.

"You've got to read this," she said.

SITTING IN THE conference room of the Hampton Inn in Pascagoula, Schnoor was getting testy. The previous day he'd been cool and confident during six straight hours of questioning by the plaintiffs' fancy New York lawyer, one Alan Howard. But today, Schnoor was starting to lose his patience.

Then came the questions about March 9—the day the firing of Jacob Joseph and his fellow troublemakers turned into a fiasco.

"Now," said the New York lawyer, "In making the determination to terminate these two workers, did you direct Mr. Snyder to handle that termination?"

"Yes," said Schnoor.

"What instructions, if any, did you give him on how to handle that termination?"

So damn much hoopla over those firings—first from the workers, then the local press, then the New York and DC papers . . . finally Schnoor had a chance to say for the record that Signal hadn't come up with the plan on their own.

"I gave him instructions based on the guidance I was given from Immigration and Customs Enforcement about how to handle this termination."

The lawyer looked up.

"You had direct communications with US officials?"

"Yes," Schnoor said.

"Could you tell me what those were, with whom, when? What was discussed?"

Four questions at once! Schnoor smirked at the big shot's un-law-yer-like confusion. Then he explained. In the days leading up to March 9, he had already decided to get rid of Jacob Joseph. Jacob was making impossible demands. So Schnoor had the camp supervisor, Darrell Snyder, call Signal's inside man at ICE's Gulfport office. They knew him from way back before the Indians arrived. His name was Lars. He'd drop in every now and then to check the papers of Signal's Hispanic contract workers.

So when it was time to fire Jacob Joseph, they asked Lars how to do it.

Over the clack of the stenograph machine, Schnoor recounted the ICE agent's reply.

"Lars told us to take them out of the line on their way to work, get them in a van, take them to the airport and send them home," he said. "The impression I was left with, to avoid the absconding of the employees, don't give them any advance notice, take them all out of the line on the way to work, get their personal belongings, get them in a van, and get their tickets and get them to the airport and send them back to India."

Schnoor watched the lawyer furiously scribble down notes.

I LOOKED UP at JJ. Schnoor had handed us a smoking gun.

"Signal's Senior Vice President admitted—"

"Under oath, in a federal lawsuit—"

"—that an ICE agent told them what to do that day."

"Exactly. Pounce on Jacob, capture him, sequester him, push him into a plane . . ."

"The company began their reign of terror over trafficked workers at the *explicit advice and direction of ICE*."

Schnoor's words were so casual that something told me it might just be the tip of the iceberg.

We printed out a mountain of transcripts from the previous depositions. It was about to be a very long night.

The revelations kept coming. After March 9, when "all hell broke loose," as Schnoor put it, Darrell Snyder's phone rang. It was the head of Mississippi's Customs and Border Patrol, a man named Richard Bryant.

He wanted to understand what he was reading in the papers. Snyder admitted that it was even worse than the press had reported. Not only had Jacob escaped, but in the commotion, *fourteen others* had made a run for it.

Bryant was more than sympathetic. As Snyder reported to his superiors in an email after the meeting, "Customs has no intention of allowing these employees free rein when they decide that they want to run." In fact, Bryant "Was certain that ICE was going to take an active role in the apprehension of the fourteen that are out there now if for no other reason than to send a message to the remaining workers that it is not in their best interests to try and 'push' the system."

In other words, ICE and Border Patrol were promising to capture Signal's fugitive migrant workers—in order to terrorize the hundreds of others still inside the man camp. Over the rest of the year, they did exactly that. When Signal fired workers or when workers escaped, the company sent their names over to ICE and Border Patrol to hunt them down.

ICE and Border Patrol knew, of course, that Signal's remaining captive workforce were all undocumented, since their temporary visas had expired. But they didn't even hint at holding Signal's feet to the fire over that. Instead, they were itching for a hunt. *I haven't heard anything from you in a while*, Bryant emailed at one point. *Have we had any additional absconders?*

And there was more. In his deposition, Darrell Snyder revealed the name of the new ICE agent that Customs connected them with, promising that he would make it his mission and ICE's to apprehend fugitive workers and send a message that the others weren't free to leave the man camps.

Alvin Ladner.

For nearly two years, the fox had been in charge of the henhouse. The very man tasked with investigating Signal had been working all this time *with* Signal to apprehend its workers.

And not just for sport—I saw all the elements of a cover-up. ICE had started by advising Signal on illegal firings and deportations, then had gone on to sanction and facilitate Signal's scheme to hold the workers in involuntary servitude. The terror of being caught by ICE agents was exactly what kept the men trapped in the man camps. Once they escaped, the men's trafficking claims implicated ICE. Which is precisely why ICE had drawn a target on their backs—and Alvin Ladner was chasing them down. ICE had made itself a link in the human trafficking chain.

I imagined how the whole sequence might have played out.

Lars and Ladner were colleagues at the Gulfport ICE office. Probably friends. Lars gets the call from Signal in early 2007 asking for help with troublemakers. Lars gives them some off-the-top-of-his-head advice about how to make the problem go away quietly, probably thinking that's the last he'll hear of it. Lars mentions it to Ladner over lunch or beers. They have a chuckle and think that's that. Then March 9 blows up in Signal's face: chaos in the yard, headlines across the Gulf Coast, workers running off in terror—all when the company is on the way to an IPO. Lars is in major trouble.

I could see Ron Schnoor on the phone with ICE, shouting his head off: *We did what you told us to do, and now we've got a riot on our hands! You got us into this mess—you goddamn well better make it go away.* So Ladner, in my version, steps up. The hunter starts hunting. Tracks down the absconders and hands them back through the Signal gates. It looks like they may have things under control.

No such luck. Our campaign launches in March 2008. Hundreds of workers marching and throwing helmets outside the Signal gates. A federal lawsuit and TV cameras and dozens of articles. And our complaint to the DOJ alleging human trafficking, hammering Signal International *for doing exactly what ICE told it to do.* DC prosecutors are about to start sniffing around the biggest screw-up in the short history of the Gulfport ICE office. They're going to be inches away from learning that, if Schnoor's testimony was right, Lars advised Signal on private deportations. And that, if my understanding was right, Ladner had been on the hunt to clean up the mess ever since.

Things look grim when the DOJ initially assigns the Mississippi FBI to lead the investigation. The only thing working in Ladner's favor is an unexpected grace period: John Cotton Richmond is finishing up his vacation before he dives into the case. So Ladner and his higher-ups find a way to convince the DOJ that *he* should be the lead investigator instead of the FBI. He succeeds—just in time. So when the DOJ man from DC does start sniffing around, he's only sniffing where Ladner points him. And day by day, week by week, month by month, Ladner turns an investigation of Signal into an investigation of the workers instead.

WITH THE DEPOSITION EXCERPTS, we had it in cold print: the evidence that might let us knock ICE out of the contest. But with the thrill of the opportunity came a jolt of fear. Buried deep in the deposition exhibits was one final revelation. The men were in greater danger than even I had realized.

We knew from our DC insiders that ICE had turned the investigation *for* the workers into an investigation *of* the workers. It wanted to build a case against them for obtaining visas to enter the US by knowingly deceiving US officials, which brought a fine of up to $250,000 and a federal prison sentence of up to five years. That's why ICE had let the workers remain in limbo in the US over the past year, rather than simply rounding them up and deporting them.

Now I discovered the deadly weapon Ladner was readying to use in his case: the testimony of other Indian workers.

In front of me was an email to Signal from an Indian worker named Yeshwant Ghadge. It was Ghadge who had shaved the beard of the Sikh priest, Giani Gurbinder Singh, back in the early days at the man camp. Ghadge was a Signal loyalist and had stayed behind with two dozen others when the rest of the men had escaped in March 2008. Eventually, though, the loyalists had returned to India. In February 2009, Ghadge emailed a Signal attorney named Patricia Bollman, pleading to be brought back to Signal somehow. "I will be very much thankful to you if you pay your precious time to this letter," he wrote.

I felt a twinge of sorrow for him. Ghadge had not been on our side, but he had debts too, and must have been desperate to come back and make enough money to pay back the lenders. But he had violated his

H-2B visa by overstaying it for more than a year. No US consulate would
grant him entry now.

Unexpectedly, Patricia replied with good news. She told him of a
"Plan that Signal has developed with ICE": former H-2B workers could
return to the US to work for Signal in mid-April—if they agreed to serve
as "ICE witnesses."

I steadied myself and read on. Patricia said that another former H-2B
worker, Gaurav, would be in touch to coordinate travel plans. I knew
Gaurav as the worker who had sold out Jacob Joseph, reporting his organizing within the camp to Darrell Snyder and even calling Sachin Dewan
in India to out him.

Incredible. We had feared that ICE's Alvin Ladner had created a drag-
net spanning half the country. Now it seemed it extended all the way to
India. According to these emails, Signal had lured seven company loyalists back to the US to be witnesses for ICE. Bringing these men back from
India was no small feat. The "Parole" Patricia was referring to was most
likely the kind reserved for people whose entry into the United States
imparted a "significant public benefit." If Ladner had managed to win
these rare permits for Signal's handpicked witnesses, even as he blocked
the T visas for the trafficking victims, we were in even more danger than
I thought.

All this had been in motion for *seven months*. The witnesses would
have earned $10,000 apiece in Signal's yards by now, living in plush
apartments provided by the company—no man camps this time!—and
each night, after shifts, they would have returned home to a smiling ICE
agent holding a microphone.

By now, Ladner would have a visa fraud case against us as solid as a
shotgun, loaded with dozens of hours of interviews with *other* Indian
workers.

He could pull the trigger at any moment.

I called Aby to gather as many of the men together as he could. It was
time for them to make the biggest decision of their American lives.

"THERE," I SAID, after I'd explained everything: the smoking gun, the opportunity, and the threat. "Now you know as much as I do."

They sat in tight rows, hunched down, consumed.

"Do we go public? You need to decide, right here, right now."

Aby was deep in the crowd, arms folded, legs crossed, in twisted silence. I hoped he would say something.

Hemant spoke up first.

"I say we go," he said. "Back to DC. And to the press. We suspected this. Now we have evidence no one can ignore."

"It's too dangerous," a man named Muthu answered from the back. He had been with us from the beginning, on the walk to Washington and the hunger strike. He had a weathered face and eyebrows that met high up on his brow, like hands folded in perpetual prayer. "That's what our lawyers are saying."

He meant Alan Howard and the other attorneys from the civil suit. They were some of the best legal minds in the country. I'd filled them in on what we pieced together. They were dead set against releasing the evidence against ICE publicly. They'd told the workers that it would be suicide.

"They are saying, ICE is upset *because of* our campaign," Muthu said. "That's why this is all happening."

I nodded. My own calls with the lawyers had been contentious. To them, our brinksmanship was why we were here in the first place. If we had let sleeping dogs lie, they argued, the workers might have had T visas by now. Instead, we had to have a high-profile march. And when we were surveilled, our outcry had provoked an internal affairs review within ICE. In retaliation, ICE had gotten USCIS to rescind the first twenty T visas and freeze the others. Now the lawyers feared us enraging ICE like never before.

"Of course it's risky," I said. "But there's risk as well in *not* going public. ICE is not a sleeping dog. It's wide awake, hunting us, right at our door."

Finally Aby spoke up.

"It is no use fighting," he said, "because we are already dead. No one can revive us."

The room halted. The others turned to look at him.

"That is what everyone is saying," he went on. "Our lawyers are tired. Our friends in Washington are tired. And we are fed up."

All eyes were on him. Other men nodded.

"Even me," he said. "Fed up with losing. Fed up with fear. Fed up with grief. Being dead is better."

Aby rose from his chair.

"But then, late at night, every night, I call India, and I talk to Bobby. My son. My life. He is almost three. I've never met him. But he knows me. He calls me Daddy. *Daddy.* So how can I be dead? If he says *Daddy,* then I must conclude that I am somehow still here."

A chill went through me. I saw I wasn't the only one.

"What about you?" Aby pointed to Muthu. "Who is your life?"

"Priya," Muthu said. "My daughter."

"And you? And you?"

He pointed to man after man around him. Each named his angel. *Aditi. Amar. Priyanka. Nitya. Nirmal. Christopher. Rajni. Lokesh. Erum. Kiswa. Glory.* The incantation lifted the room. The men stirred.

"So," Aby said, "We are not yet dead. I refuse to be buried alive. I will meet the boy who calls me Daddy. He wants me to hold him. His wish is my command."

"But do we have enough to win?" asked Muthu.

"We have each other," Aby said. "But if we have to lose, I would rather lose my life than my honor. Let Bobby inherit my honor. Let him grow up proud. So, one more time . . ."

Aby got up on a chair, stood to his full height. His chest filled and his voice rang out.

"Awaaz do!"

Give me your voices.

Every man got to his feet. Their voices joined in a full-throated chorus:

"Hum ek hain!"

We are one.

4: Brothers

A COLD MORNING drizzle covered Washington. We darted past bare January trees on our way to the Hart Senate Office Building for our first big meeting.

We had the goods on ICE. A year into the Obama presidency, ICE agents were obstructing the administration's most meager reforms. Communities everywhere were pushing Washington to rein in the deportation force, painting them as nefarious, often criminal. But its operations were very secretive. Hard evidence of intentional malfeasance was scant, so advocates and their allies in Congress could often be dismissed as shrill protesters. We'd arrived in Washington with evidence in hand.

I had my phone clamped to my ear, breathlessly narrating our new facts to Julia Preston, the unflappable lead immigration reporter at *The New York Times*. She had been on the ICE beat for a decade, and was a war correspondent before that, so when she let slip a genuinely surprised *huh*, I pumped my fist. I told her I'd have to call her back—we had just arrived at the Hart building.

Saravanan corrected me: "This is Dirksen. Hart's over there."

I smiled as I followed. These were different men than the ones I brought to Washington a year ago. They were a band of brothers now. And there was no wonderment at just being here, no lingering in the Senate's grand atrium. With purposeful strides, our delegation of twenty-four men crossed the maze toward the office of Senator Chuck Schumer.

It was a whole different Washington too. Democrats had the House and Senate. Schumer, the ambitious New York senator, was leading a new charge to overhaul America's immigration system. George W. Bush had failed at it, but Schumer was no friend of lost causes. To change the game, he had brought in a lawyer he referred to as his "Immigration genius," the Miami-born, deadlock-breaking, sweet-spot-finding Leon Fresco.

"We're here," Hemant announced. All two dozen men and I crammed into Fresco's office.

Last year, we'd met with George Miller's salad-eating intern. Today, Leon Fresco heard us out, in rolled-up shirtsleeves and a blue tie.

After I presented our evidence, an ally, Tanya Clay House, spoke up. She was the legislative director for the Lawyers' Committee for Civil Rights Under Law, the civil rights organization created by John F. Kennedy, and the architect of our DC lobbying strategy. She told Fresco that her boss, Barbara Arnwine, had just announced her support for our struggle at the National Press Club and would be calling Senate and House Judiciary Committee members all day. Then the door opened, and in slipped Hilary Shelton, the legislative director of the NAACP, America's oldest civil rights organization. He didn't say a word. He didn't have to. His presence said it all.

Then Murugan spoke. I braced myself: if he reprised T visa testimony, it would test Leon's patience. Fresco had heard all the sad tales in his day as an immigration attorney in Miami. He was in Washington to get big things done in a hurry. Like drafting America's next immigration reform proposal, an epic feat of writing and wrangling.

But Murugan skipped expertly past his trafficking journey to trace his three-year odyssey through American institutions—precisely what Fresco needed to understand. Submitting a T visa application to USCIS. Bringing a federal lawsuit. Triggering a DOJ investigation. Consenting to be placed in deportation proceedings *in order to be a witness* for that investigation. Filing a complaint against ICE misconduct after being subjected to surveillance. Testifying to Homeland Security's civil rights division about ICE misconduct.

Leon listened wordlessly but intently.

"Okay. Who else are you meeting with?" Washington-speak for *You've got my attention.* From habit, he aimed the question at the lobbyists, Tanya and Hillary. But it was Saravanan who answered: Reps. Nancy Pelosi, Zoe Lofgren, and Bennie Thompson.

Then he pointed to his watch. "It is a twenty-minute walk to the Rayburn building," he said. "Time to go."

IN THE FOLLOWING DAYS, we had a dozen meetings with different congressional offices and subcommittees, each one just as sharp and focused. The difference from our last time in Washington was unmistakable.

As pressure from Washington mounted, USCIS officials announced to us that they would, once again, consider the men's T visa applications. And to expedite things they would read only two, on the basis of which they would decide the fate of all the applicants. We were exultant. They had accepted our argument: if any one of these men was a victim of human trafficking, they all were.

The day we submitted the test applications, *The New York Times* broke the story about ICE's collusion with Signal. Two days later, the *Times* editorial board wrote a ringing endorsement of our freedom struggle.

I read the editorial out loud to the men over the lunchtime din in the basement cafeteria of the US Capitol.

"'A federal agency appears to have collaborated in an effort to silence foreign workers,'" it began. In one deft line, it embraced our trafficking argument: "'They were trapped as surely as if they were shackled.'" And it ended with hope for us and a mandate for Congress: "'The story may yet have a decent ending for the workers . . . But the broader problem remains—of immigrant workers afraid to "Push the system" and challenge abusive employers and even federal agencies when their jobs, visas and futures are at stake.'" I looked up from reading. Aby gave an impressed nod.

Murugan repeated the killer line: "'Trapped as surely as if we were shackled.'"

In eight words, three years of their lives.

Saravanan arrived with trays and set them down. They were piled with plastic-wrapped lumps. The men looked at them quizzically.

"What is this?" Aby said.

"They have hot food here," said Murugan. "I saw some kind of meat-and-tomato curry."

"If we can't get good Indian food," Saravanan said, "It is better to eat something that doesn't remind us of India at all. They call this a *wrap*." He demonstrated how to tear away the cellophane. A wilted spinach leaf hung out.

"It looks miserable," said Aby.

"Exactly! Nothing like India at all," Saravan said.

The rest chuckled and reached for a wrap of their own.

"Before I came to America," said Hemant, "I never ate cold meat. Not once. I don't understand it. If you want cold food, eat papdi chaat. Eat dhokla. But cold chicken with cold spinach? Spinach is best in the form of a saag. The kind Shruti makes. Creamy. Filling."

"By God, please. *Stop*," begged Saravanan.

Hemant continued to torment him: "With cubes of paneer floating in it. In pools of ghee. With roti."

Others laughed.

"Last night I told my daughter I met a senator," said Muthu. "All she wanted to know was if I ate Kentucky Fried Chicken!"

Aby smiled, remembering: "At Signal in Texas, I would steal out to eat that. From this gas station five miles down the road."

"Did they let you cook your own food in Texas?" asked Hemant.

"Never! There was even a local pastor there from Kerala who found out about us and tried to bring us masalas. They wouldn't let him through the gate."

The other men shook their heads.

"In Mississippi, the food was so bad that Rajan attacked the cooks," Hemant said. "Then he took over the kitchen and cooked a feast for all of us. Best daal I ever had."

"That man could cook," I said, feeling a stab of sadness. I missed him dearly.

A silence passed over the table.

"If I could eat anything, it would be Kottayam fish curry with kappa. Bincy makes it wonderfully," Aby said.

"You'll eat it again, Aby," Murugan said.

Saravanan stood up. "Eat up, brothers," he said. "We're due back in the Dirksen building in twenty minutes."

5: The Test

INSIDE THE VERMONT Service Center of USCIS, the official glanced out of her window.

Lake Champlain's coastline gleamed, reflecting the Adirondacks. Queen Anne's lace dotted the beach grass. Waves crashed against limestone bluffs and sprayed windswept cedars.

The official sat at her desk and considered the stack of T visa applications before her. The two on the top were the test cases. She picked up the first and read.

> That day, the gates of the man camp shut. After that, with each day that passed, the gate seemed to get smaller and smaller.

She finished reading with a chill, then opened the second.

> The Indian workers were given the most dangerous jobs because the supervisors know we have debt and therefore could not complain.

> I feel depressed and sick most days and forget the simplest things.

> I heard that life expectancy here is greater than in India. My own life expectancy has declined.

She couldn't stop reading. She opened one file after another.

When I saw the camp the next day in the light, I noticed a high fence enclosing the grounds.

I could never sleep more than three hours.

The smell became intolerable.

Sometimes we found bugs in the food.

They told us it was all we were going to get, so we could eat it or leave it. I survived on rice and buttermilk.

They would only take us to the Walmart. We were driven by a security guard. We had only one hour. I felt like I was an animal, always under the company's watch and control.

I had to shave my beard as they instructed. If I did not do so, they would deport me. Some men cried as they shaved.

Even when they treated us like dirt, we stayed quiet and did our work.

It was a pathetic life.

I was desperate to escape.

I remember crying . . .

If I were sent back to India, I wouldn't make it past Mumbai.

When my father-in-law passed away, I felt guilty. He died shortly after I explained to him all I was suffering here. He was devastated.

My mother's financial future will be ruined. I feel a deep shame.

My wife's family has told me that they would not have allowed me to marry her if they knew I was not going to be receiving a green card. She constantly asked me why I married her.

Only my parents, wife, and child are in my home now. There is no one there to protect them.

I crave to see my child.

I have lost my hope for the future and stand as a broken man.

6: Reunion

October 2010
Atlanta International
Airport

EIGHT MONTHS LATER, Aby stood in taut anticipation, clutching a bouquet of fresh roses in his right hand. In his left, he cradled a toy. His eyes were fixed on the escalator six yards away—as close as he was allowed. Bincy and Bobby were due to arrive in minutes. He looked down at the toy, a matchbox-sized JCB excavator. It shone yellow in his palm, bright as his anxiety.

One question had consumed him day and night in advance of his family's arrival: *Will Bobby come to me?*

He'd been in feverish preparation since Bincy's visa arrived—moving out his roommates, buying furniture, kitchenware, linens. The hardest purchase had been the toy he'd give Bobby at the airport. Bobby was shy. He might reject him. He almost certainly would. Aby's only chance was to offer a toy that Bobby wanted. Then he might peer out from behind his mother to reach for it, and him.

So Aby scoured the shelves at Walmart, and finally settled on this excavator. Bincy had described how Bobby scattered socks about the house and pretended to *be* an excavator, collecting them with a hooked arm.

But now doubt stabbed him. Was it too yellow? Too small? What if Bobby had moved on to something else?

Bincy's head rose into view. She saw him. Smiled. Shrieked. Ran to him. Threw her arms around his neck. Buried her face in his chest.

"I'll never let you go," she said.

Aby pulled her in, tight, smelled her thick hair. He dissolved in her scent. She was so soft. He felt a long-dead tenderness he'd forgotten.

Bobby was a few steps back, looking on from the arms of an interpreter who had accompanied them from JFK.

Aby took a breath, apprehension flooding back. He stepped close to Bobby. He looked just like his pictures—and, at the same time, nothing like them. He opened the palm of his hand to reveal the shiny excavator.

Bobby considered it.

He looked up at Aby. Then, ignoring the excavator completely, he leapt into his father's arms.

A welter of joy hit Aby. He squeezed Bobby, who squirmed with delight. Peals of laughter fell on Aby like healing rain.

Bincy asked Bobby if he was thirsty.

"My daddy will get me water," he said.

IT ALMOST DIDN'T HAPPEN. At the very time that Aby stood up and made his "I am not dead" speech, exhorting the men to go to Washington, the Signal loyalist Yeshwant Ghadge was presenting his testimony to Alvin Ladner, giving the ICE agent everything he needed. For months, over dozens of hours of interviews, Ghadge had been helping Ladner make his case—that the workers had committed the federal crime of visa fraud.

In Ghadge's telling, the workers *knew* they were coming to the US on temporary visas all along. They defrauded US Embassy and consular officials to get their foot in the American door. Once at Signal, they tried to blackmail company officials for green cards by threatening strikes and lawsuits. When that extortion failed, these men—shirkers who showed up to work drunk and talked back to foremen, in Ghadge's version— came up with a new ploy. They absconded en masse, went to Washington, and played Gandhi. They concocted trafficking claims to game the immigration system, fooling members of Congress with sad tales of bad food and racial slurs in the man camp. Was the food really that bad? Some people liked it, some didn't. Were the foremen really racist? Who can peer into another man's heart? In session after session, Ghadge painted precisely the picture Ladner wanted, right up until the end of December.

Then something shifted. Ghadge didn't know why, but when the interviews resumed in the new year, suddenly, there was no more Ladner. At first, another ICE agent took over the interviews, and then they stopped altogether. Even Patricia Bollman, Signal's attorney, couldn't explain what had happened. Somehow ICE's case had fallen apart.

Against all odds, our plan had worked. The evidence we'd presented of ICE's participation in a human trafficking scheme was exactly what our allies inside and outside of government needed. It gave them the leverage to push the agency to the sidelines. With ICE out of the way, DHS granted what was years overdue: a path to freedom for the survivors of one of the largest human trafficking schemes in US history.

7: Thanksgiving

November 2010
Houston, TX

SOME OF THE families arrived as soon as Thanksgiving 2010. Each week brought a new arrival, a new phone call from the airport.

Thank you, Saketji!

My wife is with me!

I'm with my daughter!

I've found my son.

I'm so happy for you, I'd always say. *No need to thank me.*

The following year, on Thanksgiving Day, I rode into Houston with my team of organizers, attorneys, and interpreters. Most of the families were reunited now, and many of them settled there. The men had invited us to a meeting. I imagined they had questions about the next phase of their lives. How to deal with the American problems that had, until now, been luxuries even to imagine: getting health care, joining a union.

A welcoming committee was waiting for us in the parking lot. I got out of the van holding a block of sticky butcher paper. Saravanan stepped up, beaming, and took it from me.

"You won't be needing that today," he said.

The other welcomers ran up and put marigold garlands around our necks. Suddenly I understood. Back in Delhi, growing up, we'd garland the "chief guests" who visited my school for annual functions. This was no meeting. It was a celebration of epic—that is, Indian—proportions.

Saravanan held my hand as he led us to the rented venue.

"Ready?" he grinned.

The doors flung open. I gasped. There were five hundred people inside, dressed for a wedding. Women in bangles and silver-hemmed saris and dazzling smiles. Little girls with bright gold ribbons in their ponytails. Boys in kurtas and light-up sneakers. A Tamil band burst alive, beating with blurry intensity on gigantic drums hanging from their necks. A dancing crowd surged around me.

Then Aby and Murugan picked me right off my feet, raised me above their heads, and passed me from man to man. The ecstatic swirl carried me to the front of the room and propped me up in front of a giant cake.

The children were summoned. They stood around me, climbed on top of me, hung off my back and my legs. I was handed a great knife. Cameras flashed as we fed each other. Smurf-blue icing was caked into my beard.

Chairs danced out of ramparts to face the stage, and a pageant of newly arrived children performed the greatest talent show of all time. Three teenage classical kathak dancers expertly avoided the toddler who had crawled up on the stage and was scooting around on his fanny. A lanky young man breakdanced in a silk kurta, jeans, and sandals. Man after man sang awful, ebullient karaoke.

Hours later, the emcee announced it was time for my speech. But I was speechless. In a daze, ears ringing from the feedback, I took the microphone and called out the only thing that came to mind:

"Awaaz do!"

Give me your voices.

Hundreds yelled back:

"Hum ek hain!"

We are one.

THANKSGIVING BECAME AN annual tradition, always with a talent show. Afterward, plate of biryani in hand, I'd tour the festooned hall, visiting with family after family, embracing the new arrivals.

"REMEMBER ME?" ASKED Jaya, Murugan's wife.

Of course! I met her during my trip to India. But I could barely recognize her. The Jaya I'd met in India was desolate. This one gleamed.

The following year, she handed me Madhav, their newborn son. *Uncleji*, Jaya taught him, pointing at me, as he gurgled in my arms.

DEBONAIR HEMANT THREW his arm around Shruti and presented her with a flourish. He recounted our campaign, a story she'd no doubt heard a hundred times in filmic detail. She valiantly maintained a look of fascination. When he was done, she asked me where in America might be the best place to put their future child in school.

Later, they moved to a Wisconsin suburb with excellent schools, and had a son, Aksh.

WHEN SHAWKAT ALI SHEIKH'S visa was approved, his wife, Mazda, came out of hiding. She and their children joined him in Texas, where he was living. He commanded his son, Mohammad, to perform, while Mazda and his daughters looked on.

"I took him straight from the airport to tae kwon do camp," Shawkat said proudly, as his son executed diligent axe kicks.

Afterward, as we talked into the night, I realized what was different in his manner. He finally had an ease about him. Later, he and Mazda had a fourth child, a feisty little girl named Raghad, "The carefree one."

WITH HIS ARM around me, Jacob Joseph announced to his wife, Lincy, "This is Saketji!"

"Ah! I've heard of you!" she said, with marvelous regard.

"I hope some of it is good," I said.

"Very much so. You're the one who sent my husband's file to the USCIS. And after that, you and he went to the EEOC. And then you brought him to the AFL-CIO! And then you went into the DOJ. And fought with the ICE, which is inside the DHS!"

Jacob called his daughters over. Donna and Donya were pretty, lanky teenage girls now. They were in high school, and worked nights in hotels.

"We've heard of you!" they said, eyes wide.

Nibu Raju, one of the bachelors, came over to get me.

"Come out to the Karo Bar?"

"Sure," I said, a little nervous. I did want to console the bachelors, who were alone without their families, but I hoped this place wasn't far. These young men could drink, and I wanted to stay present at these exquisite reunions.

The bachelors were huddled outside together, holding plastic cups. A whoop went up when they saw me.

"Get this man a drink!"

An SUV trunk opened to reveal crates of alcohol. This was the Karo Bar—or properly, the "Car-O Bar."

"One peg or two? Or *three*?"

Someone handed me a pint cup filled to the brim with Dewar's and lukewarm water. I toasted their health.

Afterward, the bachelors all applied for advance parole, which gave them special permission to go back to India for only ninety days. Not missing a moment, they got their horoscopes, found their perfect matches, had grand weddings, and fell in love—in that order, usually with days to spare. They returned to the US while their new wives waited for their own visas, usually two more years.

Back inside, I wove through the room, hugging, shaking hands, posing with children. Then I caught sight of a man whose face stopped me in my tracks. It was Giani Gurbinder Singh, the Sikh welder-priest. I had only ever seen him clean-shaven, after Signal had forced him to cut his beard. His naked face had been a picture of pain, the shame in his eyes haunting.

Tonight, his glory was restored. His beard was proud and regal. His smile was soft. He nodded at me just slightly—*Yes, it's me*—and extended his arms. As we hugged, he whispered conspiratorially: his wife had just arrived, and I wasn't to say a word about his beard. For three years, he had avoided sending photographs home—she had no idea he'd ever shaved. I promised.

Months later, cleaning out old boxes before a move to a new apartment, she found his old company ID card. She squinted at the familiar-looking man—then fell back, staggered. He held her. Gave her spoons of amrit, holy water, while he explained. In time she recovered.

IN THE IRON ARMS of Paul Konar, the hunger strike strongman, my rib cage felt close to cracking. Forgetting to release me from the hug, he told me the latest. His two younger daughters had arrived with his wife. His oldest couldn't come—US authorities granted reunion visas only to children under twenty-one. No matter, said Paul. He would go see her soon enough.

Paul presented me to Pinky, the middle daughter, whom I had met in Trivandrum. She was now going to nursing school in Houston.

She had no memory of the night I visited. Just yesterday, the moonlight had thrown our slanted shadows on walls filled with silent pictures of Paul. To her, it was a forgotten dream.

THE MORNING AFTER Thanksgiving, Bincy was making the famous fish curry of Kottayam—the one Aby had promised me for years. I leaned over her clay pot, inhaling the musk of a shimmering melange—garlic, shallots, curry leaves, coconut oil.

"Stir," said Bincy.

She threw in spice after spice. Each released its perfume. Syrupy fenugreek, floral coriander, bright Kashmiri chili. She poured water in, and when it was boiling, added something I'd never seen. Three curly, wine-dark jewels, sticky, leathery, enigmatic.

"My God," I said, "What are those?" The smell reminded me of amchur, dried mango powder, but this sweet-and-sour bouquet was more delicate.

"That's kudum puli," Bincy said. A kind of tamarind found only in Malabar.

"Time to add the fish," announced Aby, and slid it in with a flourish. A shark he caught himself, he claimed. A lid went on.

As it simmered, the kitchen filled with tangy mystery from the boiling kudum puli. I could barely focus as Bincy explained how to make the tapioca mash—the "Kappa"—that went with the fish.

Afterward, we three sat at the dining table while Bobby pushed an excavator around on the floor. Bincy spooned the fish curry over the tapioca on a plate in front of me.

I scooped up the mash with my fingers, pressing it into the glistening, pasty fish curry. The tamarind sourness was in my jaw, its fire in my nose, its sweetness in my mouth. I had never had anything like it.

It had taken us three years to bring Bincy from Kottayam. She transported us back there in minutes.

Bincy's Fish Curry

Heat coconut oil in your clay pot. Fry shallots, garlic, ginger, curry leaves. Lower the heat.

Add fenugreek and coriander. Fry until the oil rises.

Add the kudum puli, water, and salt. Slide fish in. Cover, simmer.

When it's cooked, drizzle coconut oil over it.

Serve it with kappa—mashed tapioca with spices mixed in.

It's even better the next day.

8: Good Karma

January 2015
New Orleans, LA

IN JANUARY 2015, a federal jury trial opened in *David, et al. v. Signal International, LLC,* in New Orleans. It was the first of what had become eleven separate lawsuits against Signal, Malvern Burnett, and Sachin Dewan, on behalf of more than two hundred of the Indian workers. (No individual Signal officials or employees were named as defendants in the civil suits.)

By the time the trial began in January, Michael Pol had entered bankruptcy, which stayed litigation against him.

The trial was a massive undertaking. Lead attorney Dan Werner of the Southern Poverty Law Center directed an army of pro bono lawyers from more than a dozen law firms. Signal had disclosed more than 2.5 million documents during discovery. Pretrial depositions consumed hundreds of hours. Malvern Burnett's deposition alone took five days, with the transcript running 1,055 pages.

The trial against the company, Burnett, and Dewan began on January 12.

Signal's legal team brought a kitchen-sink approach to its defense. It argued that the entire campaign was a nefarious plot by shadowy political hit men to bring down the H-2B guest worker program. It presented Signal's Indian workforce—apart from a few noisy malcontents—as a happy family, making much of a company cricket match it once held, at which a lucky raffle ticket holder was awarded a new TV. As for the malcontents, Signal's lead attorney, Erin Hangartner, minced no words: "So you take that money out, and you make the grown-up decision as a grown man [that] you are going to borrow the money. And now, even though you liked your job, unfortunately, you have to get up every morning and you have to go to work. So, I think that I am a victim of forced labor because all these years later, the [lenders] still want my money. . . . Again, I'm not being snarky, but this is the real world."

Signal's team cast aspersions on the character of campaign leaders, suggesting that the jury should dismiss Hemant's testimony because his credit card statements showed evidence of a visit to a Mississippi massage parlor. They pursued a strange historical inquiry with a Sacred Heart Catholic Church parishioner who had helped transport Indian workers to Sunday Mass. ("Do you believe in your personal experience and knowledge that slaves are typically paid?" "I guess not.") And they repeatedly cast Signal as a touchingly naive victim of devious recruiters and a dishonest lawyer.

Burnett's attorney, Tim Cerniglia, insisted that Burnett had acted with exemplary honesty, and had just tried to do right by everyone. "Mr. Burnett did the best he could for these people. He did the best he could for Signal to get the workers in because they needed them desperately. He did the best he could for the Indians, the workers, because they wanted to come and make some wages. . . . And now he's caught by crossfire because these two want to duke it out." If anyone was a victim, in Cerniglia's telling, it was Malvern. "Caught in the middle is Mr. Burnett. . . . Why is it always the way? *Why is it always the way?* It's the little guy's fault."

Dewan's attorney, Steve Shapiro, after introducing "Anita, [Dewan's] beautiful wife," praising Dewan's "Wonderful family, really close-knit family," and insisting, "Mr. Dewan is really a good person," took a nearly identical approach: "The workers were told exactly what to expect. Mr. Dewan didn't mislead anyone, at all, at any time. He was following his direction from Signal. . . . But those instructions were based on advice given by Mr. Burnett." Dewan "Was caught in the crossfire. Caught in the crossfire."

But the workers' testimony was devastating for all the defendants. On the eleventh day of the trial, Signal's lead attorney Hangartner suffered a stroke and was hospitalized.

On February 18, 2015, the jury found that Signal International, Malvern Burnett, and Sachin Dewan had committed forced labor, trafficking for forced labor, mail fraud, wire fraud, immigration document fraud, a Racketeer Influenced and Corrupt Organizations Act (RICO) conspiracy, negligent misrepresentation, breach of contract, and promissory estoppel against all five named plaintiffs. It found that Signal had subjected the workers to discriminatory terms and conditions of employment, and to harassing living conditions. It also found that Signal had subjected Joseph Jacob to false imprisonment and intentional infliction of emotional distress.

The jury awarded the plaintiffs $14.1 million in damages: $12.25 million from Signal, $915,000 each from the Law Office of Malvern Burnett and Dewan Consultants.

Dewan and Burnett appealed the verdict, then reached a settlement with the five named plaintiffs, as well as the plaintiffs in the other ten cases, for an undisclosed amount. Burnett and Dewan refused further comment on the cases.

In July 2015, Signal settled the remaining ten lawsuits on behalf of other Indian workers for $20 million. It also filed for bankruptcy.

In December 2015, Signal agreed to settle an additional lawsuit, by the Equal Employment Opportunity Commission, over alleged racial discrimination toward the Indian workers, for $5 million. In an unprecedented move for a company implicated in human trafficking, Signal CEO Richard Marler issued this apology as part of the settlement:

On behalf of Signal International, Inc., its management expresses their sincerest apology and regret for the treatment its guest workers from India received while living and working at Signal to help in the rebuilding effort on the Gulf Coast after Hurricane Katrina and Rita. Signal was wrong in failing to ensure the guest workers were treated with the respect and dignity they deserved. Signal deeply regrets the living conditions the guest workers were subjected to, and is sorry for its actions on March 9, 2007. Signal knows this treatment caused hardship to the guest workers, and, in many cases, their families. Signal has learned from its mistakes and is committed to ensuring the experiences of the guest workers and their families will not be repeated.

Signal is pleased to have recently achieved bankruptcy court approval of the July 12, 2015 settlement agreement and, although pursuant to the agreement, Signal is obligated under the circumstances not to admit legal liability, Signal is pleased the settlement will ultimately result in a meaningful recovery to those who have been affected. Signal looks forward to confirming its chapter 11 plan and completing its bankruptcy case so that the guest workers will begin to receive the benefits of the settlement agreement.
Sincerely,
Richard L. Marler
CEO and President
Signal International, Inc.

SIGNAL'S ASSETS WERE SOLD off in a bankruptcy auction to the Teachers' Retirement System of Alabama and the Employees' Retirement System of Alabama. The company was reconstituted as World Marine, LCC. It retained Signal's logo; its CEO, Richard Marler; and Senior Vice President Ronald Schnoor. Camp manager John Sanders wasn't around for the reorganization, having been fired by Signal in 2007.

MALVERN BURNETT CONTINUED his immigration law practice in New Orleans, with three satellite offices in Mississippi. He never stopped dealing in H-2B visas. The Burnett law office website featured the blog articles "How to Get a Green Card" and "Help Wanted: U.S. Desperate for Qualified Foreign Workers."

But in the years that followed his firing by Signal, he seemed to have found his way back to the role he had pictured for himself as a young idealist. In 2019, I heard from the colleagues that he defended an undocumented poultry worker snared in President Donald Trump's ICE raids on

Mississippi poultry plants. When President Trump announced plans to "Dump illegal immigrants in sanctuary cities" that same year, Malvern sparred with a conservative local radio host in New Orleans, saying that the undocumented were "Providing lifeblood to their communities."

MICHAEL POL LEFT his primary job at the police force of Ocean Springs, Mississippi, in 2009. He acquired the radio station WMXI FM in Hattiesburg, MS, where he hosted a conservative morning talk show called *Pine Belt Daybreak*. His shows featured interviews with local entrepreneurs and conservative figures such as Corey Lewandowski, and espoused complaints about cancel culture and its victims, including Aunt Jemima.

SACHIN DEWAN'S ORGANIZATION, Dewan Consultants, continued to recruit workers for placements in multiple countries, and maintained a robust online presence. The company profile featured Sachin's father, "Late Mr. Jadgish Dewan," looking venerable in a framed portrait, and listed Sachin as Managing Director besides two Dewan brothers as Directors.

As the website said: "Having operated internationally for over four decades, Dewan Consultants prides itself on having set the standards for world-class recruitment both in India and globally." Dewan Consultants "Has pioneered fast and efficient recruitment and remains the accolade for being the leading Indian consultancy providing personnel Globally."

YESHWANT GHADGE, the Signal loyalist who nearly brought the entire campaign down, had a strange epilogue of his own.

Shortly after Signal lost in the courts, it fired Ghadge. By this time, he had no papers. The legal status Alvin Ladner arranged for him had long since expired. So had his driver's license and his passport. On paper, he was no one.

He knew a Krishna temple deep in the woods of Gulfport, Mississippi, where he sometimes went to pray. He fell to his knees at the gates, and the prabhu—the priest—granted sanctuary, in exchange for work around the temple.

Ghadge swept, cleaned, collected flowers for the temple. He chopped vegetables at the temple's restaurant, Good Karma.

But mostly Ghadge prayed to Lord Krishna. He had a wife and two kids, a boy and a girl, in Pune, his hometown. He hadn't seen them in seven years. He prayed for a way to bring them to America, so his kids could earn engineering degrees in US universities.

Ghadge had a good singing voice. His fervent devotional songs to Krishna earned him the priest's admiration. One day, the priest rewarded him with a treat: a trip up the road to the farm Good Karma sourced from. There, Ghadge saw cows, grazing, transcendent, like Lord Krishna's own. He turned to the priest and asked if he could build them a cowshed. The hands that had built oil platforms went to work erecting a humble barn. Atonement.

His devotion was rewarded. An associate of the campaign—the very freedom movement he had shunned, then attempted to destroy—found him and offered to file a T visa application for him. For the first time, Ghadge told the truth about his own troubles and others' at Signal. His T visa was approved.

Ghadge's family arrived, and settled in Victoria, Texas. His son and daughter earned engineering degrees from US universities.

AFTER OUR PAINFUL parting in Kentucky, Rajan returned to India and vanished from my life. A few years later, I got a flurry of calls from workers all at once: Rajan was dead. *How?* I asked. No one knew for sure. He had been gloomy, unsettled, but apparently healthy. Then one day, it seemed, his heart just gave out.

It was a terrible shock, but in a way, it wasn't a surprise. Rajan was made for journeys. It's what he lived on. Taking cooking classes in Saudi labor camps. Picking up Russian in Azerbaijan. Walking in giant strides from New Orleans to Washington. The restless, happy exile. Once it was over, he died of a broken heart. Rajan died of being home.

While we were friends, Rajan sometimes asked me to tell him a story. He was equally fascinated and baffled that I'd studied literature at university—including Indian folk tales. ("You come here from India, then you pay to learn stories . . . *from India*?") He would invent mock folk tales about himself as a superhuman worker hero, crossing continents in a single step, setting the world right with a wag of his eyebrows.

But he also had a great appetite for the stories I found fascinating, some of which I'd heard from home, some of which I had to cross the world to learn. One in particular he would ask me to tell him again and again. It has haunted me since he died.

THERE WAS ONCE a great king. One day a foreign magician visited his court. "Cast a spell! Do a trick," the king invited. The magician waved his wand. The king fell asleep and dreamed.

In the dream he was wandering through a forest in another country, hungry and penniless. After weeks in the wilderness, he arrived in a town. People asked: "Who are you?" He didn't remember. They took pity on him and let him stay. He met a good woman, had two daughters, grew old, and in time, he died.

The dream ended. The king woke up with a start.

"How long have I been asleep?"

"Ten minutes, Majesty."

"Impossible! I lived a whole life. Did I vanish from the court?"

"Majesty," the magician said, "You were here the whole time."

"It was real. If felt too true not to be."

The king gathered his army. Marched through the forest, invaded the next country, kept marching, until he arrived in a town. It looked familiar. He asked a local:

"Does someone live here—someone who looks like me, but older?"

The man pointed to a plume of smoke rising from a cremation ground. The king ran over. By the side of a funeral pyre, there was an old woman. He knew her. It was his wife from the dream. The two young women with her were his daughters.

That's the story of the king who dreamed he was an exile and woke up to find it was true.

9: Alvin Ladner's America

Summer 2021
Waveland, MS

IT WAS ONLY in writing this book that I let myself feel my grief and anger over Rajan's death. He had been a beloved friend during our three years together, but once he left for India, I forgot him the way only a migrant can—as completely as I once cherished him. As I wrote, the memories came back, first in flickers, then in floods of light. Rajan in his blazing orange overalls. Rajan garnishing a one-pot meal with crunchy green cilantro stems. His hairbrush mustache. His equine smile. His grim thumbs-up okays, like he was fixing a thumbprint on a will. How he inspected cashews like gemstones before popping them in his mouth. His misty adoration of his wife, Shamitha, who he vowed would one day see Niagara Falls. His disbelief that my Indian parents could countenance my romantic life. His discomfort at hugs. ("Where'd you pick up that habit?") And more than anything, his mind for dreams. He was a dreamer of futures, for himself, for Shamitha, for the children he was sure they'd have.

Most painful was the memory of how I'd abandoned him. The first time he called me from India, in the summer of 2010, he hurried past my pained greeting. Now that we had won the T visas, he wanted to know, could he return to the US? *Can the door open back up for me?*

I told him I was sorry, but the door had shut tight. The government's rules, not mine. But I promised to call him back.

I never did. When he called again, I never picked up. I was in the middle of a million things, and what could I offer him anyway? A flurry of unanswered calls came in the autumn of 2013, when he must have wanted to tell me about the birth of his twins. (Daughters, like he'd always wanted.) His last call came on their third birthday, in September 2016, two weeks before he died.

While writing about him, I cooked the daal he had shared with me the last time I saw him. Canary-yellow stewed lentils tempered with fried mustard seeds. Eating it, I felt his presence, and finally cried over his death. He was the best man I knew.

THE MORE I wrote and learned, and the fuller my picture became, the more my anger and grief focused on one man. Of all the actors in this drama, one had never had a reckoning of any kind. Without him, Rajan would have had an entirely different fate—he might well be alive today. Yet this man had faced no jury, met no justice. It was the ICE agent Alvin Ladner.

We had survived the assault of Ladner's bringing handpicked witnesses back from India to testify against our campaign. Our workers got T visas, reunited with their families, set about reestablishing their lives. In our relief and elation, I lost track of how Ladner had succeeded in his ultimate purpose: to ensure that Signal International never faced federal criminal charges.

If the system had functioned as it should have, I thought, the DOJ's Human Trafficking Prosecution Unit would have brought indictments against Richard Marler, Ronald Schnoor, and the other responsible parties at Signal, along with the recruitment trio of Burnett, Pol, and Dewan. John Cotton Richmond would have prosecuted the case before a jury. Instead, even after *The New York Times* reported that "a federal agency appears to have collaborated in an effort to silence foreign workers," even after congressional allies again pressed the DOJ on our behalf, Richmond shut down his investigation. No criminal charges were ever brought against Signal or any of its officers or employees, or against Signal's agents—Burnett, Dewan or Pol. In a long-form closing memo, the conclusive record of his three years on the case, Richmond wrote that he couldn't establish Signal's culpability.

Why not? Because of those very handpicked witnesses. ICE had flown the seven men back from India to testify that they were perfectly happy in the labor camp, that they'd never felt trapped or coerced. This muddied the waters of our trafficking complaint to the DOJ. And if Richmond couldn't establish Signal's culpability in trafficking, he couldn't bring charges against Burnett, Pol, and Dewan as traffickers either.

How could I be sure that Ladner was the one behind this? At first, I couldn't. The Signal lawyer's emails didn't name the ICE agent she was coordinating with. Then during the writing of this book, I tracked down Yeshwant Ghadge, Handpicked Witness No. 1, in Victoria, Texas. I asked him if he remembered the name of the ICE agent who had picked him up at the airport when he came back as an ICE witness in 2009, who had brought him to the furnished apartment Signal rented for him, who had met with him and the Signal lawyer at Chinese buffets to prepare him to testify against his former coworkers to the DOJ. Even more than a decade after the events, Ghadge recalled the name like he was remembering an old friend.

"Ladner," he said.

The closing of DOJ's investigation had been Ladner's victory. It was a masterful one. When I met with John Cotton Richmond during the writing of this book, he revealed that he'd known virtually nothing of Ladner's real role, even while the two worked side by side. I documented for Richmond why I'd concluded that Ladner had been hunting runaway workers for Signal for a full year before becoming the investigator on Richmond's trafficking case. Richmond said he'd had no idea.

I showed him emails proving that Ghadge and the other final witnesses he'd interviewed had been part of "The plan that Signal has developed with ICE," as Signal lawyer Patricia Bollman called it. That testimony, as much as anything else, left Richmond unable to bring an indictment. I relayed to Richmond what Ghadge had shared with me: that Ladner had told him not to reveal the circumstances of his return from India. As I read Bollman's emails, Richmond cradled his head in his hands, his face flushed red. After a long silence, he could manage only one whispered word: "Wow."

Richmond asked me if we'd made Ladner a defendant in the workers' civil suit. We hadn't: we'd learned about Ladner's role far too late for that. A *New York Times* story had condemned ICE for "appear[ing] to have collaborated in an effort to silence foreign workers," but Ladner was so well shielded that his name had never been made public. Instead he had been promoted to a position in ICE intelligence. Several years later, he retired. Now he was fishing speckled trout in Mississippi.

Did he understand what he had done? The human cost of turning trafficking survivors into targets? How many of them never made it to our Thanksgiving reunions, had suffered self-deportations, broken marriages, suicide attempts? Without him, all the men should have received Continued Presence weeks after escaping from Signal. Work permits in hand, they would have set about paying off their debts, and T visas would have followed soon after, letting their families join them. Shamitha would have joined Rajan. I would have held their twins. I wanted him to face what he had done, to understand his impact on these people I loved. So I set out to confront him.

LADNERS ARE UBIQUITOUS in Mississippi. I found several Alvin Ladners in the white pages, one of whom lived in Waveland. I knew I would have only one chance to get him to agree to meet, so before I reached out, I looked for every way possible to understand the man and his context. In my hunt, I found *The Ladner Odyssey*, a remarkable genealogical account, starting in 1710 with Christian Ladner's sea voyage, through the "Dreams, ambitions, toil, defeat, and triumph of five generations of Mississippi's colonial families . . . [from the] French, Spanish, and then British colonial eras, to statehood, through a destructive Civil War and into the modern era." It was over nine hundred pages long. I devoured it.

An amateur historian who was one of the contributors to *The Ladner Odyssey* confirmed that I'd found the right man. He made an introduction for me. Alvin agreed to take my call.

I told him I was writing a book about migrant workers after Katrina. I wanted to talk to him about his role as an ICE agent after Katrina. I could hear the wheels turning on the other end of the line. Was he recalling my name from when we were opponents? Was he curious to suss me out face to face?

He agreed to meet on the steps of the Waveland Public Library.

THE LIBRARY WAS a broad brick house with green shutters and a pastel blue roof, quietly grand atop a five-foot elevated platform built after Hurricane Katrina. The porch was lined with white rocking chairs set out in pairs. When I got there at eleven o'clock, pelicans were flying overhead. In a chair at the far end of the porch, sitting perfectly still, was Alvin Ladner. Silver-haired, in a polo shirt and slacks. My body buzzed with nerves as he got up to greet me. He was six feet tall, a well-built man with a jawline sunken into his neck. He gave me an iron handshake.

"Presents from New Orleans," I said, handing him a bag. Deer sausage, andouille, and tasso.

"Oh, I wish you hadn't done that," he said with a gracious smile. "But deer sausage! I'm fresh out. So I do appreciate it."

He pointed me to a rocking chair as though the porch were his own, sat back with his hands clasped over his belly. I gathered my courage as our small talk found points of rapport. Our mutual taste for South Louisiana's smoky hog meat, which Ladner enjoyed on French bread. The remarkable story of his ancestor, Victor Ladner Jr., who was released as a Confederate POW and went right back to fighting. The unforgettable mud left by Hurricane Katrina, which felt like wet concrete and smelled like death. As we talked, Ladner's bright blue eyes studied me from behind his silver rims.

"How did you get my name?" he finally asked in his tinny twang.

We started to negotiate the rules of our porch summit. I explained I was writing a book about the Signal story. He was familiar with the story, he said, but wasn't going to be able to talk about it. I pressed on: he was already a character, based on information that was public.

"I don't remember a whole lot about it," he said. "But the part that I do remember I'm not going to share."

I needed a foundation to build on, a way to gain his trust for the real conversation. I steered him from more talk of Katrina to the start of his career in law enforcement. That's when he threw his first curveball.

"I never thought of myself as an immigration agent," he said. "I was a customs agent. Worked drugs my whole career. Big narcotics cases." I asked what had set him on that path. He leaned forward. His silver rims gleamed as he told of his boyhood role in blowing up illegal whisky stills. Then carefree days hanging out with customers at his parents' grocery store. Wading through warm Gulf waters with his first crush in the summer of 1969, "Fishin', crabbin', flounderin', swimmin'."

Then his description of idyll took a disturbing turn. On August 17, 1969, his childhood ended when the most powerful storm ever to hit American shores roared into the Gulf: Hurricane Camille. The Ladners fled to the highest point in the Gulf of Mexico, in Bay Saint Louis, to wait it out. They returned to piles of debris and craters with bodies in them. Their house was flooded. So was the store. They pushed Alvin through a window to fish out canned goods that were still edible—all they had to subsist on for weeks. Martial law was declared. The rest of that year, Alvin slept in an open-air camp on a government cot. Without the grocery store, his parents slid into penury. Alvin attended class in a tent. His sweetheart had moved away, probably forever. And though the Ladners fixed up their house, the flood had destroyed most of what was in it, including their family photo albums. No record of Alvin Ladner's childhood exists today.

This story of trauma threw me into confusion. On one hand, I felt the pull of his humanity. Part of me was growing closer to him, feeling grateful for what he was sharing. Another part screamed: *Remember why you're here!* We were two hours in, and I was no closer to my real purpose: getting him to talk about Signal.

The path to that was through his career. I encouraged him to recount his glory days as a customs agent, and it invigorated him. He told of chasing "The bad guys" on the "big narcotics cases." But when I asked him how his work changed after 9/11, he seemed to anticipate where I was leading him. He derailed me in advance with a narrative about his time at ICE that completely contradicted my picture of him. He portrayed himself as a man who couldn't possibly have done the things I knew he'd done.

First of all, he'd never believed in the agency. He was as much in favor of catching the terrorists as anyone, he said. But when DHS was invented, and US Customs was merged with INS to create ICE, Ladner quickly came to the conclusion that "ICE was a terrible agency," inefficient and misguided at best, when it wasn't downright dishonorable. He described being forced to pick up an undocumented man in his fifties to deport him over a decades-old drug offense. The man had been brought to the US as a child, and now owned a company and spent his free time putting Bibles in motel dressers. But "The immigration gods" deemed that he should go. Ladner described being furious, and fighting the decision, stalling the arrest as long as possible. "I had this pit in my stomach," he said. "It was like, God, you gotta be kidding me. I hate this job!"

He presented his own analysis of how private employers used ICE agents to exploit immigrant reconstruction workers after Katrina, calling in raids on payday to avoid having to pay them. "These big companies, after they have their roofs put on, want the Mexicans gone. Which is not really fair."

My mind reeled. How could this be the same man I'd pictured hunting us, surveilling us, plotting against us, nearly destroying us?

Then Ladner's story turned flat-out unbelievable. Not only was he a reluctant ICE officer, in his telling, he was a barely functional one. He'd only managed his immigration qualification exam because it was "open book, call-a-friend, look in your neighbor's page." Even so, "I don't know how I passed it." In spite of being at the agency during peak deportation years, "I can honestly say I never processed anybody." He'd never learned to operate the office computer, he said, and the only time he tried, he broke it.

His time at the agency ended when he was forced to travel to DC for a pointless briefing with "The immigration gods," after which he told his boss's boss, "I think y'all are a bunch of clowns. I'm going home and retiring."

Ladner leaned back in his rocking chair and smiled. The wind blew through his silver hair. His version of himself was as far from mine as it could possibly be. I had no choice, and little time left. I had to come at him head on. As I gathered my thoughts, he got a faraway look:

"Still miss the chase. I still miss the big smuggling deals," he said. "Nothing against Hispanics, but back in the seventies and eighties, and sometimes the nineties, if you saw a group of Hispanics around here, that was a sign of something. Today there's a bunch of 'em. It's a sign of *nothing*. Other than them looking for work! Work. They do a lot of work Americans tend not to want. In fact, I got some work I need done and I'm scared to hire anybody because of my job. I don't want to get into any trouble. But you can't get the Americans to do it!"

He laughed. Spoke admiringly of "Those Mexicans" who had replaced his neighbors' roofs in a day, while locals from Waveland—"nothing against people from Waveland"—would take two weeks.

By the time he was grumbling about needing to move "My camper and my two boats" to take some trees down, "and that's a pain in the rear end," my blood was boiling.

I confronted him directly. I struggled to keep my composure during a twenty-minute blow-by-blow of how I understood his role. Every time these men's futures were obstructed, I charged, he was the one who had done it. He had hunted Signal's runaways. Helped the company hold the men captive in the labor camp. Blocked the protections they were due when they escaped. Yanked back their T visas when they were first granted. Hijacked the DOJ investigation and upended any potential indictments. No authority would investigate him now, but I was going to hold up a mirror to him. Make him face the reality of what he'd done.

As I spoke, I could see the avuncular retiree transform into the hyper-focused federal agent. When I took a breath, Ladner shifted.

"Let me ask you a question," he said. "You've been asking all the questions. What is the point of revisiting the Indian worker issues? I mean, it's been to court. I assume the statute has run out on any criminal charges that could be filed. So what's the purpose?"

I could feel them there with me, waiting and listening—Aby and Hemant and Shawkat and Jacob Joseph and Murugan and Saravanan all the rest. And Rajan.

"*These are real lives,*" I said.

Ladner took up the pose of the ICE reluctant who'd barely passed the test. "It's unfortunate for you that—at least on paper—I got assigned the case. At least that's what they're saying. I don't know enough about immigration to talk intelligently about it."

I channeled my anger into focus. I gave names and dates, quoted emails from memory. He continued to dodge and stonewall. I refused to let him slip away.

He'd been the lead investigative agent. The futures of these men had depended on him.

"I don't have a clue."

He'd had witnesses arrested.

"Did I do that?"

He'd insisted on it. The DOJ emails proved it.

"See, I think that's the law."

I barked a laugh. The law is to protect witnesses during investigations—*he'd* decided to target them instead.

"I can tell you Alvin Ladner didn't make the decision!"

Four hours in, I'd backed him into a corner. He looked like he might lunge right back at me.

Then, abruptly, his face softened. His guard went down again. He seemed to age a decade in front of my eyes. His next question I never could have imagined.

"So," he said, "Whatever happened to 'em?"

He was diminished, but unmistakably sincere. These men, whose lives he'd nearly destroyed, seemed to become real to him for the first time. It took me a moment to catch my breath to answer.

"They're still here," I said. "We won."

I'd come here to do battle, but a new possibility opened in my mind. I told him that I would be passing through Mississippi again soon with a group of former Signal workers. I asked him if he'd be open to meeting them—maybe sitting down to share a meal.

"I'd have to think about that," he said. Then he mentioned there was an Indian man in town who he actually thought might be one of the workers. His family ran a convenience store. "They're good people, they're friendly people." Ladner went there for gas, lottery tickets, and fried chicken. "It's excellent." When I said I would go and give it a try, Ladner gave me directions, but made a request: that I not tell the man who Ladner was. "Because I enjoy going there. And I love his fried chicken."

I turned my phone on as Ladner walked to his truck. Text messages poured in from my partner, Marielena. Was I okay? Safe? Alive? She'd heard too many stories of my having guns pulled on me in Southern towns before. I called her from the porch and reassured her. My mind whirled while we talked. The strangest thing had happened in my conversation with Ladner. I hadn't won from him the admission of his role that I came for. But I had made the Indian men human to him. They were people like him, with lives of consequence, with futures. It wasn't a reckoning, but it was recognition.

Ten minutes had gone by, and I suddenly realized Ladner's truck hadn't moved. He had his hands on the wheel and was staring ahead.

He got out, hesitated briefly, and started walking back toward me. The hair on the back of my neck stood up. I didn't know what to expect. A revelation? A recantation? A threat? I told Marielena I'd call her right back, and climbed down the porch to meet him.

When he reached me, his face was a mix of pain and resignation.

"There's something else," he said. "I have dementia."

A doctor had first diagnosed it a few years ago, he said, after Ladner had found himself sitting helpless in his truck, unable to remember how to turn on the wipers.

I struggled to find a reply. I told him I was sorry to hear it. Asked him how he was managing.

"There's good days and bad days," he said. "But I thought you oughta know. It's probably why I can't be much help to you. I've just forgotten."

EPILOGUE **FORGETTING**

I THINK ABOUT Alvin Ladner every day. He haunts me—because I know he was telling the truth. The claim of dementia wasn't a crowning evasion. Nor was it a fig leaf, protecting him from the embarrassment of owning up. It was an admission.

The Ladner who came back out of his truck was a different man from the one I had spent five hours with on the porch. His gait was hesitant. He shrank back and offered to wait until I finished my call. As if I, not he, were the patriarch of Waveland, and this were my porch. And when he told me about his dementia, we shared a deep sorrow.

He'll never express remorse for the role he played because he'll lose all memory of it. And he'll forget so much more. Reuniting with his childhood sweetheart, the one who moved away after Hurricane Camille, years after his first marriage fell apart. Getting down on one knee in the grotto of Saint Clare Catholic Church, still standing by the Gulf shore after Katrina, to ask her to marry him. Camping. Grandkids. And everything that came before. All this will be lost, like the childhood photos of him washed away by Hurricane Camille.

I'm one of the lucky ones. I haven't yet had a parent disappear into forgetting. But I'm terrified by the knowledge that their memories will one day go there. That eventually, mine will too. Aren't we all afraid of that void?

I'm sad not just for Alvin, but for the country we share. His forgetting is part of a bigger forgetting. It's an American project. It's what lets us be shocked by the story contained in these pages. In fact, what happened to these men wasn't an aberration. It was deferred action on an impulse almost as old as America.

After the end of American chattel slavery in 1865, Mississippi leaders sought new ways to continue plantation production without sharing land and political power with newly freed Black workers. Many looked to the British Empire's coolie system as a model. After British abolition, the empire imported indentured laborers—nearly a million Indians, half a million Chinese—to its colonies to replace slave labor. The coolies were immigrants on labor contracts, given wages and work, but excluded from the ability to bargain or vote. American leaders of industry and politics in the post–Civil War South envisioned a similar solution. Newspaper editorial boards were their tribune. "Let the Coolies come," Mississippi's *Vicksburg Times* proclaimed in 1869, "and we will take the chance of Christianizing them."

Forgetting allowed large parts of the American economy to run on unfree labor even after the end of slavery. It allowed Congress to create, after World War II, the "bracero" program, which imported almost a million Mexican laborers into California's fields. After that program was abandoned as a national shame, forgetting allowed it to be replicated in the 1980s in the form of the "guest worker" programs Malvern Burnett mastered.

Each time, the same impulse under a new name: give us workers, not full human beings.

It's forgetting, too, that lets us blame Alvin Ladner entirely for the role he played. Each time America's immigration system has imported migrant workers, it has appointed wardens to keep them at work. When captivity clashes with dignity, as it always will, laborers will run, and Ladners will be sent to hunt them down. Ladner presents a continuity: a twenty-first-century captive worker's scourge whose ancestors chased runaway slaves.

But forgetting can also mean survival, just as survival can mean forgetting. I think about the range of reactions I got from the Indian men themselves as I started to interview them for this book. Some preferred not to revisit their fugitive years. "We're Americans now," one said to

3

me. "Why do we need to remember?" Others, like Shawkat Ali Sheikh, were willing to recall and be written into this account, but wanted to shield their children from their memories. Shawkat cried through interviews out of earshot from his family, with the door shut tight, and then emerged with a smile. He told me he'd give the book to his daughters only when they turned twenty-five, the age at which he believed they'd be able to bear the pain of their father's plight.

But some wanted to remember. Aby and Bincy sat with me at their dining table for hours, narrating the pain of their separation, as Bobby scampered about, now with his younger Georgia-born brother, Benji. At one point Bobby asked what we were doing.

"Writing a book about your dad," I said.

"So we can get rich!" Bobby exclaimed, wide-eyed.

"No," Aby said. "So that when we grow old, we can remember."

MERCIFULLY, MOST OF us have some choice in what we remember, and equally in what we forget. I think back to a story I heard as I was leaving Waveland. After Hurricane Katrina, county leaders decided to install a monument on the I-10 overpass, where the floodwater had left its mark. It was twenty feet high. The monument bore the words KATRINA HIGH WATER 2005 to serve as a reminder of what the community had endured, long after the flood line had faded.

A year later, the county leaders decided to paint over the words. First they chose to remember, then they chose to forget.

Notes On Sources

THE MOST IMPORTANT SOURCE in the writing of this book was the workers themselves. Over the course of three years, many workers shared with me enormously detailed personal recollections—that must often have been painful to retrieve—on the record during in-person, recorded interviews. It was never lost on me that these were working people who were living paycheck to paycheck, and the dozens of hours they devoted to our conversations meant giving up weekends, rare time with their families, sometimes even work shifts. This was a measure of their investment in their stories being told through this book. Together with their recollections, they often shared wonderful meals.

My second primary source was the mountain of documents produced by the workers' federal civil suit, *David vs. Signal International, LLC*. This included thousands of pages of depositions of the recruiters, Signal officials, and the workers themselves; pleadings; trial transcripts; and exhibits, from John Sanders's workplace diary to the trio's alternately chummy and poisonous emails.

Much of the dialogue in the book involving company officials and recruiters has been reconstructed from these court documents. Where the dialogue involved workers and it was necessary to rely primarily on their memories, I used court records and/or other eyewitness accounts for corroboration. For example, the extensive dialogue during the scene of Jacob Joseph's captivity (Part Two, Chapter 9, Captives) relies on Joseph's recollections, the depositions of William Bingle and Darryl Snyder, a pair of interviews I conducted with Breland Buford, and Buford's trial testimony in the civil suit.

Buford is one of numerous non-worker subjects I am grateful to for agreeing to be interviewed for the book—some recorded and on-the-record, others on background. Buford spoke in detail about the events of March 9, 2007. William Bingle spoke about Signal's evolution, his travels to India during the recruitment process, and his relationship with the recruiters. John Cotton Richmond spoke about his early career experiences in detail, and cautiously, though helpfully, about his work on the case at DOJ. Malvern Burnett spoke about his childhood and his experience with the Cuban refugees his family took in, but refused to speak about his work with Signal or the Indian workers. I reached Signal CEO Richard Marler by telephone, though once he learned about the subject of the book, he refused to be interviewed.

Subjects I attempted but failed to reach for interviews include Ronald Schnoor, Michael Pol, John Sanders, Darrell Snyder, and Sachin Dewan. In the absence of direct interviews, I relied on their depositions, as well as the other sources previously mentioned. Schnoor's deposition runs 447 pages, Pol's 400 pages, Sanders's 508 pages, Snyder's 303. Dewan and Burnett were deposed most extensively, with Burnett's transcript totaling 1,055 pages and Dewan's 924.

In constructing the sections of the book that are primarily from my point of view, I was able to draw on years' worth of contemporaneous field notes I kept, from a daily campaign diary to jottings after particularly inspiring conversations with Rajan.

The organization I directed at the time, the New Orleans Workers' Center for Racial Justice (NOWCRJ), produced its own trove of sources. These include a daily campaign blog about the public portion of the workers' fight, contemporaneous media releases, evidence packets for Congressional allies and advocacy organizations, and a detailed memorandum on ICE's interactions with Signal that became the basis for the *New York Times*'s reporting on an editorial condemnation of "an effort to silence foreign workers." I also drew on archived email correspondence between NOWCRJ's then legal director Jennifer J. Rosenbaum, the DOJ's John Cotton Richmond, and ICE's Alvin Ladner.

Workers generously shared with me the personal narratives they prepared for their T visa applications, together with exhibits such as receipts for their payments to recruiters.

Among the extensive press coverage of the workers' fight, none was more valuable than the articles by the *New York Times*'s legendary immigration reporter Julia Preston.

One of the joys of being a labor organizer is that you meet and form friendships with the unlikeliest people. You may not share views, but you nevertheless build connections as they let you peer into their lives and they peer into your own. The greatest surprise in writing this book was the emerging friendship I formed with Alvin Ladner. When I first reached out to him in early 2021, he was reluctant to speak. Eventually he agreed to meet, then had a series of conversations that ran as long as six hours. I am grateful for his agreeing to these being recorded, on-the-record interviews, the transcript of which runs over 32,000 words.

NOTES

PROLOGUE: THE CALL

Based on my notes and recollections.

For more on Hurricane Katrina, its devastating impact, and the disastrous policy decisions that followed, see *Katrina: A History, 1915–2015*, by Andy Horowitz (Harvard Univ. Press, 2020); *Katrina: After the Flood*, by Gary Rivlin (Simon & Schuster, 2015); *Breach of Faith*, by Jed Horne (Random House, 2006); and *The Great Deluge*, by Douglas Brinkley (William Morrow, 2006).

For a fascinating account of how migrant workers like Javier went on to become America's new "Resilience workforce," traveling to climate disaster sites around the US to rebuild, see "The Migrant Workers Who Follow Climate Disasters," by Sarah Stillman in *The New Yorker*, Nov. 1, 2021.

PART ONE: DREAMS

All of Part One is based on 2018–21 worker interviews.

1 Schemes

The "Migrate to USA" ad is Plaintiffs' Exhibit 524 in the civil suit David, et al. v. Signal International, LLC, 37 F. Supp. 3d 822 (E.D. La. 2014).

3 Supplicants

"Of course he paid!": Malvern Burnett testified in David, et al. v. Signal International, LLC, that he explained this sequence to workers precisely as Murugan understood it: "I told them that the deal was that the initial H-2B period would be . . . a ten-month visa. . . . Signal had the intention, though, to file their immigrant visa petitions." (David, et al. v. Signal Internatio-nal, LLC, trial transcript, pp. 4,455–56.) "Q. And, in fact, you understood that Signal had committed to sponsor all of Indian H-2B workers for green cards, correct? A. Yes. Q. Okay. And you made that promise to each and every worker, correct? A. Each and every worker with whom I met." (David, et al. v. Signal International, LLC, trial transcript, p. 4,499.)

"He remembered Sachin saying that the most important thing": Sachin Dewan himself testified in *David, et al. v. Signal International, LLC*, that in spite of the fact that workers had been promised green cards and paid the trio up to $20,000 apiece in recruiting fees, they should tell the US officials they would return to the US after the ten-month H-2B term, and that they had paid only a nominal filing fee. "Q. You instructed them what to say when they were questioned, right? A. Yes, right. Q. You told them to tell the U.S. consulate that they had paid 33,500 rupees, right? A. Yes." (*David, et al. v. Signal International, LLC*, trial transcript, p. 4,684.) "Q. And did you also instruct them to tell the consulate when they would be returning to India? A. Yes. As per the validity of the visa, the validity was, I believe ten months at that time. So we informed them to say whatever the fact was, the validity of the visa." (*David, et al. v. Signal International, LLC*, trial transcript, p. 4,684.)

In *David, et al. v. Signal International, LLC*, a jury found that Sachin Dewan had committed forced labor, trafficking for forced labor, mail fraud, wire fraud, immigration document fraud, a RICO conspiracy, negligent misrepresentation, breach of contract, and promissory estoppel against all five named plaintiffs.

4 Eid

"But the American lawyer Malvern Burnett said he had to tell the consulate": See Malvern Burnett's trial testimony in David, et al. v. Signal International, LLC: "And then I would go over each of the [application] packets with each of the individuals. . . . How long do you intend to stay in the United States, the duration of the requested [H-2B] visa. Through 7/31/2007 . . . To do anything else, you know, it wouldn't—it would cause immediately that the consulate would say, well, how long—we don't understand. How come it's not the validity date of the visa?" (David, et al. v. Signal International, LLC, trial transcript, pp. 4,460–61.)

In interviews I conducted and in trial and deposition testimony, multiple workers described how Dewan held their passports, enabling him to coerce payment. See, for example, trial testimony of Andrews Isaac Padvevettiyil in *David, et al. v. Signal International, LLC* (Day 8, pp. 1,393–94); deposition of Sony Sulekha (p. 174); trial testimony of Hemant Khuttan (Day 12, p. 2,380); and deposition of Palanyandi Thangamani (pp. 309–10). Dewan himself testified in *David, et al. v. Signal International, LLC*, that he routinely held workers' passports, and inadvertently described having the power to cancel workers' visas: "That's a—number one, that's a general practice in India for all the recruitment agencies. . . . And also, once the visa is completed . . . if and the candidate chooses not to go, if he changes his mind, then I have to take the passport back to the consulate to get the visa canceled."

As noted above, Sachin Dewan himself testified that in spite of the fact that workers had paid up to $20,000 apiece in recruiting fees, they should tell the US officials that they had paid only a nominal filing fee of 33,500 rupees (about $400). (*David, et al. v. Signal International, LLC*, trial transcript, p. 4,684.)

"Sachin had Shawkat sign an affidavit": Dewan himself admitted to having workers sign these affidavits in an email to Signal officials produced as Plaintiffs' Exhibit 822 in *David, et al. v. Signal International, LLC*. One of these affidavits was entered into the court record as Plaintiffs' Exhibit 853, as was John Sanders's concerned email to William Bingle: "Bing, this is an example of the affidavit which the workers from Dubai must sign for Dewan Consultants. It says they paid no money which is false. They paid the same 14,000 or so as everyone else. Their signatures were the price Sachin charged to give their passports back." (*David, et al. v. Signal International, LLC*, trial transcript, p. 4,691.)

PART TWO: MAN CAMP

1 The Immigrant's Best Friend

Based largely on Malvern Burnett depositions taken September 10, 2009; November 17, 2009; and January 12–13, 2010; as well as Burnett's trial testimony in the civil suit David, et al. v. Signal International, LLC.

In that suit, the jury found that Burnett had committed forced labor, trafficking for forced labor, mail fraud, wire fraud, immigration document fraud, a RICO conspiracy, negligent misrepresentation, breach of contract, and promissory estoppel against all five named plaintiffs.

"In 1962, when Malvern was a young boy": Burnett tells the story of the Cuban refugees who lived with his family in "Pensacola to Havana Race Starts Today," by Susan Langenhenning in *Havana Live*, Oct. 31, 2015; as well as in his November 17, 2009 deposition in *David, et al. v. Signal International, LLC*, pp. 221–22.

The Cuban refugees were "a topic of conversation at the family dinner table for years afterward," Malvern Burnett recounted to me in a May 2021 telephone interview.

Many of the children airlifted into the US as a result of Operation Peter Pan went on to write about their experience. See, for example, Carlos Eire's *Waiting for Snow in Havana: Confessions of a Cuban Boy* (Free Press, 2003), winner of the National Book Award for Nonfiction.

For basic background about the 1986 immigration law and amnesty, see the US Library of Congress Research Guide "1986: Immigration Reform and Control Act of 1986," at http://guides.loc.gov/latinx-civil-rights/irca.

For information about the 1996 immigration bill, see, for example, "The Disastrous, Forgotten 1996 Law That Created Today's Immigration Problem," by Dara Lind in *Vox*, Apr. 28, 2016.

For a discussion of "The conflation of immigration and terrorism" in the wake of 9/11, see, for example, *The 9/11 Effect and Its Legacy on U.S. Immigration Laws*, by Penn State Law and the Pennsylvania State University School of International Affairs, based on a symposium of legal and immigration scholars held by the schools in September 2011, available at https://pennstatelaw.psu.edu; and "Two Decades after 9/11, National Security Focus Still Dominates U.S. Immigration System," by Muzaffar Chishti and Jessica Bolter, Migration Policy Institute, Sept. 22, 2021, available at http://migrationpolicy.org/article/two-decades-after-sept-11-immigration-national-security.

For more comprehensive treatment of the decades-long efforts to reform American immigration policy, see *Immigration Matters: Movements, Visions, and Strategies for a Progressive Future*, edited by Ruth Milkman, Deepak Bhargava, and Penny Lewis (The New Press, 2021); *Immigration Reform: The Corpse That Will Not Die*, by Charles Kamasaki (Mandel Vilar Press, 2019); and *Americans in Waiting: The Lost Story of Immigration and Citizenship in the United States*, by Hiroshi Motomura (Oxford Univ. Press, 2006).

The story of the business partnership between Burnett, Pol, and Dewan draws on the depositions of Michael Pol and Sachin Dewan, as well as correspondence between the trio produced as evidence in *David, et al. v. Signal International, LLC*.

"The men gave each other nicknames": Burnett, Pol, and Dewan all discuss the nicknames they gave each other and used for years in their depositions and trial testimony. See, for example, Deposition of Malvern Burnett, taken November 17, 2009, p. 172.

"Some were even applying for H-2Bs for jobs that didn't exist": See Deposition of Malvern Burnett, taken November 17, 2009, p. 344: "Frauds. There were people that got involved in bringing in foreign workers when there weren't even . . . H-2B employment available, you know, for them once they got to the United States."

A summary of the PERM program titled "Permanent Labor Certification Details" is available at the US Department of Labor's Employment and Training Administration website at https://www.foreignlaborcert.doleta.gov/perm_detail.cfm. Burnett describes the trio's PERM recruitment plan and his delays in filing the PERM applications in his November 18, 2009, deposition, pp. 321–23.

"In late August 2005, a warm wind rose out of the Bahamas": The account of Hurricane Katrina's impact on the Burnett family is drawn from the *New*

York Times article "Searching for the Living, but Mostly Finding the Dead," by Abby Goodnough and Kate Zernike, Sept. 1, 2005.

"He was still in a fog": Burnett testified about his experience of what University of Tennessee professor of psychiatry Kenneth Sakauye dubbed "Katrina brain": "So, you know, my memory ain't as sharp as it used to be. And I've gone to a couple of psychologists at the request of family members. . . . Well, you know, my memory ain't what it was and it probably will never be. And, so, when you're asking these questions, I'm doing the very level best that I can at responding, and you're just going to have to be patient with me. Alright? I'm not asking for sympathy. I'm just laying it on the line. I continue to live with what I think is a disability of having gone through this, like the rest of this freaking city." (Deposition of Malvern Burnett, taken November 17, 2009, in *David, et al. v. Signal International, LLC*, p. 95.)

"Why can't you make the dolts understand": Email from Malvern Burnett to Sachin Dewan on February 3, 2006, introduced to *David, et al. v. Signal International, LLC*, as Plaintiffs' Exhibit 564.

The email in which Burnett forwarded the racist article "The Border Control Game" from Resist.com to Michael Pol, where you pretend **"To shoot immigrants as they tried to cross the border,"** is Plaintiffs' Exhibit 564 in *David, et al. v. Signal International, LLC*. A Plaintiffs' attorney asked Burnett, "Do you see any inconsistency between your practice as an immigration lawyer and playing a game shooting immigrants as they cross the border?" Burnett answered, "No, I don't see anything inconsistent." (Deposition of Malvern Burnett, taken November 17, 2009, in *David, et al. v. Signal International, LLC*, p. 217.)

For further background on the H-2B visa program, particularly its vulnerability to abuse, see Daniel Costa's excellent work at the Economic Policy Institute, including the fact sheet "Frequently Asked Questions about the H-2B Temporary Foreign Worker Program," June 2, 2016.

For more on the Avondale Shipyard, see *Avondale, A Model for Success: The Story of a Great American Shipyard, 1938–1999*, by Philip J. Meric and Rene Pierre Meric Jr. (Philip J. Meric Consulting, 2015).

For an account of the battle for a union at Avondale Shipyard, see the *New York Times* story "Five Years After Workers' Vote, Shipyard Holds Off a Union," by Steven Greenhouse, July 10, 1998.

"For it to work, everyone would have to lie": Signal, according to William Bingle's own testimony, filed labor certifications with the Department of Labor that had been prepared by Malvern Burnett, and that falsely stated Signal only planned to employ workers for ten months. "Q. So they were inaccurate statements to tell the government this in July 2006? A. Yes." (Deposition of

William Bingle, taken November 10, 2009, in *David v. Signal International, LLC*, p. 57.) Burnett acknowledged at trial that he prepared this certification (*David, et al. v. Signal International, LLC*, trial transcript, p. 4,436). Bingle said he expressed concern to Burnett and Ronald Schnoor that this was a lie but relied on Burnett's assurance. Bingle testified: "I had a problem with it, but it's what the immigration attorney who was versed in the H-2B process told us this is how the process works. Q. So you just said Mr. Burnett says, you know, it is okay to lie to the US Government, that's the way it works, and you accepted it? A. Yes." (Deposition of William Bingle, taken November 10, 2009, in *David v. Signal International, LLC*, pp. 60–61.)

Burnett himself admitted at trial that he advised Signal officials not to reveal that they were seeking workers for two to three years at a minimum, claiming instead that they were seeking workers for only the ten-month time frame the H-2B visa allows. (*David, et al. v. Signal International, LLC*, trial transcript, p. 4,439.) Burnett warned John Sanders in a September 2009 email exchange, "We do not want to publicize the fact that Signal may have a need for temporary workers for the next two or three years because it could jeopardize the granting of temporary work visas for the requested ten-month period." When Sanders objected that "Two to three years is reality and our saying so up front gives our request greater credibility," Burnett replied: "It is important that the embassy/consular staff not be advised that the work will extend beyond ten months regardless of how long Signal may believe the temporary need will exist." (Plaintiffs' Exhibit 568 in *David, et al. v. Signal International, LLC*.)

In depositions, Burnett described instructing workers to claim non-immigrant intent at their consular interviews: "I said [to workers] the H-2B visa is a temporary non-immigrant visa, and you must express the intention to return to your home country at the expiration of your H-2B status." (Deposition of Malvern Burnett, taken January 12, 2010, in *David, et al. v. Signal International, LLC*, p. 638.) This came after the workers had been promised green cards by Burnett, Michael Pol, and Sachin Dewan repeatedly, starting at the 2006 recruitment seminars, as testified to in the depositions of Soni Sulekha, Hemant Khuttan, Andrews Isaac Padvevettiyil, Palanyandi Thangamani, Kurian David, Sachin Dewan, and Michael Pol in *David, et al. v. Signal International, LLC*; and as Burnett himself told Joseph Jacob via email: "Sir: You will come as a lawful permanent resident also known as a green card holder. Your wife and under 21 children, unmarried, can join you after that date. Regards, Malvern Burnett." (Plaintiffs' Exhibit 570, *David, et al. v. Signal International, LLC*.)

Michael Pol wrote to John Sanders that if the workers told the truth about promises of green cards at their interviews, they would be denied H-2B visas. "One of us (Mal, Sachin or I) needs to be with each and every candidate going into the consulates before their interview. They sometimes say the dumbest things and need to be coached on the proper way to interview. They need to have the proper documents with them and more importantly there are some things that should not be known to the consulate personnel, such as the fact that we are going to process them for a green card. If one of these guys says he's going to the U.S. for immigration and Signal is sponsoring him for permanent residence . . . he's a goner." (Plaintiffs' Exhibit 550, *David, et al. v. Signal International, LLC.*)

Signal's labor provision contract with Michael Pol's company was Plaintiffs' Exhibit 423 in *David, et al. v. Signal International, LLC.*

2 Giani

Based on 2019–21 interviews with Giani and other workers who were in the first wave of arrivals to Signal's Pascagoula man camp, as well as the deposition of William Bingle, taken November 10, 2009, in David, et al. v. Signal International, LLC.

This chapter's telling of Sikh history, including the account of Baba Deep Singh's heroism, is loyal to the account narrated to me by Giani Gurbinder Singh. For a comprehensive study of Sikh history, see *A History of the Sikhs, Vols. 1 & 2*, 2nd ed., by Khushwant Singh (Oxford Univ. Press, 2005).

3 Signal

Based on depositions of John Sanders taken November 19–20, 2009, and January 20, 2010; as well as excerpts from Sanders's diary, internal Signal emails, and trial testimony in David v. Signal International, LLC.

No Signal officers or employees were named as defendants in the civil suit *David v. Signal International, LLC*, nor did any of them face criminal charges. In that civil suit, a jury found Signal liable of forced labor, trafficking for forced labor, discriminatory terms and conditions of employment, harassing living conditions, fraud, a RICO conspiracy, negligent misrepresentation, breach of contract, and promissory estoppel against all five named plaintiffs. The jury further found that Signal responsible for retaliation, false imprisonment, and intentional infliction of emotional distress against Joseph Jacob in connection with the events of March 9, 2007.

"But Signal's safety director said everything was good to go": Pat Killen, Signal's director of environmental health and safety, described at trial the discovery of lead at the man camp building site: "And in that, they discovered they had lead contamination in that. And there is a plan that you submit . . . to basically seal and cap the site so that no further dredge spoils would go into that" (*David v. Signal International, LLC*, trial transcript, p. 2,491). Killen also admitted at trial that he failed to apply for state approval until construction was months underway. "Q. Now, you first went to the Mississippi Department of Environmental Quality to ask for permission to build the man camp on this lead-contaminated site during the second week of October of 2006; is that correct? A. Yes, sir. Q. And, in fact, you'd already started building the man camp? A. Yes, sir, we had." (*David v. Signal International, LLC*, trial transcript, p. 2,553.)

4 The Mix-up

Based on 2018–21 worker interviews, contemporary marine construction industry media reports on Signal International, and depositions of Signal employees in David v. Signal International, LLC.

5 Rot

Based on John Sanders's deposition, diary, and correspondence; the depositions of Ronald Schnoor, taken December 16–17, 2009, and William Bingle, taken November 10, 2009; and internal Signal correspondence produced in David v. Signal International, LLC.

Sanders's comment about **"serious, endemic plumbing problems in the trailers"** is taken from his diary, quoted at his November 20, 2009, deposition (pp. 20–21), and entered into the court record as Plaintiffs' Exhibit 621.

Details about the state of Signal's business are drawn from contemporary industry media coverage of Signal, including "Acon Investments Find Big Value in the Undervalued," by Terence O'Hara in *The Washington Post*, May 23, 2005; "Signal International Positions to Capture the Gulf," by David Paganie in *Offshore*, June 1, 2006; and "Labor Unrest," by Christopher Helman in *Forbes*, May 19, 2007.

"Well, that just wasn't true": As detailed above in endnotes to Part Two, Chapter 1, The Immigrant's Best Friend, Burnett himself admitted at trial that he advised Signal officials not to reveal that they were seeking workers for two to three years at a minimum, claiming instead that they were seeking workers for only the ten-month time frame the H-2B visa allows. Burnett acknowledged warning John Sanders in a September 2009 email exchange, "We do not want to publicize the fact that Signal may have a need for temporary workers for the next two or three years because it could jeopardize the granting of temporary work visas for the requested ten-month period." When Sanders objected that "Two to three years is reality and our saying so up front gives our request greater credibility," Burnett replied: "It is important that the embassy/consular staff not be advised that the work will extend beyond ten months regardless of how long Signal may believe the temporary need will exist." (Plaintiffs' Exhibit 568 in *David, et al. v. Signal International, LLC.*)

Signal, according to William Bingle's own testimony, filed labor certifications with Department of Labor that had been prepared by Malvern Burnett, and that falsely stated Signal only planned to employ workers for ten months. "Q. So they were inaccurate statements to tell the government this in July 2006? A. Yes." (Deposition of William Bingle, taken November 10, 2009, in *David v. Signal International, LLC*, p. 57.) Burnett acknowledged at trial that he prepared this certification (*David, et al. v. Signal International, LLC*, trial transcript, p. 4,436). Bingle said he expressed concern to Burnett and Ronald Schnoor that this was a lie, but relied on Burnett's assurance. Bingle testified: "I had a problem with it, but it's what the immigration attorney who was versed in the H-2B process told us this is how the process works. Q. So you just said Mr. Burnett says, you know, it is okay to lie to the US Government, that's the way it works, and you accepted it? A. Yes." (Deposition of William Bingle, taken November 10, 2009, in *David v. Signal International, LLC*, pp. 60–61.)

"Well, Schnoor had plenty of other things to worry about": Based on Ronald Schnoor's deposition on December 16, 2009, in *David v. Signal International, LLC*: "Q. So why would you continue to bring in workers when you'd known they'd paid an unreasonable amount of fees? . . . A. We needed the workers." (pp. 40–1) "Q. Mr. Schnoor, did the fact that Signal had invested $7 million in building man camps to accommodate H-2B workers and needed to recoup those costs . . . factor in any way, shape, or form into your decision to continue bringing workers from India after November 2006, despite knowing the extent of the fees they were paying? A. It was part of the investment. Certainly, our investment was there, and our desire to find a long-term solution was still there, and the need was still there. Absolutely." (p. 150)

Schnoor also described his discovery of the exorbitant fees the trio charged, his confrontation of them over it, and his firing of Pol in his deposition on December 16, 2009, pp. 41, 109–10. Pol described Schnoor's fury at the meeting: "He said, 'You're going to refund half the money or I'm going to blow this goddamn deal up.'" (Deposition of Michael Pol, read into the trial record at *David v. Signal International, LLC*, p. 1,737.)

"In the meantime, Schnoor sent Sanders back": Sanders details the "Very firm" warnings Schnoor instructed him to give the workers, that "They must act like adults and that there would be no next time: we would shut down the camp," in his November 20, 2009, deposition in *David v. Signal International, LLC* (pp. 194–96).

6 Tea

Based on 2020–21 interviews with Jacob Joseph and depositions of John Sanders taken November 19–20, 2009, and January 20, 2010.

7 The Secret Catholic Church

Based on my notes and recollections and 2019–21 worker interviews.

8 Winter

Based on 2019–21 worker interviews and depositions of John Sanders taken November 19–20, 2009, and January 20, 2010.

"To his surprise, Mr. Schnoor already knew": The role of Signal's "Inside man" was described in detail to me by multiple workers in interviews. William Bingle also testified to Signal's reliance on a number of worker "Moles" to monitor potential labor unrest. "Q. 'What are the moles saying?' What is that a reference to? A. Just some of the guys in the camp who were happy with everything that was going on would sometimes go to Darrell [Snyder] or Rhonda [George] and give them some information about what the other guys were talking about." (Deposition of William Bingle, taken November 10, 2009, in *David v. Signal International, LLC*, pp. 208–9.)

"Which is why Schnoor had a plan": Darrell Snyder testified that he recommended Ronald Schnoor fire Jacob Joseph and Sabulal because "They were creating unrest" by enlisting other workers "To participate in making more petty complaints. . . . I was told they were going bunkhouse to bunkhouse to recruit workers. I was also told that they were meeting with the immigrants' rights people at the church." (Deposition of Darrell Snyder, taken October 1, 2009, pp. 54–59.) Schnoor testified that he agreed to the firing, and added as an additional reason his impression that Jacob Joseph was meeting with outside lawyers and considering a lawsuit against Signal. "The termination had nothing to do with their skill level," Schnoor admitted. (Deposition of Ronald Schnoor, taken December 16–17, 2009, pp. 270–71, 313–14.)

9 Captives

Based on my notes and recollections; 2019–21 worker interviews; deposition of Darrell Snyder, taken October 1, 2009; depositions of William Bingle and Ronald Schnoor; Breland Buford's deposition in David v. Signal International, LLC (read into the trial record on January 20, 2015, in the trial's Day 6 a.m. session); and a telephone interview with Buford in October 2021.

"'If you ever shake hands'": Snyder's "Joke" about Indians not using toilet paper is related by Buford in the trial transcript of *David v. Signal International, LLC*, Day 6 a.m. session, pp. 804–5: "A. They did tell me to wash my hands if I ever shook their hand. I guess because they didn't use toilet paper or something. Q. Who told you that? A. That was—it was a guy that worked at Signal. Darrell . . . Snyder, that's it."

10 Carrot and Stick

Draws on the depositions of Burnett and Schnoor, as well as 2019–21 worker interviews.

"'This company is going to be here for a long time'": All direct quotes in this chapter are from an audio recording of the "captive worker" meeting produced as evidence in *David v. Signal International, LLC*, and transcribed on pp. 310–13 of Ronald Schnoor's deposition, taken December 16–17, 2009.

PART THREE: ESCAPE

1 Get Out

Based on my notes and recollections.

Malvern Burnett described being fired by Signal at trial in *David v. Signal International, LLC* (trial transcript p. 4,510).

For more on Continued Presence, see Authority to Permit Continued Presence in the United States for Victims of Severe Forms of Trafficking in Persons, 28 C.F.R. § 1100.35 (2022).

United States Citizenship and Immigration Services (USCIS) has a similarly useful resource on T visas titled "Victims of Human Trafficking: T Nonimmigrant Status," last updated Oct. 20, 2021, at https://www.uscis.gov/humanitarian/victims-of-human-trafficking-and-other-crimes/victims-of-human-trafficking-t-nonimmigrant-status.

For number of T visas issued in 2006, see the Department of Justice annual report, "Assessment of U.S. Government Efforts to Combat Trafficking in Persons in Fiscal Year 2006," September 2007, available at https://www.justice.gov/archive/ag/annualreports/tr2007/assessment-of-efforts-to-combat-tip0907.pdf.

2 Big Man

Based on my notes and recollections, and 2019–21 worker interviews.

3 Genius

For background on United States v. Kil Soo Lee, see the Department of Justice media release "Garment Factory Owner Sentenced to 40 Years for Human Trafficking," June 23, 2005, available at https://www.justice.gov/archive/opa/pr/2005/June/05_crt_335.htm; and "Anatomy of an International Human Trafficking Case, Pt. 1: Kil Soo Lee and the Case of the Samoan Sweatshop," July 16, 2004, available at https://archives.fbi.gov/archives/news/stories/2004/july/kilsoolee_071604.

"They joined him in making their own promises of green cards": Ronald Schnoor admitted that Signal repeatedly promised workers green cards in his December 16, 2009, deposition in *David v. Signal International, LLC*: "Q. And as we discussed yesterday, the fact that these workers were promised green cards was problematic in two respects: First, because you can't guarantee what the U.S. government's going to do, right? A. Correct. Q. And, second, because Signal had not even determined for itself that it was going to even file for green cards for any or all of these workers, right? A. Correct." (p. 232)

4 Elders

Based on my notes and recollections, as well as 2019–21 interviews with Hemant Khuttan and Yeshwant Ghadge.

5 Freedom Papers

Based on my notes and recollections, as well as 2019–21 interviews with workers and Ted Quant.

6 The Last Cashew

Based on my notes and recollections.

7 The Day Time Stopped

Based on my notes and recollections, 2019–21 worker interviews, and contemporary press coverage. See, for example, "Revolt in Mississippi: Indian Workers Claim 'Slave Treatment,'" by Joseph Rhee, ABC News, Mar. 7, 2008; and "Workers Sue Gulf Coast Company That Imported Them," by Adam Nossiter, New York Times, Mar. 11, 2008.

Many public campaign activities are detailed at the New Orleans Workers' Center for Racial Justice's (NOWCRJ) blog at https://nolaworkerscenter.wordpress.com.

Ted Quant—a talented photographer on top of his gifts for historical analysis, organizing, and oratory—published a beautiful album of photos from the satyagraha launch at https://www.flickr.com/photos/tedquant/sets/72157604061490756.

8 Paradise

Based on my notes and recollections, correspondence between the NOWCRJ legal department and the Department of Justice, and 2019–21 worker interviews.

The Department of Justice has a thorough overview of standards for trafficking investigations and protections for victims, including temporary immigration relief, at its Human Trafficking Prosecution Unit page at https://www.justice.gov/crt/human-trafficking-prosecution-unit-htpu.

"Ted and I had sprung citizen's arrests on Southern bosses before": CNN reported on "Bimbo" Relan and recorded his worldview in the blog of Anderson Cooper 360°: "Bimbo's Point of View," by Drew Griffin, Feb. 25, 2008, at https://ac360.blogs.cnn.com/2008/02/25/bimbos-point-of-view/?hpt=ac_bn2.

9 Restless

Based on my notes and recollections, as well as correspondence with the Indian Embassy.

PART FOUR: TRUTH MARCH

1 Satyagraha

Based on my notes and recollections, 2019–21 worker interviews, and contemporary press coverage. The satyagraha and campaign activities in Washington, DC, are detailed at the campaign blog of the NOWCRJ https://nolaworker-scenter.wordpress.com.

Though the quote "First they ignore you. Then they ridicule you. Then they attack you. Then you win" is often incorrectly attributed to Gandhi, it is likely derived from a speech by trade unionist Nicholas Klein in 1918: "First they ignore you. Then they ridicule you. And then they attack you and want to burn you. And then they build monuments to you."

2 Surveilled

Based on my notes and recollections.

"They had arrested over a thousand people without warrants": ICE's warrantless arrests were reported in *The New York Times*, "No Need for a Warrant, You're an Immigrant," by Julia Preston, Oct. 14, 2007. The 2007 deportations are recorded in the Department of Homeland Security's *2007 Yearbook of Immigration Statistics*, which lists the total number of "aliens removed" in 2007 as 319,382.

3 Greensboro, USA

The 1979 Greensboro Massacre continues to be a contested and highly sensitive topic for North Carolinians, as does the work of the Greensboro Truth and Reconciliation Commission (TRC). In February 2005, the Greensboro City Council divided along racial and party lines over whether to approve a memorial plaque at the site, with two Republican members pressing to replace the word Massacre on the plaque with Shootout. The plaque was eventually approved with Massacre.

My telling of the events relies significantly on the perspective of Rev. Nelson Johnson, but also draws on extensive outside sources, including the well-documented account at the online civil rights archive of the University of North Carolina (see https://gateway.uncg.edu/islandora/search/%22Greensboro%20Massacre%22?type=edismax) (search results for "Greensboro Massacre"), the Final Report by the Greensboro TRC (available at https://greensborotrc.org), and *Learning from Greensboro: Truth and Reconciliation in the United States*, by Lisa Magarrell and Joya Wesley (Univ. of Penn. Press, 2008), transitional justice experts who provided technical assistance to the Greensboro commission.

For more on the Greensboro Massacre, see *Civilities and Civil Rights: Greensboro, North Carolina, and the Black Struggle for Freedom*, William H. Chafe (Oxford Univ. Press, rev. ed., 1981), and *Through Survivors' Eyes: From the Sixties to the Greensboro Massacre*, by Sally Avery Bermanzohn (Vanderbilt Univ. Press, 2003).

4 Alarm

Based on my notes and recollections, as well as correspondence between the legal departments of the NOWCRJ and the Southern Poverty Law Center.

5 Department for Justice

John Cotton Richmond's professional biography is available on the website of the US State Department, at https://2017-2021.state.gov/biographies/john-cotton-richmond/index.html.

After his work on the Signal case, Richmond would write an excellent scholarly article on trafficking law for the *Saint Louis University Law Journal*, "Human Trafficking: Understanding the Law and Deconstructing Myths," Volume 60, Number 1, Fall 2015. See pp. 34–35 for Richmond's views on T visas and Continued Presence.

The horrific attack on Jessie Lee Williams Jr. by Mississippi corrections officers is detailed in a Department of Justice press release, "Former Mississippi Corrections Officers Sentenced for Role in Abusing Inmates," Nov. 6, 2007, available at https://www.justice.gov/archive/opa/pr/2007/November/07_crt_898.html, as well as the civil suit filed by his estate, *Estate of Jessie Lee Williams Jr. v. City of Long Beach, Mississippi et al.*, No 1:09-cv-00144-LG-RHW.

6 The Diplomat and the Coolies

Based on my notes and recollections, the campaign blog at https://nolaworkerscenter.wordpress.com, and contemporary Indian press coverage of the meeting. See, for example, "After March to Meet Sen, Workers Seek CBI probe," Press Trust of India, Mar. 28, 2008; and "Sen Cancels Travel Plans to Meet Indian Workers," Times of India, Mar. 21, 2008.

The story about Sen's mistake was documented extensively (and gleefully) in the Indian press in 2007. See, for example, "Ronen Sorry for 'Headless Chicken' Remark," *The Indian Express*, Oct. 29, 2007.

For background on the controversy surrounding the nuclear deal, see "The U.S.-India Nuclear Deal," by Jayshree Bajoria and Esther Pan, Council on Foreign Relations, updated Nov. 5, 2010.

For more on the coolie system, see *A New System of Slavery: The Export of Indian Labor Overseas 1830–1920*, by Hugh Tinker (Oxford Univ. Press, 1974).

7 A Conditional Resident

Based on my notes and recollections, as well as contemporary US and Indian media reports. See, for example, "Indian Workers Find Ally in US Politicos," Hindustan Times, updated Mar. 13, 2008.

The process of removing conditions from permanent residence is detailed at "Conditional Permanent Residence," USCIS, https://www.uscis.gov/green-card/after-we-grant-your-green-card/conditional-permanent-residence.

For a sense of John O'Neal's five-decade career as a playwright, storyteller, and civil rights leader, see *Don't Start Me to Talking: The Selected Plays of John O'Neal* (Theater Communications Group, 2016).

For a history of the Southern organizing tradition that Hollis Watkins, John O'Neal, and others were part of, see *I've Got the Light of Freedom: The Organizing Tradition and the Mississippi Freedom Struggle*, by Charles M. Payne (Univ. of California Press, 1995).

8 Food of Wanderers

Based on my notes and recollections.

9 Hunger no

Based on my notes and recollections, correspondence between the NOWCRJ legal department and the Department of Justice, 2019–21 worker interviews, and the campaign blog at https://nolaworkerscenter.wordpress.com. For coverage of the hunger strike, see "Workers on Hunger Strike Say They Were Misled on Visas," by Julia Preston, New York Times, June 7, 2008.

For Gandhi's own account of one of his earliest fasts on behalf of textile workers striking for wage increases at the Ahmedabad Mill, see *An Autobiography or The Story of My Experiments with Truth*, M. K. Gandhi, trans. By Mahader Desai (Yale Univ. Press, 2018). For a more comprehensive treatment of the strike, see *Gandhi's Truth: On the Origins of Militant Nonviolence*, by Erik H. Erikson (W.W. Norton & Co., 1969).

For Gandhi's quote beginning **"Suffering even unto death"**: See *Non-Violent Resistance (Satyagraha)*, by M. K. Gandhi (Dover, 2001).

10 Breakdown

Based on my notes and recollections, as well as correspondence between the NOWCRJ legal department and the Department of Justice.

PART FIVE: HUNTED

1 The Hunter

Based on telephone and in-person interviews I conducted with Alvin Ladner in summer 2021, as well as *The Ladner Odyssey*, a family history compiled by Nap L. Cassibry and published by the Mississippi Coast Historical and Genealogical Society in 1988.

"Christian Ladner of Lucerne was a tobacco smuggler": The semilegendary origins of Christian Ladner were told to me by Alvin Ladner—with a laugh—as family lore.

2 Notice to Appear

Based on my notes and recollections, 2019–21 interviews with Murugan Kandhasamy, and correspondence between the NOWCRJ legal department and the Department of Justice.

US government policy on when and why undocumented immigrants should be issued Notices to Appear—effectively the beginning of deportation proceedings—has changed significantly with each new presidential administration. See, for example, "Practice Advisory for Immigration Advocates: The Biden Administration's Interim Enforcement Priorities," National Immigration Project of the National Lawyers Guild, available at https://www.nationalimmigrationproject.org/PDFs/practitioners/practice_advisories/gen/2021_24Mar_pekoske-memo.pdf.

3 Damage

Based on my notes and recollections, 2019–21 interviews with Aby Raju, and the text of Aby's T visa application.

4 Fargo

Based on my notes and recollections, 2021 worker interviews, and contemporary press coverage. See, for example, "India Workers: 14 of 'Cass 23' plead guilty in Fargo," Grand Forks Herald, Dec. 18, 2008.

As for the assertion in *The New York Times* that the men were victims of trafficking, see "North Dakota: Immigrants Arrested," by Julia Preston, *New York Times*, Oct. 29, 2008.

"'Everyone knows this isn't a real trafficking case'": This detail was recounted in a March 2019 interview with Minnesota-based attorney Amanda Bortel, who represented some of the men in their criminal proceedings.

5 Death of a Friendship

Based on my notes and recollections, as well as 2020 interviews with Shamitha Rajan.

That the S in *S visa* stands for "snitch," see the USCIS information page "Green Card for an Informant (S Nonimmigrant)" (detailing informant visas) at https://www.uscis.gov/green-card.

6 India

Based on my notes and recollections, as well as 2019–21 interviews with workers and family members.

From 1870 to 1920, indentured emigrants from Tamil Nadu staffed British Empire's plantations, including Malayan rubber plantations, the sugar industry in Fiji, and plantations in Ceylon, Burma, Mauritius, British Guiana, the Straits Settlements, and beyond. See *A New System of Slavery: The Export of Indian Labour Overseas, 1830–1920* by Hugh Tinker (Oxford Univ. Press, 1974).

PART SIX: FAITH

1 Revoke

Based on my notes and recollections, as well as 2020–21 interviews with workers.

2 Belief

Based on 2020–21 interviews with Shawkat Ali Sheikh about the episode. John Cotton Richmond details his early anti-trafficking work and struggles in India in an April 21, 2020, podcast interview "John Cotton Richmond: Dreaming for Justice," on the Dream Big Podcast with Bob Goff and Friends, available at https://www.accessmore.com/episode/John-Cotton-Richmond---Dreaming-for-Justice. Richmond also recounted various elements of the story to me in an in-person interview in Washington, DC, summer 2021.

3 The Smoking Gun

Based on my notes and recollections; the deposition of Ronald Schnoor taken December 17, 2009; and the deposition of Darrell Snyder taken October 1, 2009.

"I imagined how the whole sequence might have played out": This imagined reconstruction of events relies on correspondence between Signal, ICE, and US Border Patrol produced in *David v. Signal International, LLC*, as well as my 2021 in-person interview with Alvin Ladner in Waveland, MS.

Deposition excerpts that detail the interactions between ICE and Signal, including Ladner's participation, are collected in the NOWCRJ legal department memo "Timeline and Evidence," prepared Jan. 18, 2010. This memo was shared with the *New York Times* and served as the basis for their reporting on and editorial condemnation of ICE's actions: "Suit Points to H-2B Program Flaws," Feb. 1, 2010; and "A Bitter Guestworker Story," Feb. 4, 2010.

Darrell Snyder testified: "[The head of Mississippi Customs and Border Patrol] introduced me to an ICE agent . . . Alvin Ladner . . . because he felt there might be an issue of immigration fraud. . . . [I met with Mr. Ladner] maybe four, three, four [times] . . . from maybe late March [2007], early April on into after [about December 2007]." (Deposition of Darrell Snyder in *David v. Signal International, LLC*, taken October 1, 2009, pp. 244–45.) On March 19, 2007, Snyder sent an internal Signal email memorializing a meeting with the head of Mississippi Customs and Border Patrol: "He also states that he was certain that ICE was going to take an active role in the apprehension of the 14 that are out there now if for no other reason than to send a message to the remaining workers that it is not in their best interests to try and 'push' the system." (Excerpted in "Timeline and Evidence.")

The emails quoted between Signal lawyer Patricia Bollman and worker Yeshwant Ghadge were also produced as Plaintiffs' Exhibits in the civil suit. Bollman wrote: "The plan that Signal has developed with ICE is that all of the former H-2B workers who are ICE witnesses will return to the U.S. to work for Signal in mid-April." (Excerpted in "Timeline and Evidence," SIGE 0237302.) Further corroboration came from my recorded interviews with Yeshwant Ghadge, who described meetings between himself, Bollman, and Ladner, in which Ladner prepared him to testify against the other workers.

4 Brothers

Based on my notes and recollections and 2019–21 worker interviews.

Attorney Leon Fresco's role was later profiled in the *Miami Herald* story, "Miami's Leon Fresco: The Immigration Mover and Shaker You Don't Know," by Franco Ordonez, updated July 22, 2013. The breaking story about ICE's collusion with Signal was "Suit Points to Guest Worker Program Flaws," by Julia Preston, *New York Times*, Feb. 1, 2010; and the editorial "A Bitter Guestworker Story," *New York Times*, Feb. 4, 2010.

5 The Test

Excerpts are taken directly from the workers' T visa applications.

6 Reunion

Based on my notes and recollections and 2019–21 worker interviews.

7 Thanksgiving

Based on my notes and recollections and 2019–21 worker interviews. These Thanksgiving reunions with workers and family members continue to be an annual tradition.

Kudum puli, the Malabar tamarind in **"Bincy's Fish Curry,"** is a specially treated tropical fruit that's pulled from the vine, dried in the sun, and smoked. It's hard to find outside of Kerala, though it is sometimes sold under the name "Fish tamarind." If you can't find it, try the recipe with the more common tamarind pulp or tamarind concentrate, though they won't give you the funky, smoky quality of kudum puli.

8 Good Karma

Based on my notes and recollections, trial transcripts, and contemporary press coverage of David v. Signal International, LLC. See also, for example, "In Bankruptcy Filings, Maritime Company Says It Settled Labor Case," by Barry Meier, New York Times, July 16, 2015.

Quotes from defendants' attorneys are taken from the trial transcript in *David v. Signal International, LLC*: Hangartner's on pp. 4,904–10; Cerniglia's on p. 4,950; Shapiro's on pp. 4,955–59.

The EEOC settlement and apology by Richard Marler are available on the EEOC website, in the December 18, 2015, press release "Signal International, LLC to Pay $5 Million to Settle EEOC Race, National Origin Lawsuit," available at https://www.eeoc.gov/newsroom/signal-international-llc-pay-5-million-set-tle-eeoc-race-national-origin-lawsuit.

In December 2019, **"He defended an undocumented poultry worker"**: See coverage of this case at "4 poultry plant execs indicted after 2019 immigration raid," by Emily Wagster Pettus, *Associated Press*, Aug. 7, 2020.

When I first told the story of the King Who Dreamed He Was an Exile to Rajan, he was astonished by it, and amused that I heard it not growing up in India but in an American classroom. It was first told to me by the Sanskrit scholar Wendy Doniger, probably in 1999. In writing this book, I found Doniger's version of it in *Dreams, Illusion and Other Realities*, by Wendy Doniger O'Flaherty (Univ. of Chicago Press, 1984). Doniger cites the *Yogavasistha*, a Sanskrit epic, "Probably composed in Kashmir, sometime between the sixth and twelfth centuries," where the story appears as "The King Who Dreamed He Was an Untouchable and Awoke to Find It Was True." That story is followed by "The Brahmin Who Dreamed He Was an Untouchable Who Dreamed He Was a King," another tale in the shape of a Möbius strip.

9 Alvin Ladner's America

Based on in-person interviews with John Cotton Richmond and Alvin Ladner in summer 2021, as well as The Ladner Odyssey.

The *New York Times* story exposing the collusion is "Suit Points to Guest Worker Program Flaws," by Julia Preston, *New York Times*, Feb. 1, 2010.

EPILOGUE: FORGETTING

The quote about Christianizing "'**the Coolies**'" is from the *Vicksburg Times*, June 30, 1869, excerpted by James W. Loewen in *The Mississippi Chinese* (Waveland Press, 1971). Loewen notes that the proposed importation of indentured servants "Was intricately tied to the continuing and unequal struggle" between whites and formerly enslaved African Americans. "The apolitical noncitizen coolie, it was thought, would be a step back toward the more docile labor conditions of slavery times and would also destroy all arguments about the indispensability of Negro labor to the Southern way of life."

The story of the high-water mark was first told to me by Shawntel May, who operates Blue Eyes Taxi and Limo in Mississippi, as she was driving me around Hancock County in 2021. The high-water mark monument and its erasure are described in "Hancock Co. Katrina high water markers now painted over," WLOX, July 13, 2012, updated July 14, 2012.

ACKNOWLEDGMENTS